Walking with Wildlife

Alan Stewart spent all of his early years in the countryside, where he learned about farming, fishing, gamekeeping and, most importantly, the wildlife that surrounded him every day. He worked on a farm for a short time while awaiting a position in Perth and Kinross Constabulary, where he began as a police cadet in 1964. In due course he served in Dunblane, Perth, Headquarters (Dundee), Kinross and Crieff. Much of his service was as a CID and Drug Squad officer. Throughout his service he took an interest in dealing with poaching offences, particularly salmon and deer poaching. From 1993, in the rank of inspector, he was given the additional responsibility as the force wildlife crime officer. Alan retired as a serving officer in 1997 and was re-employed in a civilian capacity in the full-time role of force wildlife and environmental crime officer. Later, from 2011, he was employed by the UK National Wildlife Crime Unit as an intelligence officer, finally retiring in 2015. Since then he has augmented his knowledge of our precious wildlife by regular walks in the countryside. He has been presented with many prestigious awards during his 50-year policing career, including, in 2001, the MBE for services to policing wildlife crime. He is the author of six books on that subject plus one earlier book on wildlife seen during a year walking on a Highland Perthshire estate. Alan lives with his wife, dog, ducks and hens on the edge of a Perthshire village.

previous books by the author

Wildlife Detective (Argyll 2007)

The Thin Green Line (Argyll 2009)

A Lone Furrow (Argyll 2011)

Wildlife & the Law (Argyll 2012 and repr. Thirsty Books 2019)

A Wealth of Wildlife (Thirsty Books 2015)

Killing by Proxy (Thirsty Books 2017)

Walking
with Wildlife

a year on a Scottish estate

ALAN STEWART

THIRSTY BOOKS
EDINBURGH

British Library Cataloguing-in-Publication Data.

A catalogue record for this book is available from the British Library.

ISBN 978-1-9161112-0-2

Printing & Binding
Bell & Bain Ltd, Glasgow

For the Robb family, past and present, of East Lamberkin Farm on Dupplin Estate who, in my formative years, helped inspire my love of the countryside and were an extremely positive influence on my life.

Contents

Foreword

Alan Stewart has spent a lifetime observing and protecting Scotland's wildlife in Perthshire. That interest was sparked in his early life on East Lamberkin Farm and then more widely across Dupplin Estate.

He is therefore well placed to reference the past as he revisits the places of his youth. The patient observations set out across these pages chart a landscape in three dimensions, drawing historical comparisons into wildlife sightings and a narrative of walks in the different habitats.

Land managers have a responsibility to safeguard the natural heritage they inherit. Our passage in time is temporary but our legacy may be long lasting. The economic pressures of running an estate must not lose sight of the social and environmental impacts of decision making. Politicians sometimes assist but sometimes short-term and well-meaning policies and incentives run counter to longer-term sustainability.

While Alan's book *Walking with Wildlife* celebrates the varied wildlife that he encountered on his wanderings, it also highlights the decline in the diversity of the wildlife. In my lifetime capercaillie have disappeared from the mature pine woodlands on the estate. This absence is not clearly linked to forestry management where formerly their previous habitat had been preserved but is no doubt impacted in part by the combination of commercial management of the land, the encroaching urban population, highway construction and increased human activity in this secretive bird's world.

The grey partridge, once a fairly common resident is now a rare and special sighting; similarly the curlew. The period of industrialisation in farming practices is acknowledged to be linked to this decline where the demand for greater output has been at the expense of conservation. The environment and climate change have now gained due recognition and land managers across Scotland have an important role to play in reducing our impact on the land over which we are temporary guardians. It will be important that the long-term impact of headline grabbing policies are considered alongside the immediate benefits; examples include rewilding the uplands and reducing livestock farming in favour of plant-based foods.

It is naïve to think that increasing human pressures on the land can happen without affecting the wildlife that shares the land with us. To protect some species sometimes requires intervention that impacts on others, examples being the removal of grey squirrels to safeguard our native red squirrel, the removal of non-native mink to allow the recovery of water voles and the control of foxes to assist the breeding success of ground-nesting birds. Alan met many of the people on the estate for whom restoring wildlife of conservation concern as near as possible to their former level is their vocation. This also means minimizing the use of chemicals, allowing some land to become wild, waterlogged, flooded, or to plant hedges, native trees and to sow wild bird seed crops. Hopefully it can be seen through Alan's observations that this estate has a genuine desire to protect the fragile rural ecosystem and our natural heritage alongside the support of rural livelihoods.

Alexander Dewar

The Dewar family have been owners of Dupplin Estate since 1912

Introduction

In the early summer of 2018 I was relaxing in the evening with a glass of red wine along with my wife, Jan, and daughter Janet. Janet asked if I had any more books planned, but at that point I had considered myself retired from writing. As it turned out, that conversation encouraged me to write a further two books, of which this is the second.

Janet had particularly enjoyed my book, *A Wealth of Wildlife*, that related to wildlife encounters on my walks on a Highland Perthshire estate and thought that I should write a similar one relating to another part of Perthshire. We discussed possible estates but one was most definitely at the head of the list: Dupplin, an estate lying to the west of the city of Perth.

I had spent many years of my life on Dupplin Estate: my early years with my lifelong friends Jimmy Robb at East Lamberkin Farm and Gerry Oliphant at Cairnie Toll Cottages; about ten years trapping rabbits over the whole estate in the 1970s and 1980s; and a few days beating on pheasant shooting days with a variety of headkeepers over intervening years. I knew the 13,000 acres of the estate intimately and, even though I had seen very little of the estate since the mid-1990s, Dupplin was ideal for the purpose of a book, giving me the chance to compare the farming, forestry and wildlife of the estate over the course of nearly 60 years. Importantly, given my background in policing, I knew that the estate was run within the law and that I would certainly not be coming across poisoned raptors or illegally-set traps. An added bonus was that the estate boundary is less than two miles from my house.

In late July 2018 I met with the factor, Alexander Dewar, who is the son of the estate owner, Lord Forteviot, and outlined my plans to him. He was immediately supportive and gave me the run of the estate for the purposes of gathering material for the proposed book. Over the course of the year I liaised on a regular basis with Stewart, the sole gamekeeper for the estate, and with Bill, the retired gamekeeper and John, the farm manager.

My walks over the estate began in mid-August, each visit covering approximately five miles, and normally running from about 8.00 am until midday. The estate is exceptionally varied, comprising ancient woodlands, new woodland areas of native trees, mature conifer forests, farmland with crops and livestock, a river, two lochs, several ponds and some wild boggy areas. The contrasting habitats support a magnificent variety of birds and mammals.

During my walks I like to stop regularly and sit quietly, allowing wildlife to come to me. Unfortunately this is not very practical when everything is wet and I often found myself not sitting but standing with my back against the trunk of a tree. It is amazing how often animals accept a lone person sitting down quietly or even walking slowly. I regularly got close to wildlife that in most circumstances are very wary of humans. In return, when I saw them and they did not see me, I tried when I was finished observing them, to sneak off and leave them undisturbed.

I thoroughly enjoyed my year of walking with wildlife. I would like to think that you, the reader, as you go through the chapters, can imagine to some degree that you are walking with me.

A wet-looking Back Hill

CHAPTER 1

Monday 13 August. Persistent, moderately heavy rain. Slight mist. 16°C.

Back Hill, East Drive

The black water-laden clouds above Dupplin Estate are releasing their cargo in the form of heavy rain. It is also misty, with visibility substantially reduced. It is certainly not a morning to be out and about, far less to be starting out on my year walking over this estate in search of the variety of wildlife I know to be here, walks to which I am so looking forward. I have planned my first walk in advance and there is no way that the weather is going to put me off, after all we're well-used to wet weather in Scotland; we would not have over 30,000 freshwater lochs if it were otherwise. My mind is made up; I am still going out!

My plan for the first few walks is to stay in the centre of the estate until the start of the pheasant shooting season. This officially begins on 1st October, though on this estate is usually delayed till mid-October. Most of the pheasant shooting takes place in the much more wooded central part of the estate and come October I will avoid being there on shooting days, keeping to the outer parts, the River Earn and the various lochs and ponds.

I start out, as planned, at Back Hill, a strip of land about three quarters of a mile in length and two hundred yards wide, running between two areas of woodland. The fences on either side of Back Hill have been netted since my many visits some years back. The crop in the fields between the woods is wheat, which is ripe and ready to harvest; it looks a decent crop considering the very dry summer. When I was a regular visitor in the 1970s and 1980s this area had been permanent pasture. In the early mornings and in the evenings the fields were alive with rabbits encroaching from the woodlands on either side; a tide of them, some black and with an occasional orange-coloured one, would run off the field in front of me. This was repeated the further along the field I walked.

Around 1980 the then farm manager decided to plough the grass up and sow barley. This was a major mistake and it was evident from the minute the barley briered – a Scots term for the seed breaking through the ground – that the crop was doomed to failure. The sweet barley shoots were a treat for the rabbits and they munched their way towards the centre from both sides. It was like providing a supermarket for a community and saying, 'Come on, help yourself folks, it's all free'. Needless to say, the services of the combine harvester were not required and the rabbits of Back Hill were rolling in fat and well set up for the winter.

What a difference today with the fences netted. The crop is standing tall right up to the track on which I am walking. No doubt there will be some damage from other wheat munchers – roe deer and hares – but nothing that was obvious. Just to make the point an adult brown hare pops out of the wheat just in front of me, shakes itself so that for a moment it is enveloped in a cloud of fine spray, flicks water droplets off its front paws, takes half a dozen lazy hops in my direction, then returns to the wheat field, this time keeping to one of the tractor tramlines where it will be infinitely drier than battling through soaking wheat.

As I walk slowly along the track between the wheat field and the topmost strip of woodland I am noting the variety of mature trees inside the fence. Strangely, I'd never really taken much notice of them up to this point. Beech and oak are the main species, though there is a good sprinkling of birch, ash, sycamore, rowan, lime, various conifers and chestnut. I wonder how there could have been chestnut trees right beside that track, all of them now hanging with large round green knobbly fruits which would contain the horse chestnuts that were so sought after when I was young, and this was the first time I had been aware of them.

What I do notice is that the grass inside the wood is quite long, evidence that the rabbit population has either died out or at least very few remain. There is no doubt that if the other side of this strip of woodland was also netted many of the rabbits would have starved to death. They would have finished off whatever grass there was first of all, possibly started eating the bark of some of the trees, especially beech, but that would not have sustained any more than a fraction of the numbers that had been there.

While I am pondering the fate of the rabbits, a bird of prey flies through the trees in the centre of the woodland and lands briefly on a branch. I only have a brief glimpse and think initially, probably because it is flying fast and low to the ground, that it is a sparrowhawk. The bird sees me and flies off, identifying itself with its brief *peee-uu* as a juvenile common buzzard. This is a frequent sound for the rest of the journey along Back Hill and it is clearly the home range of a family of

buzzards. Had it been a decent day weather-wise they most likely would have been circling and mewing in the sky above me. The weather hasn't deterred four or five swallows, all adults with long streamers of tails, from swooping and diving just over the tops of the ears of wheat in their relentless hunt for insects. Most likely they have families to feed in the steading of Windyedge Farm at the other side of the strip of woodland.

At the end of Back Hill I turn right and head towards the Pond Wood, where I can see that forestry operations are underway. The conifers are being thinned and there are high piles of logs along the side of the track. The lovely smell of resin fills my nostrils and is one of the delights of being amongst newly cut conifers. The smell is probably exaggerated by the heavy, damp air. If so, that is the only advantage of the weather, since drips of cold rainwater from the back of my bonnet are by this time running down my neck. As I pass one pile of logs I disturb yet another very bedraggled immature buzzard which has been perched on a recently-cut tree stump. Its soaking feathers mean that its flight is exceedingly laboured but it manages to flap across in front of me and takes refuge half-way up one of the still-standing conifers.

Woodpigeons are landing on the

field just outside the strip of woodland on my left. I stop to watch pigeon after pigeon landing in the same area of the field and wonder what is attracting them. I look through the binoculars and can only assume, since it is a grass field, that there is a decent sward of clover. To go closer to confirm this means disturbing the drookit buzzard again, which I decide against.

Further ahead there is a man on a tractor unloading logs from a trailer, three or four at a time in his massive mechanical grab, and placing them in yet another pile at the side of the track. I need to walk past but am wary in case I get hit by the swinging grab. The tractor cab door is open and I shout up to the operator high above me but he doesn't hear because of the noise of the machinery. I tap on the window with my stick. Still no response. I touch him on the arm with my stick. There is a response now: he nearly jumps out of his skin! I apologise for giving him such a fright and chat a while, discovering that he is a friend of Joan, the woman who cuts my own and my wife's hair. No doubt he will have a tale to tell when he sees Joan later.

I continue on, admiring a few hundred metres of hawthorn hedge that is new since I had last been in that part of the estate. It is now around six feet high and, as well as providing nesting places for many species of birds, is a perfect corridor facilitating the movement of wildlife between two separate woods. From the end of this hedge and towards the main (east) drive to Dupplin Castle, the estate has planted a line of lovely light green conical and symmetrical conifers which I understand are a variety of cedar. Further along the drive, on both sides, are ancient yew trees, giving a perfect blend of the old and the new.

As I approach Dupplin Castle I see three or four small brown birds (apart from the swallows, the first wee birds I have seen all day) flying between a fence and a tree in the field. From the birds' activity and their upright stance while perched on the fence, I guess what they are and this is confirmed through the binoculars. The family of spotted flycatchers are having a brief foray to catch flies, then either returning to the fence or flying to the nearby tree, where they continue their brief but invariably successful aerial sorties. It is quite surprising that they and the swallows are the only birds at work today. Both species only visit us for the summer. They need to build up their strength before winging the long way back to sub-Saharan Africa.

Hawthorn hedge running towards The Parsonage

I watch these long-distance migrants for five or ten minutes, noting in the background on the Lawn Park the skeletons of half a dozen mature oak trees that were destroyed in the great storm of 1987. I saw these on the morning after they were toppled. It was really sad to see so many oak trees cut down in their prime, trees which could easily have survived another century. My thoughts are then disturbed by the very brief single *kew* of what might have been a green woodpecker behind me. Since there is only a single note it could equally have been the quiet call of an osprey. I stand and listen for a while but unfortunately the bird has gone quiet. I've never seen a green woodpecker in this part of Perthshire so if that's what it is, it would be lovely to meet it in due course.

I continue round past the stables and the gamekeeper's house on my route back to the car, completing the circle – or at least the square. I pass yet another new (to me) connecting corridor of hawthorn hedge, a large rowan tree with more berries than I have ever seen on a rowan, two whitebeam trees, several discarded pine cones from which red squirrels had eaten the seeds and – at last – a rabbit run. A very clear run with separate hops made by rabbits extend from the gully behind the stables out to the field on the west side of Dupplin Castle. Rabbits are now scarce but not totally gone.

Birds identified:
common buzzard, swallow, woodpigeon,
spotted flycatcher.
Mammals identified:
brown hare

19

CHAPTER 2

Wednesday 22 August. Sunny, light wind. 20⁰C.

The Parsonage, Beech Alley

What a difference the weather makes to a walk! Today was a lovely warm summer day when I parked my car at The Stables, right in the centre of the estate. High in the sky there was a mix of around 40 swallows and house martins. Strangely, their location meant that there seemed to be more flies above the buildings than above the surrounding trees. Typically, on a hot day, their food source was much higher than it would have been on a dull day. Pity there were no swifts; by this time of year they were more likely to be winging their way back to their winter haunts in sub-Saharan Africa.

I walked westwards, past the sawmill and towards the large mixed woodland known as The Parsonage. The names of fields, woods and hills on farms and estates are fascinating and it would be great to know the history behind them.

Just before The Parsonage a field has been re-sown with what appears at first glance to be grass seed. I am assured that this is a crop of kale that has been sown as winter feed for sheep but there are still no signs of kale to be seen above ground. As I leaned over the tubular steel gate where the field meets the woodland an adult robin flew down

View from Factor's Strip towards the Earn valley

from a birch tree to the field. It was followed by another adult robin then a willow warbler. The slightly larger and more aggressive robins took exception to this incursion to their territory and both flew at the willow warbler, which retreated into a rhododendron bush.

I watched this scene for about 15 minutes and these robins continued to harry any other small bird that landed in that part of the field. I suspect it was the newly-sown kale seed that was attracting the birds, and the area from about 25 to 50 yards from me and for about 15 yards into the field was the part that was of particular interest to the birds. A delightful but unusual mix of birds tried their luck in the robins' patch: a dunnock, a wren, a female chaffinch, some immature robins, the willow warbler again, and even a female redstart with the loveliest red tail. Most were seen off by the robins either immediately or after a few minutes. A spotted flycatcher had no interest in what the field offered but tried its luck at catching flies, darting out from a perch on an elder bush hanging over the fence. Meanwhile a wren rattled its *tic, tic, tic* call from within a rhododendron beside me, annoyed at my presence. It was a veritable feast of wee birds.

Reluctant to leave the area of the gate in case yet another species of small bird showed up at the kale seed party, I eventually tore myself away and continued to walk westwards along the estate road at the top end of The Parsonage. I was accompanied by a jay which, though always unseen and

Red squirrel busy either burying or unearthing some morsel

morsel less than 10 yards from me. It was still busy with its task as I got the camera from my pocket but by the time I had switched the camera on it had spotted me and scurried to the base of a distant tree. I managed a couple of photographs, but they had lots of background and minimal subject matter.

screeching intermittently, appeared to be keeping pace with me inside the wood. The oaks this year seemed to have a bumper crop of acorns. The jays will not go hungry and will no doubt bury many acorns which then have the potential to develop in time into a new tree. There was also much evidence of a subterranean dweller along the edge of the woodland, with a series of brand-new molehills. Moles are busy fellows in their quest for earthworms and a dozen new molehills may well have been the work of only one mole.

At the corner of The Parsonage I turned left (south) down the western edge of the wood. Ahead of me a mistle thrush was having a bath in a pool of water in the middle of the estate road. It was reluctant to leave its ablutions and only flew off when I came within about 15 yards. A few yards further on I surprised a red squirrel which was busy either burying or unearthing some

I passed the former factor's house and walked down the west side of The Factor's Strip. This narrow woodland had been almost clear felled with only the mature deciduous trees still standing. I was delighted to see that it had been replanted with a mix of native trees and was protected by a deer fence, netted on the bottom half against rabbits. As I turned left along the bottom of the woodland I could see that its width had also been doubled. Since these protected woodlands now have much more cover they will hold an increased number of voles so the owl population on the estate should be thriving. The voles should also replace young rabbits as food for buzzards and in time may increase the number of red kites and kestrels.

I always found it difficult to decide which wood on the estate, for its size, would have had the most rabbits. The Factor's Strip must have been a contender. One winter day back in the late 1970s I had noticed that there were rabbit runs, albeit quite faint, coming diagonally the whole length of the ploughed field to the west of The Factor's Strip down to a turnip field which was over the farm track at the bottom. I had set snares along the banking between the ploughed field and the turnip field and in two mornings had caught nearly 200 rabbits. All of these had come from The Factor's Strip and were beginning to seriously damage the turnip crop.

The field I was walking through, adjacent to the wood, was young grass sown the previous year. It was a lush growth and the sheep in the field had probably just been put on to it. Because of the temperature the sheep were nearly all sheltering under a handful of oak trees scattered throughout the field. A hare rose almost at my feet. I was wishing I had seen it beforehand as I'd have had my camera ready. It is always a challenge to photograph a hare running away. This may well have been the chance; it just loped away quite slowly as if it sensed that I was no danger and that in any case it had plenty of speed in reserve.

I walked to the east end of Beech Alley and sat for about 20 minutes looking along the ride that runs lengthways through the wood. Not a thing moved during that time apart from an odd butterfly. This wood, formerly alive with rabbits, appeared

A brown hare runs off

now to be completely devoid of the wee furry bodies that used to criss-cross the grassy ride with such regularity. Their absence detracted from its splendour, though farmers might disagree.

As I was finishing for the day I met Stewart, the keeper. I was pleased with what I had seen during the couple of hours I had been out. Unfortunately Stewart beat me hands down, having seen a red kite, peregrine and a goshawk that morning.

New birds identified:
house martin, robin, willow warbler, dunnock, wren, chaffinch, redstart, jay, goldfinch, mistle thrush.
New mammals identified:
mole, red squirrel.

CHAPTER 3
Wednesday 29 August. Sunny, light wind. 19⁰C.

Milton Den, Munday

Another lovely sunny day as I drove down through the estate. I was surprised as I drove past the sawmill to see a flock of about 60 birds pouring in from the adjacent grass field and making for the trees behind. They looked like fieldfares until I thought of the date – a bit early for fieldfares, which don't arrive here from Scandinavia until mid-September or even October. One or two were still in the grass field and I could see the spotted breasts, brown backs and brown heads. They were mistle thrushes; fieldfares have chestnut backs and slate grey heads. I'm not sure how unusual this is to see such a large congregation of mistle thrushes. So far as I am aware they don't migrate to this country from colder climes, at least not in great numbers, but they do move about within the UK. It was a first for me and certainly an interesting encounter.

The area of the estate I made for was Milton Den, which lies just west of the picturesque hamlet of Aberdalgie. I parked near Munday House, a large house surrounded by a few cottages, and I headed off with rucksack and walking stick. I disturbed a cock sparrow bathing in a puddle. It was absolutely soaking and barely recognisable as a wee sparrow. I was surprised in fact that it was able to fly away. Its line of flight took me to the roof of one of the cottages where, typical of human habitation, a collared dove sat on a television aerial and a jackdaw was poking around the base of a chimney. A wisp of wood smoke curled up from the chimney and wafted towards me. It was a lovely smell, reminiscent of the autumnal days still waiting patiently in the wings.

When I first knew Munday House it was unoccupied with a largely unkempt garden apart from the lawn, which was manicured daily by rabbits. Rabbits had burrowed under many of the trees in the large garden and yet again I was amazed that in all these years I had never noticed that one of the very old trees in the garden was a walnut tree. It was a huge tree with several trunks rising from the same base, and was

Milton Den

Walnuts on the ancient tree

absolutely laden with clumps of round, green walnuts. I've no doubt this tree would be really old and it would be interesting to know its history. To think that so often I had walked past it and even under it and this was my first realisation of its species. When I mentioned this later to Stewart, the keeper, he commented, probably correctly, that I would always have had my head down looking for rabbit runs and snares.

I walked through a field of quietly-grazing sheep towards Milton Den, following the line of yet another new hawthorn hedge. Behind the hedge and running along its length was a strip of

25

Game/wild bird crop about 30 yards wide

game/wild bird crop about 30 yards wide. I scanned the crop for small birds but only saw a small group of goldfinches feeding on some teazels near the hedge. The mix of flowers, grains and vegetables is a real source of winter food for a variety of birds but as yet, in this year of unusual bounty, there is an abundance of seeds, berries and insects for birds everywhere.

Seven or eight rooks were feeding near the bottom of the grass field, no doubt gorging on invertebrates attracted by the sheep dung. They were joined by a further three which flew over from a harvested barley field at the other side of the den. When looking at the crow family from a distance a rough guide is that a large number of black birds are normally rooks, while pairs and single black birds are normally carrion crows. Far better though is to look at the wing beats if the birds are in flight. Carrion crows have a much slower, almost lazy, wingbeat as if there

is no rush to reach their destination, while rooks are more business-like and beat their wings faster. While I was meditating these differences a pair of carrion crows flew into the west end of Mlilton Den and landed on a tree near a small pond. When they landed they flicked their wings a couple of times, which is typical of carrion crows and is yet another identifying feature. I'm surprised this was my first sighting of these ubiquitous corvids.

I sat on the edge of a water trough to view the scene and to have a drink of water – no, not from the trough! There is a great mix of trees, bushes, rushes and rough grass in the den, plus the pond and the burn which feeds into it, all of which create an exceptional habitat for a wide variety of wildlife. The hawthorn hedge and game/wild bird crop provide a wildlife corridor from the south, a strip of trees provides a corridor to the woodland to the north, and similarly a strip of trees does likewise to the west. I'd forgotten what a fantastic estate Dupplin is, and of course it's even better now with the various new hedgerows and trees. As I sat there I thought I heard a single *prukk* from a raven. I listened for further sounds to confirm but all was quiet. Frustrating.

I walked along the south side of the den which, like almost all the woodlands, is now netted. The short grass which I remembered inside the fence has now been replaced by much longer and courser grass and yet again I lamented the absence of rabbits. As a

A roe doe stepped daintily out of some bushes

farmer would do while studying his relaxed and ruminating beef cattle, the growth on his Texel cross lambs or the readiness of a field of barley to harvest, I leaned over a gate that led to a track cutting across the den giving access to farm vehicles. Almost immediately a roe doe, in resplendent summer coat of foxy red stepped daintily out of some bushes and surveyed her surroundings. I doubted that she would see me as I was motionless and to a degree blended in with the gate. There was little wind but it blew from the south east from me towards the deer. She lifted her head, looked in my direction, clearly got my scent and retreated, albeit without panic, back into the bushes. She looked a yearling, which is possibly why there was no fawn or fawns alongside.

Suddenly three young pheasants about 100 yards from me jumped in the air and began to *cuck, cuck, cuck* in alarm. I thought they'd been spooked by a fox but seconds later a female sparrowhawk landed in a small rowan tree just in front of me. She had lovely slate-grey and white bars on her breast and leg feathers and was close enough that I could see her yellow, piercing, eye. She had most likely flown low over the pheasants, as hunting sparrowhawks do, and was unseen by me until she landed. I slowly reached into my pocket for the camera but the sparrowhawk, much persecuted for centuries and in fact the last of the raptors to be protected by law, was having none of it and flew off to the other side of the den. The pheasants, still alarmed by the sudden appearance of this stealthy predator, continued to *cuck cuck cuck* for some time after it had gone. Even the much smaller male sparrowhawk has the same effect on my domestic ducks at home: they often dive into the pond if a sparrowhawk flies over and quack in alarm, often for a good 15 minutes afterwards.

Female sparrowhawks are approximately 15% larger than the male and have a 20% longer wingspan. The female can even weigh almost twice as much as the male. The prey species of sparrowhawks is almost entirely made up of birds. The male specialises in taking small birds, with birds at the smallest end of the spectrum such as wren, tits and goldcrest almost always taken by males. The female, on the other hand, can take birds up to woodpigeon size with even a pheasant poult an occasional prey species.

Amazingly the next birds I saw were much bigger versions of the sparrowhawk: goshawks. I had walked further westwards along the den and was sitting on a stile having a sandwich when three birds appeared in the air above the den and a quarter of a mile further west. I thought of the oft-quoted tale about buses: you wait for ages for one and then three come along at the same time. So it was with the goshawks, with the last one I'd seen being around seven years earlier. They are normally pretty secretive birds, mostly keeping to woodlands where they hunt small mammals and birds up to the size of an adult pheasant. In the springtime they display with an undulating skydance above their woodland nest site but what I was being treated to today was, I am sure, a form of training.

Of the three, one was much larger and clearly a female. The other two were male. I suspected they may have been this year's youngsters though – maybe less likely – could have been the female's partner plus one youngster. Unfortunately they were just out of the range needed to make this differentiation. The three were diving at each other in mock aggression, with the main player being the female. They were probably about 150 yards high and at one point the female closed her wings and plummeted towards the ground in a stoop that would have done credit to a peregrine. She rose again and this mock sky battle continued for at least five minutes until they were lost to my view behind trees. It was interesting to note their underwing colour, which was much lighter and much more even than that of buzzards – birds of a similar size, and which normally have dark and light patches under their wings. The goshawks' wings were broad and short, which facilitates their fantastic manoeuvrability through the narrowest gaps in trees in their more usual environment: woodlands.

This was a fantastic display by top avian predators. I thought of the prey species in the den underneath the trio of raptors and wondered how they were reacting. All was quiet and I suspect the pheasants had hidden out of sight. Rabbits would have been perfect prey for the goshawk family but I doubt they would have any better luck than me in locating one. I spoke later to Stewart the keeper, who told me that the

The survivors of 100 mallard ducks bathing in a large puddle

goshawks had 'knocked hell' out of 100 young mallard ducks he had released on to a pond in the den. There were no ducks on the pond when I had passed it but I saw the survivors of the 100 later bathing in a large puddle on one of the farm tracks near the den. Only around 25 remained. The difficulty of course with having supermarket-scale numbers of prey species is that they attract higher than normal predator numbers.

As I headed homewards along the East Drive of the estate I watched a flock of finches at the top of some high conifers. They were sadly just silhouettes against the sky but their size and the shape of their forked tails suggested they could be chaffinches, greenfinches or common crossbills. They left the trees and flew past me, still at tree-top height. At that stage, had they been crossbills, I would have seen the orange-coloured males. I could therefore rule out crossbills but frustratingly still couldn't be sure what they were.

Nearer Dupplin Castle a single red-legged partridge tried to hide from me in a tuft of grass, while a pied wagtail searched for invertebrates on the shorter grass of the castle lawn. To finish the day a flock of wee birds rose from the far end of a hawthorn hedge opposite the sawmill and flew to The Parsonage. They were nearly a quarter of a mile away and could have been any one of a number of species but it was good to see that birds are making use of the hawthorn hedges either for feeding or cover.

New birds identified:
house sparrow, collared dove, jackdaw, rook, carrion crow, sparrowhawk, goshawk, red-legged partridge, pied wagtail.
New mammals identified: None

CHAPTER 4

Wednesday 5 September. Sunny, light wind. 19⁰C.

Lochs

Magical. That is how I would describe today's fairytale-like walk. I walked up the forest track to the Dupplin lochs. These are two man-made lochs, one named Dupplin Loch and the other Pitcairnie Loch. Beside Pitcairnie Loch is a natural pond surrounded by rushes. The last time I was here would have been around 2008, when I accompanied RSPB staff to ring three young red kites that had been reared successfully in a tree nest near the smaller of the lochs, Pitcairnie Loch. I'd forgotten how old many of the trees are in this sylvan paradise. They are real goliaths and easily match the trees in what is known as Big Tree Country around the Dunkeld area of Perthshire. Many are Douglas fir, noble fir, Lawson's cypress, larch, possibly silver fir with their mass of cones on the uppermost twenty or so feet of the tree, almost gold-coloured in the morning sunshine, and some are really ancient Scots pines. Lastly there were some that I could not identify and which were tall, slim conifers. In equal number are elderly beech, oak and, nearer the lochs, birch and alder.

Because of the age of the trees many have long-since died, but their skeletons defiantly remain upright, making interesting milieus for great-spotted woodpeckers to visit for insects, to announce their presence by drumming – the sound of which I will no doubt hear in the spring – or to peck out their neat circular nest holes. One of the dead trees still sports an osprey nest on the top, though it looks dilapidated and has not been used for some years. Some trees have given up their struggle to remain upright and now lie prone and rotting, though they are even better in this condition to sustain insect life. I was amazed at the number of huge dark brown fungi *Phaeolus schweinitzii* which are pathogens of conifers and were growing near to some of the trees. Some were over 12 inches in diameter and I imagine could be quite common in woodland of this maturity.

Making the most of the mature trees and their food supply was a wee red squirrel, which ran across my path into some bracken. I suspected it was away either to cache some food or to look for something to cache. Sure enough within a few minutes it re-crossed the path and made for a beech tree. I was hoping it would stop but it disappeared behind the tree. I waited to see if it would peep round the tree to see what I was up to but it had gone. It looked to be a young squirrel so hopefully there would be enough food over the leaner winter months for it to survive, as young red squirrels have a high mortality rate.

One of the dead trees
still sports an osprey nest

Dupplin Loch

I'd now reached Dupplin Loch and left the path to walk the short distance down to the boathouse. At one time this was a great fishing loch with decent-sized trout regularly being caught. Around 1980 pink-footed geese started to come in to the loch in the evenings to roost. Their numbers built up and I remember coming to the loch one October evening just before dark along with the then head gamekeeper Peter Nicol to witness the spectacle of many thousands of these Icelandic visitors, skein after skein, piling in to the loch just above my head. Their high-pitched cackling and the whoosh of thousands of wings was almost deafening.

The effect of the guano from the geese acidified the water in the loch and unfortunately many of the trout died. I keeked around the corner of the boathouse and saw that the boat was still there but it didn't look like it had much recent exercise, nor was there any disturbance of the lilies and other water plants at the boathouse entrance. With the general increase in otters, their presence now on the loch disturbs the roosting geese and the numbers roosting there has dropped dramatically.

Three quarters way across the loch there were 30 or 40 mallard, mostly with their bums in the air and feeding heartily. It seemed from this that the loch is quite shallow, which would mean that a change in acidity could take place quite quickly. Twenty-one mute swans were scattered around the loch and a small flotilla of black female and black and white male tufted ducks were impossible to count as they alternated between bobbing on the surface and diving for food. There were one or two other smaller wildfowl in the distance, possibly grebes of some sort, but they were too far away for identification. The scene was completed with a sunlit heron at the edge of the reeds waiting for its lunch to pass by.

Both ends and the far bank of the loch had extensive reed beds. It is an ideal setting for wildlife and I expect that reed buntings and sedge warblers may be present here in the spring. Meantime a pair of greylag geese hugged the reeds at the west end of the loch. There seems to be more and more of these large grey geese remaining to breed in the UK, particularly on the Western Isles. It will be interesting to see if these two stay until the next breeding season.

I moved on towards the smaller loch, Pitcairnie Loch, and became aware

Pitcairnie Loch through a hollow tree trunk

of a roe doe with a well-grown fawn on my left-hand side. The doe was engrossed in nuzzling the fawn and licking its neck and was as yet unaware of my presence a mere 40 yards away. They began to move forward, still without having seen me. They were beside a deer fence and seemed keen to get to the other side. I moved forward with them. The doe eventually saw me and stopped and stared. There was still no panic and she trotted on again, followed by the fawn. They went briefly behind a rhododendron, giving me a chance to overtake them and carry on up the track without disturbing them.

Pitcairnie Loch is dammed at the east end. I could see three small waterfowl at the far end of the dam but my attention was attracted by an osprey which had come from the direction of Cairnie Wood on the far (south) side of the loch and was now flying over my

Roe doe with a well-grown fawn

head. Unbelievably, following on the same parallel course but slightly higher was a goshawk. The colouring of its underside showed that it was an adult and, since I had the osprey to give a size comparison, I suspect the goshawk was a male, being much smaller than the female. It was remarkable that I'd never seen a goshawk for years and here was one for the second time in a week.

I walked the width of the loch behind the dam to give some cover so that I could get closer to and identify the birds at the far side. Despite my caution (or maybe because of the presence of the goshawk) two of the birds had disappeared and the third was at the edge of the rushes bordering the loch. In any case it was close enough for me to see that it was a little grebe, or dabchick to give it its other name. Though this dumpy wee bird was still some distance off I could clearly see its white tail, sometimes referred to as a 'powder puff' and there was still some chestnut around the neck, though this seemed to be fading towards the light brown of its winter plumage. I could now see up the loch. In the centre there were one or two small birds, divers of some sort since they kept disappearing

33

but they were too far off for identification. At the very far end I could see 20 or so mallard, two adult mute swans and possibly some young swans.

I made my way back to the track, noting piles of droppings from roe deer which had no doubt been attracted to the sweeter grass on the dam. There was also a dead red admiral butterfly among the grass. To get back to the track I had to negotiate, for the second time, a gate in the top half of a deer fence which was hinged at the top and swung rather like a letter box. I managed with some effort to post myself through it and continued along the track towards the top end of the loch.

The pond is on the opposite (right-hand) side of the track and I heard the grating *kaark* call of a heron. I looked but was unable to see it. It may have been among the rushes at the side of the pond nearer to me, in which case it would be out of my vision, or it may have seen me approaching and made its alarm call as it flew off.

I passed the graves of a former laird of the estate, John, Second Baron Forteviot of Dupplin, and his wife, Marjory. Without going into the fenced area I could see that he died in 1947, the year I was born. The first Lord Forteviot whom I knew would have been his son and it was he who regaled me with his fishing tales of Dupplin Loch during one of the many times he would appear when I was trapping on the estate. He was always interested to see how many rabbits I had caught. I could quite see why a former laird would wish to be buried overlooking the loch, though I believe that the late Lord Forteviot who showed interest in my rabbit catching prowess is buried in woodland near the castle.

At the point where the loch and the pond are closest there was an obvious run crossing the short distance between the two. Initially I suspected it had been made by an otter or otters, but had that been the case it would have been more defined. I checked at either end where the track met the water to see if there was any otter spraint or footprints but there was none. There was an extremely fresh fox scat on the run but I think this was coincidental. There were also three white splashes of bird droppings, which made it much more likely that the run or track was made by waterfowl moving from pond to loch or vice versa.

While I was studying the signs on the run I could hear an osprey making a *pieu, pieu, pieu* call above my head. Its shadow passed over me but despite that I was unable to see the bird. I did, though, see the beautiful grey heron which rose at the side of the loch as I made my way further up the track. It gave the usual *kaark* call and flew across the loch to resume its patient and stealthy hunting in the rushes beside the far shore.

I was now near the top of the loch and could see that there were indeed four fully grown brown cygnets with the two adult mute swans. The mallards, being less tolerant of the presence of humans, were already swimming towards the far shore, and a pair of Canada geese, which seem to be on almost every inland water these days, was following in the wake of the swans. Completing the wildfowl picture a lone coot was skulking at the edge of the rushes.

I continued on past the end of the loch but the track had come to an end and the waist-high bracken was making progress difficult. I decided to leave exploration beyond this point until the winter, when the bracken would be flattened by frost and snow and the walking would be much easier. Even more importantly the ticks that lie in wait for the unwary on the bracken would by that time be dead or dormant. As I turned to go back I heard the rush of wings as a large bird, possibly a buzzard, flew off a tree above me. I watched the gaps in the canopy but never managed to see it.

I ventured out into Blairbell moor, a huge rough grass area with a clump of hawthorn bushes in the centre. The bushes were absolutely laden with berries. Winter migrants from Scandinavia would have a bonanza this year. I disturbed a single meadow pipit, which flew off, its two white outer tail feathers helping the identification. The return journey to the woodland took me past a multi-catch corvid trap which, as should be the case when not I use, was minus the door, which had been removed to ensure any bird entering

had an easy means of exit. This is exactly as the legislation dictates and I would have expected no less from this estate, which has a well-deserved reputation for staying within the law.

There were many more buzzards on my return journey, with two or sometimes three and once five circling and giving their plaintive mewing *peee-uu* call as they kept in touch with each other. A great-spotted woodpecker gave its presence away with its *tick, tick* call but remained out of sight. Shortly after, a family of jays screeched their displeasure at a human intruder in their domain. The screeching shifted from tree to tree but the origins of the sound, as is often the case, remained unseen. As I walked down past the edge of Pitcairnie Loch an osprey flew towards me carrying what appeared to be part of a fish. It saw me at the last minute and veered down the loch.

When I was nearly back at my car I came to a lovely sunny clearing where I sat down against the bole of a large conifer to watch, to listen and to enjoy the sunshine. About 100 yards away I could hear the *pieu, pieu, pieu* of an osprey. This sound, like that of the jays, was mobile, sometimes to the side, sometimes in front and sometimes behind. Now that the female ospreys have left for warmer climes and this year's offspring are being taught by dad how to catch fish, I suspect this would be a youngster calling for the parent either to deliver fish or to pay better attention to the offspring. I would not be surprised if the ospreys had nested in this area. In 2017 the birds nested not 400 yards from this point but for whatever reason did not return to that nest in 2018.

Half-way through my walk I had met Gordon, still referred to as the rabbit trapper though he is semi-retired. Gordon works a three-day week on the estate cutting grass and trapping grey squirrels, of which he told me he has eliminated around four hundred. Gordon started on the estate about thirty years ago, just about the time I gave up catching rabbits. His was a different method to mine; Gordon mainly gassed the rabbits with Cymag while I snared them, unfortunate bunnies whichever way you look at it. While gassing burrows certainly cuts down numbers I don't like the method since it is wasteful of what would otherwise be perfectly good food. Cymag was also extremely expensive and I'd be surprised if the gassing regime cost the estate any less than £1000 a week.

Cymag is a white power which, if exposed to moisture, gives off a gas which can cause severe poisoning, heart problems, fitting, fluid accumulation in the lungs and death. I have seen a rabbit bolt out of a burrow which is being treated with Cymag, run off for 100 yards and drop down dead. Gordon told me that after the years of

gassing and while the fences were being netted he used drop boxes. Dropbox rabbit traps are a type of multiple live catch trap that work in conjunction with rabbit-proof fencing. These traps allow free passage through the fence line via a tunnel system over a buried holding box. As soon as a volume of rabbits become accustomed to using the tunnel system, the door system can be set so that instead of being able to pass freely over the box the lid tilts and the rabbits fall into the box. These are extremely successful and Gordon once caught 33 rabbits in one drop box overnight, a number which is not too unusual where there is a large population.

Nevertheless none of the methods used by Gordon, or the snaring or night-shooting methods that I used to carry out would eradicate rabbits. I strongly suspected that while Gordon's gassing and live trapping seriously reduced the population, my experience suggested that the complete extermination of rabbits over an area is caused by viral haemorrhagic disease (VHD). VHD is a very serious, highly contagious disease that can spread through a population extremely rapidly. There is no cure once a rabbit is affected. Unlike myxomatosis, where most rabbits die on the surface (and from which a high proportion now have sufficient immunity to recover), rabbits affected by VHD mostly die in their burrows. It is as if a whole colony of rabbits has disappeared without trace overnight. The disease was first diagnosed in the UK in 1992 and can also be spread by insects such as flies and also by birds. Death usually occurs 12-36 hours after the onset of fever. Post-mortem examinations show haemorrhages throughout most of the internal organs, the liver being the most severely affected.

Returning briefly to Cymag and since it is relevant to this discussion I'll repeat an incident that I narrated in an earlier book, *A Lone Furrow*:

Cymag was taken off the market in late 2004. Its legitimate use in the gassing of rats and rabbits had come to an end, probably because of the real risk to the health of those using it. Its effects are of course fatal, though if caught early enough the drug amyl nitrate can sometimes ameliorate its effects.

Its effects were demonstrated in an incident in 2005 when a Perthshire gamekeeper found several part-filled Cymag tins left behind by his predecessor. For whatever reason he decided to put all the powder into one tin, and in so doing was badly affected by the toxic sodium cyanide fumes. An ambulance was called and, as is the case with fatal or potentially fatal accidents at a workplace, the police were informed. For my part, as force wildlife crime officer, I arranged for experts from Science and Advice for Scottish Agricultural (SASA) in Edinburgh to collect and make safe the Cymag. Meantime I phoned the previous manufacturer of the substance, Zeneca, a company based in Grangemouth. I spoke to a woman there, explained the incident that had just taken place, that a man was seriously ill from the effects of Cymag and was being taken to Ninewells Hospital in Dundee. Was there any further information she could give on Cymag that might be of assistance to the hospital?

She said she would need to speak with someone else first and could I hang on. I hung on. She came back to the telephone after a few minutes, and I must confess I was more than a little stunned by what she had to say. Very politely and in a matter-of-fact manner she said, 'I have to ask you first of all if the man was prescribed the Cymag by his doctor?'

New birds identified: mute swan, mallard, greylag goose, Canada goose, little grebe, tufted duck, osprey, heron, coot, meadow pipit, great-spotted woodpecker.
New mammals identified: None

CHAPTER 5

Wednesday 12 September. Mostly sunny, stiff breeze. 14⁰C.

Wester Cairnie, Nether Keir

I moved away from the centre of the estate today, slightly further west, to Wester Cairnie, one of the estate's tenanted farms. I've known this part of the estate well since I was at primary school and regularly visited a school friend of mine, Gerry Oliphant, at his parents' cottage at Cairnie Toll on the side of the old A9 now by-passed by a dual carriageway. I intended to park halfway down the Wester Cairnie Farm road at the Cairnie Strip, a narrow belt of conifers running north to south and which is now effectively doubled in width by a game/wild bird crop. A belt of sunflowers ran beside the farm road from the public road to the game/wild bird crop. Their cheery nodding yellow heads were in full bloom and all facing south-east to take advantage of the early morning sun. A dozen or so chaffinches flew across in front of me from the sunflowers to a hawthorn hedge at the other side of the farm road. Further chaffinch-sized birds perched on telephone wires above the sunflowers, maybe resting between feeds.

The area at the top of the Cairnie Strip had been widened since my last visit so my parking there would not in any way block the combine harvester if it needed access along the farm road. Harvesting is still in full swing, with much of the spring-sown wheat still to be cut. The fence at the top of the strip had also been removed and I could already see that the fence between the strip and the game/wild bird crop was in a very poor state. This had been a woodland with an unbelievable number of rabbits during the 1970s and 1980s, though it was a rabbit refuge that would have been relatively easy to clear through the use of Cymag.

I walked down the track between the strip and the game/wild bird crop. No rabbits and, surprisingly since there is a pheasant release pen at the bottom end and the strip, no pheasants either. The reason for the lack of pheasants became clear when I reached the pen. There were two extremely loud shotgun blasts which seemed to have gone off very close to me. Simultaneously I saw a woodpigeon change its flight path rapidly as it approached a single tree in the centre of a stubble field. There was a hide beneath the tree and despite the pigeon shooter being a good 200 yards from me the brisk south-westerly wind blew the sound in my direction, exaggerating the effect.

I cut diagonally left across a field of recently-sown tares or winter turnips to the top of Glenhead Den. This is – or at least was – a mature mixed woodland also running north to south and leading almost down to the River Earn at the Forteviot bridge. There had been changes here as well: the centre of the woodland had been almost clear-felled, and the fence between the wood and the field had been replaced by a deer fence, though without netting. Glenhead Den had been replanted with Scots pine and Douglas fir, though Himalayan balsam has spread through the wood and will need to be controlled until the young trees are strong enough to take over.

On my many walks in this area with my school friend Gerry, probably in the late 1950s, we found a chestnut tree in the centre of this wood with probably the biggest chestnuts I have ever seen. We visited it regularly in the autumn to collect conkers which, when we took them to school, almost always beat our pals' conkers in the competitions which seem now to be a thing of the past. I also saw that another tree, an ash this time, which had a broken and hollow limb and had been just outside the

bottom end of the wood, had finally succumbed to winter winds and had fallen over. This tree had been of particular interest as almost every year while I was rabbit trapping on the estate it hosted a goosander nest in the hollow limb. I noticed the female going in to the nest hole one day while I was checking snares and, while I never saw the goosander itself again, I saw evidence of down at the ragged edge of the hole every spring. I always wished I had been there when the wee downy goosanders were jumping out of the hollow limb and making their way down to the River Earn.

The walk westwards along the River Earn was extremely disappointing. It was no longer possible to walk right beside the river as there was a thick growth of Himalayan balsam keeping me at least five or six yards from the water's edge. Himalayan balsam, with its dark pink flowers, is not an unattractive plant but it is an invasive non-native species that has infested our waterways. It is quickly spread downstream by the dispersal of seeds or the careless movement of soil from one place to another. Even worse, the stretches of balsam were intermittently broken by patches of even more insidious invasive non-native plants: Japanese knotweed and giant hogweed.

Himalayan balsam and Japanese knotweed on the riverbank

The giant hogweed, being the worst of the unwelcome trio, seemed to be being tackled by the estate. They were quite small and were dying back, probably by the result of spraying, though it takes several years of specialised treatment to finally get rid of this unwanted plant. Formerly, when these river-side fields were in grass, sheep and cattle cropped the grass almost right to the riverbank, which made the riverside walk much more pleasant.

I watched a heron flying down to the river. The sun was shining on its blue-grey feathers as it banked away from me, giving them a lovely sheen. The bird was an adult with long black feathers on its crown and a yellow dagger beak that seemed to sparkle in the sun. My eyes were then drawn to what I thought were two brown birds jumping into the air about 20 yards ahead. I walked forward slowly, looking into a dip in the ground. Suddenly

three grey partridges exploded from the dip and flew close to the ground up the field. Grey partridges are one of my favourite birds, possibly because they are now so rare, but also because of their splendid looks: brown and grey plumage, orange face and chestnut horseshoe on their breast. I loved it most to hear their *kerr-ick* call from the edge of a field at dusk as the birds made contact with one another before going to roost, which is simply a matter of bedding down with other grey partridges on the ground, often in the open. I often found a covey of them bedded down for the night in a small group, most often with very little cover around them so that they could spot danger in the form of a prowler approaching. When I spoke with Stewart the keeper later he assured me these are wild-bred birds, which is great news and their nesting success may well

A young roe deer gazed at me through the long grass

have been assisted by the proliferation of new hawthorn hedges on the estate, with their undisturbed cover on either side.

I now had to crawl through one of these hawthorn hedges to get to the next field, possibly the only disadvantage of a hedge as compared to a fence. On its south side this field bordered an area of long rough grass, rushes, bog and (unfortunately) more Himalayan balsam which extended to the river. This was an area that formerly held several pools of water which were a great attraction in winter for teal and wigeon. I was always fascinated by the *wee-ooo* calls of the male wigeon, giving rise to their name as the whistling duck. If I happened to disturb them at the pools I was also amazed by how the teal just shot almost vertically up into the air. Unfortunately there were none today as the pools were almost dried up and in fact were full of balsam. This may

just have been due to the extremely dry summer but whether they will fill up in winter remains to be seen.

The hedge I was now walking alongside was not one of the new hawthorn hedges but a mix of older rowan trees, elder and of course, some hawthorn. A small bird flew in front of me landing near the top of one of the trees. It was a bird that seemed slightly out of place with the absence of wetlands: a male reed bunting. Maybe, like me, it was hoping the pools would fill up and the rushes would thrive again.

Two brown birds fluttered to the ground not far from me in the stubble field. Just before they landed I momentarily saw their crests through the binoculars, confirming them as skylarks. Like the grey partridges, skylarks are having a hard time and

41

their numbers are only a fraction of what they were. Dupplin Estate used to have a lot more permanent grass that was ideal for nesting skylarks, but the farming system has changed and there is now a lot more grain grown. Maybe leaving odd small squares unsown in the cereal fields at sowing time thereby creating 'skylark plots' where they can access the tall crop to nest would help. This seems to be working on some environmentally-friendly farms and is certainly worth a try, especially since the cost in lost grain is negligible. I noted that at the top of the field there was yet another strip of sunflowers augmenting a narrow den to create not just another pheasant drive but more winter feed for wild birds.

Before I left this field for the next I had a look inside a small brick building in the corner. It was beside a ditch and adjacent to a square of concrete with a drain cover on top. Though there was nothing in the building to indicate its purpose, I think it at one time housed a water pump. Since the door was open I wondered if it might be a place that a barn owl would frequent or even nest. There were no signs inside of barn owl use but there were two new swallow nests. One had definitely been used this year as there was a pile of droppings underneath and droppings down the edge of the nest. Another nest was in pristine condition and looked as if it had never been used. The swallows had bedfellows in the form a huge wasp bike just beside the small window. It was a real work of art, about eight inches in diameter and rather like a white turban which had been squeezed in between the lintel and the window frame. The wasps must have taken ages to chew the wood for its immaculate construction but they appeared no longer to be in residence.

I walked past a brown hare clapped down into its form. It was in a stubble field about 40 yards on the other side of the fence and, with the dividing fence, maybe felt safe. I wondered about crossing the fence to get a photo but it would have seen this change of direction as a threat and would have made off. Instead I took a couple of distant photos of what I thought was the hare but turned out to be a molehill that had been near to the hare. Damn!

I was now at the bottom of Cairnie Den, a deep den – almost a ravine – with mature trees on either side. Yet again a game/wild bird crop widened the den and its appeal to wildlife. The fencing had not changed on the den since I was last there over 30 years earlier. As I walked up the west side of the den I looked in vain for any signs of rabbits as this had been yet another stronghold. Not a dropping, not a scrape, not a rabbit run, not a rabbit. With its steep sides and tree roots this is most certainly not an area that could be successfully gassed and yet again supports my theory of VHD.

Half way up the den there were the remains of a toppled ash tree in the form of a sharp spike about 15 feet high. I had a pang of conscience as I remembered Gerry and I coming across a pile of logs just inside the fence that the farm workers, Jock Kettles and Geordie Begg, no doubt in their farm 'uniform' of dungarees, denim jacket and bunnet perched jauntily on the side of the head, had laboriously pulled up from the bottom of the den with a tractor and rope or chain. As typical boys we rolled all the logs down to the bottom again. It was probably when they were all at the bottom of the den that the realisation dawned that the farm workers would know perfectly well who had been responsible. We certainly got a row but the men, in time, saw the funny side and ribbed us about our misdemeanour for years afterwards.

My mood lightened when a family of blue tits flew from the sunflowers to a small rowan tree at the edge of the den. They flitted about the tree for several minutes while I hoped they would return to the sunflowers. They'd maybe had enough food for the time being as suddenly they were gone. The interest was replaced a minute or two later as I rounded a bend in the fence and disturbed a young roe deer which bounded a few steps then gazed at me through the long grass, with not much more visible other than its eyes and ears. Like the blue tits, it also vanished into the den.

I walked further west, now on to the former Nether Keir Farm, also farmed by the tenant of Wester Cairnie. I passed by the top of a conifer strip and was astonished to find a cherry tree. My astonishment turned to delight when I saw that the tree was laden with black cherries. Strange that all the red cherries on my cherry tree at home had been scoffed by birds, as were all the cherries on the gean (wild cherry) trees in my garden. The cherries that I could reach or pick off the ground tasted lovely, but it seemed as if black cherries are disdained by birds.

The old farm steading that I knew at Nether Keir was gone and all the grass fields had been made into one huge field that had held a cereal crop but has still to be re-sown. The remnants of a strip of phacelia, a plant with a blue flower used to attract pollinators, covered an area near the river at the east end of the field. At the far end of the field a group of common gulls plus a single immature gull, which was either a herring gull or a lesser black-backed gull, rested. They had been following a plough at the other side of the river but were relaxing in between meals of worms, other invertebrates and maybe even some mice and voles. The River Earn formed a great loop but as I could see with the binoculars that the banks were still covered with Himalayan balsam I decided to cut the corner to the far end. A cormorant had the same idea and flew high over my head. It was followed shortly after by three goosanders, all either female or immature birds with their brown heads rather than the black head of the mature male.

I checked out a new conifer strip but saw nothing more interesting than a few chaffinches that rose from the thistles at the side of the strip. I climbed back up to the top of the field where there are the remains of a wood that probably had held more rabbits than anywhere on the estate. I'd had a bumper day catching rabbits from this wood, with a total of just under 400.

I sat in the sun for a while trying to work out where the various fences had been in this now vast field. Times and farming practices change but the former Nether Keir Farm is certainly now more barren in terms of wildlife. I was slightly cheered up when two ravens flew overhead, their sheer size and wedge-shaped tails the main identifying features, and shortly after reinforced by a single and rather quiet *krukk* as they disappeared over the wood.

I followed a track back towards my car, passing a pond with the sound of quacking ducks. I knew they would be reared mallard and, since there was a banking between me and the pond, I sneaked past without disturbing them. Further along there was a very sick red-legged partridge at the side of the track. I'd no idea what was wrong with it and doubted that it would survive. I thought that would be my last interesting sighting of the day since I was nearly at my car but a blackbird chattered from the depths of (yet another) hawthorn hedge. Hardly a rare bird but the first I had identified on the estate up to that point.

New birds identified: grey partridge, reed bunting, skylark, blue tit, common gull, cormorant, goosander, raven, blackbird. New mammals identified: None

CHAPTER 6

Friday 21 September 2018. Sunny though became dull later. Light wind freshening later. 14⁰C.

Upper Cairnie

Today the area covered was Upper Cairnie farm, another of the estate's tenanted farms. I planned to park at Cairnie Toll cottages, my school pal Gerry's former house (now just Cairnie Toll cottage as the two houses have been combined into one). I drove slowly down the remaining section of the old A9, which is a curved piece of road, its juxtaposition to the new dual carriageway resembling an ox-bow lake in tarmac.

Just before the cottage there were some bushes on my left and gigantic piles of logs on my right. A flock of birds flitted from bush to bush and across in front of me to the log piles. They were mostly yellowhammers, but of the birds that landed on the logs and were more easily seen, a couple were linnets, one was a greenfinch and one was a robin, though I doubt that the robin, normally a solitary bird, would have been part of the flock. They kept in front of me as I drove at a snail's pace down the road, with some landing on telephone wires to my right and all eventually making for a group of birch trees beside the cottage.

I parked and walked up the track on the east side of the cottage which led to Cairnie Wood, a conifer plantation a few hundred yards further on. I checked among the group of birch trees adjacent to the cottage for some thick bushes which used to grow from a wet and boggy area there but they had been replaced by the trees. These had been interesting bushes in that they used to support a colony of nesting house sparrows. There were probably half a dozen nests every year and occasionally they were joined by a nesting moorhen. This was the first and only time I had encountered a moorhen which nested off the ground.

As I walked up the track I could see that the fields on either side had been expanded. On my right one field had replaced two, and on my left one field had replaced three. It seemed odd that in the centre of the estate on the land that was farmed 'in hand', miles of lovely hawthorn hedges had been planted, yet on these two tenanted farms that I had visited so far fences (though not hedges) had been ripped out. The original field immediately on my left had been really interesting for two reasons. Firstly it had a great attraction for lapwings and dozens nested in it. In a walk in a straight line across any part of the field in late March or early April at least three nests would be found and these lovely, crested, black and white and iridescent green and orange birds would be swooping and tumbling over the field with their haunting *peee-weep, weep-weep, peee-weep* calls. Secondly, many years ago, probably in the early 1960s when we were teenagers, Gerry and I watched a pure black hare in that field. It hopped about for fifteen or twenty minutes, gradually making towards the wood, then jumped the dyke and was lost among the trees. No-one else saw the hare that we were aware of and we were well enough acquainted with wild black rabbits (and many other colours of wild rabbits) that we certainly hadn't mixed up the two lagomorphs. It was strange that the hare was never seen again in the field or in nearby fields but its brief appearance and vanishing trick will remain one of life's mysteries.

In real time I had reached the wood by this point and turned right (east) along the woodland track. There had been heavy rain and gale-force winds two days earlier as remnants of Storm Ali and I was interested in the puddles

on the track that were starting to dry out and might reveal what animals has passed that way over the last 48 hours. There are few if any pheasants on this part of the estate but one puddle revealed the earlier presence of a woodpigeon. It had probably come down to drink and had left its footprints in the mud round the remaining water in the puddle. Further on, a roe deer had come out of the wood through a hole in the netting fence and crossed the track to a stubble field. Further round – I had turned left (north) by this time and was heading for the fields and house at Blairbell – there were much larger footprints on soft earth at the side of the track. These would most likely be from red deer as there are quite a number of these in the woodlands on the north of the estate now.

Just before the end of the woodland track and the entrance to Blairbell fields I spotted scattered white feathers on a grassy knoll. A closer look confirmed it had been a woodpigeon which had been eaten by a predator. All that remained of the carcass was the head. I examined some of the larger feathers and they showed signs of being plucked out of the body but no signs of being chewed. This gave the clue that the predator was a bird rather than a mammal. The most likely was a

Red deer footprint at Upper Cairnie

Single footprint from a feral cat in the tattie field

Woodpigeon eaten by a predator at Blairbell

peregrine, (or goshawk since this is only 100 yards from the west end of Pitcairnie Loch where on an earlier visit I'd seen one) though a buzzard or a female sparrowhawk could not be discounted. I have watched a buzzard chasing a woodpigeon for almost a mile before catching it and on the day of Storm Ali there were several of the wing feathers of a woodpigeon in my garden. A female sparrowhawk had been visiting and the day before had taken a collared dove. I suspected it had tried its luck with a woodpigeon though I'm not convinced it had managed to make a kill. Working out 'whodunit' in the countryside is fascinating.

I turned and retraced my steps, passing a group of shaggy inkcap toadstools that varied from young and pristine white cylinders coated with off-white roughcast to those that had been above ground for a few days and whose shape had altered to resemble policemen's helmets on stalks. They are edible when they are at an early stage though I'm never too sure of eating wild toadstools or mushroom unless they are the delicious yellow chanterelles. A single bird quite high in the sky caught my attention. I watched it for a while through the binoculars. Initially I thought it was one of the larger gulls but then realised it was a curlew. I also remembered that this was not the first time I had been in this identification quandary with a curlew. It is sometimes difficult to appreciate scale when a bird is in the sky and a curlew is in fact a sizeable bird almost equalling a lesser black-backed gull.

I made my way back along the field (now one field, formerly three) on the southern edge of Cairnie Wood. The last field had always been grass and had ridges running lengthways from the wood. It was termed the 'riggit field,' originating from the ridge (or rigg) and furrow method of ploughing. The ridges in this particular field were about five yards in width, with the height between the bottom and top of the ridge being about eighteen inches. When I snared in this field I always put the line of snares on the downward slope of the riggs for rabbits coming out of the wood. To have put them on the upward slope meant that the rabbits may have been able to see them silhouetted against the sky. These undulations may have survived for a century or more but this area is now regularly ploughed and cropped and the riggs are no longer visible.

I turned left (south) at the end of what had been the 'riggit field' down the edge of what I remember as a young coniferous wood which has now matured to tall evenly spaced trees. At

most gaps in the broken-down dyke roe deer and red deer had been coming from the wood into the newly sown field, their footprints telling the tale of their nocturnal perambulations. At the end of the 'young' wood there is a pond which always held a few mallard. When I peeped over the banking I expected it to be as it was but it had all but dried up and was now mostly mud. I was tempted to climb the fence, jump the ditch and scramble through the whin bushes to examine the mud for footprints. Twenty years, maybe even ten years ago, I would have tackled this but at 71 as I write this I'm beginning to know my limits.

Reluctantly I started off up the muddy edge of a tattie field which was bounded by a 40-yard-wide strip of ancient oak and beech trees, some of which showed recent serious storm damage, with recently-broken limbs joining the many already on the ground from previous storms. Roe and red deer had been coming from this strip and visiting the tattie field. As well as foot prints there were gaps in the tattie shaws (haulms to give them their posh name) where deer had been scraping to get at the tatties. The large round red Rooster variety of tatties had been damaged pretty severely with many munched or missing. In addition, potatoes were exposed to the sunlight where red deer had been tramping around on the drills with their large cloven hooves carrying, in the case of stags, maybe 150-200 kilos of body. Many of the tatties would now turn green before they were harvested and would be discarded either on the tattie harvester or when they were dressed to separate out damaged or small tatties (brock) from the main (ware) crop later in the year. A single footprint from a mammal much smaller in stature at first looked as if it had been made by a fox, but a closer inspection revealed that there were no claws visible at the end of the toes. It had been a feral pussy cat, which retracts its claws when walking, but it was odd that I could only see the one print.

At the end of the tattie field I crossed a fence into a steep field of permanent pasture. I walked along the top of the field, which is lined with elderly oak trees and hawthorn bushes. Burrows under the roots of these trees used to harbour many hundreds of rabbits but today there was not a sign of a rabbit. Like other parts of the estate this was not an area where the rabbits could be gassed with any great success since there were always unseen boltholes among the roots, many rabbits lay out in the rough grass and there were plenty of replacement rabbits just over the march fence on Gask Estate. This was another element in the rapidly building case that viral haemorrhagic disease had been the principle reason for the annihilation of Dupplin Estate rabbits.

Near the end of the grass banking two hawthorn bushes has succumbed to Storm Ali. They may well have been a hundred years old with trunks of at least 15 inches diameter. Both had been broken about two feet from the ground by the gale. One was still partially attached to the bottom of the trunk while the other had been blown over a fence and finished up 30 yards into the tattie field. The fence had been flattened, with the high tensile wires now as tight as bow strings and the top strand of barbed wire snapped. The damage certainly made it easier for me to cross the fence and shortly after to reach the old A9. It was strange walking up the old road, this tarmac ox-bow road, that I had driven on so often when it was a busy, if dangerous, steep and winding road, and now walking back to my car with no risk from traffic. It had been an unusual day. Some days are of sightings, some days of sounds, some of smells. This was definitely a day of footprints.

New birds identified:
yellowhammer, greenfinch, linnet, curlew.
New mammals identified:
red deer, feral cat.

CHAPTER 7

Friday 28 September 2018. Sunny and calm. 13⁰C.

River Earn at Sauchie Farm

I always enjoy a walk beside water, whether loch, pond or river. In this case it was a walk predominantly by the River Earn below Dupplin Gardens. As I parked my car a grey squirrel ran across the road from the field, climbed the high wall with ease and disappeared into the gardens. This was one yet to be caught by Gordon's traps.

There were a couple of anglers' cars beside the river at a part known as The Minister's Pool, and I met them downstream of their vehicles before too long. I had just returned from a few days in Speyside and during that time had been discussing Spey casting. A Spey cast was developed to deal with the number of trees and other obstructions on the River Spey compared with the open background for casting on many other rivers. The looped Spey cast can be executed in places with little or no room for a back cast and is also inherently much safer because the fly never goes behind the person casting. I could now see ordinary casting being executed by the first angler before I could see the actual

person with the rod. It was very amateurish but as I got closer (not too close to be hooked on a fly) I could see it was a young woman receiving tuition from possibly her father. I chatted for a minute but they had not hooked either a salmon or a sea trout as yet.

I had fished this same stretch of water, although almost forty years earlier, in the 1980s. My fishing had been for brown trout with a brown trout rod and a light line. I was lucky enough one day to catch a sea trout of about two pounds, and on another occasion hooked a salmon, which promptly broke my line.

I walked slowly down the riverbank, stopping regularly and looking ahead through the binoculars. In 2009 the previous gamekeeper for this part of the estate, Bill McIntosh, took me to a beaver lodge near this part of the river, though on the other bank. There is a strong chance beavers will still be in the area since they are now well spread out over the River Tay catchment, with numbers in the hundreds. I had been quite amazed at the size of the beaver

Beaver lodge on bank of River Earn in 2009

lodge and the amount of work its building had entailed. There were hundreds of short willow branches that the beaver or beavers had chewed from the many trees behind the lodge and all were worked into its design and structure, making a safe haven with an entrance under the bank of the river. I noticed at the time that a beaver had even climbed up the sloping branch of a willow tree and chewed off some branches about 6 feet from the ground. Nothing is so true as the axiom 'as busy as a beaver', but the chance of seeing a beaver in the river in the middle of the morning was slim and if any were around they were in bed.

The river then took a sharp left-hand bend and the far bank consisted of a vertical clay face around thirty feet high. I scanned this with the binoculars looking for any signs that sand martins had nested there. There were no sand martin nest holes but there was a single hole well up the bank and under an overhang. White splashes of dropping under the hole gave a good indication that this was most likely a kingfisher nest hole from earlier in the season.

Further along the river, on a patch of sand and shingle that was quite wet in places, I was on the lookout for footprints that might tell me who had recently visited. There were footprints of pheasants, many of smaller birds which could have been waders and one webbed set which was most likely a mallard duck. There was also a footprint of a fox; in fact two footprints, one overlapping the other, very fresh and clear and probably made during the night. If walking in a straight line the rear paw of a fox lands almost exactly in the place that the front paw has just been, hence the almost double print. The odd thing was – like the cat's print

Whooper swans, newly arrived from Iceland

in the tattie field at Upper Cairnie – that I could find no other fox prints.

The river went to the left again and it obviously flooded from time to time into a dip in the field, as there were willow trees and some Himalayan balsam growing in the dip. These were probably generated by seeds washed in by the flooding river. I went around this group of willows to see if there were any signs of beavers having snacked on the thin wispy stalks. As I emerged at the other end I saw four swans in the river. A quiet stalk got me closer and I was pleased to see they were whooper swans, newly arrived from Iceland after their breeding season. Whoopers are lovely swans, with black and yellow bills and straight necks, making them completely different from our own mute swans with their black and orange bills and curved necks. They also make a haunting whooping or trumpeting call, often when in flight. These were

four adults and as I gradually showed myself they slowly drifted off down the river.

Slightly away from the river and on my left was a small square wood of six or seven acres. It had some mature oaks and willows, including one really tall willow. I knew there was a pond, Sauchie Pond, in the centre of the wood, so I crossed the field to walk round the wood to get near it. The fields in the area were mostly grass which had been partly cut for silage or haylage. It was a desperate attempt to increase winter feed supplies since the grass was no more than 9 inches high. Nevertheless in times of necessity, and after the extremely dry summer, every blade of grass counts for winter fodder.

Though I could hear mallard quacking and chattering on the pond

Overlapping footprint of a fox on sand near the River Earn

the trees in the wood had grown so much that I couldn't see the water, far less the ducks. A buzzard overhead mewed as it circled above the wood, a delightful sound at any time of year but particularly in autumn when young buzzards are keeping in touch with their parents and vice versa. I disturbed a hare which had been resting inside the fence and it hopped off through the trees to find another spot in which to spend the remainder of the daytime hours. It will be surrounded by much more sweet young grass than it can eat shortly once the newly cut grass starts to grow again.

I walked across the field at the other side of the wood towards another area of woodland. This time it was one of a series of strips running down towards the river and consisting mainly of oak trees with a good sprinkling of ash, lime, birch, rowan, alder and some conifers. Yet another magnificent hawthorn hedge, new since I was last here, ran from the wood up to the little-used Sauchie Farm steading. As I was photographing the hawthorn hedge a roe doe appeared in the middle of the grass field I had just walked through, and exactly on the route I had taken. It had shed most of its foxy red summer coat and was now almost into its much

Nest box for barn owls at Sauchie Farm steading

53

darker winter coat. It was as if it had been following me. To reward its unusual interest in me I took its photograph before it trotted into the strip of woodland just down from me.

The doe had obviously gone through the strip and out the other side as it now viewed me from a dip in the next grass field as I crossed to the next woodland strip. Initially only its forward-facing ears down to just below its eyes were visible as it listened intently and watched my movements with interest. It then came fully into view, stared for a minute, and trotted across the field into the next strip of trees.

I walked up the side of the strip of trees where the doe had taken refuge, finishing at the Sauchie Farm steading. One of the sheds which had formerly housed sheep and cattle formed an L shape with another shed which had probably been used to store hay, straw or machinery. I had earlier noticed from the fields below the farm that the buildings were open and thought that, with the amount of rough grass and bog forming part of the half dozen or so strips of trees, that there would be plenty feeding in the form of mice and voles for barn owls. Since the steading looked an ideal nesting or roosting

place for owls I had a look inside.

Someone else had been thinking along the same lines and there were two nesting boxes for barn owls fitted inside the buildings. One even had a spattering of cement on the outside to replicate bird droppings. I looked under each of the boxes hoping to find some owl pellets but there was nothing to suggest that barn owls were present. There were plenty jackdaws though, and ten or twelve flew out of the building as I entered. They could certainly make good use of the nest boxes but they are messy nesters and there was nothing sticking out of the entrance holes to suggest jackdaws had hijacked boxes intended for *Tyto alba*. There was a jackdaw's nest high in the metal framework of the roof which had been constructed of sticks and sheep's wool. It was a large scruffy construction, though I'm sure the eggs and subsequent chicks would have been cosy in a nest with a wool lining. I found a jackdaw's nest years ago in a ruined house a field-width over the Dupplin Estate boundary. The jackdaws had dropped stick after stick down the chimney to the extent that the fireplace underneath was full of sticks. These continued right up the chimney to the eventual nest cup, which must have been near the top of the chimney otherwise the jackdaws would never have managed to come and go from the nest.

I suspect that these boxes would have been put up by retired gamekeeper Bill McIntosh some years earlier. He had reared and released a number of barn owls under licence from Scottish Natural Heritage. They had been successful in the wild and had colonised the area, regularly being seen up to ten miles from the release area.

As I passed through the old steading I suddenly spotted a freshly-dug rabbit burrow. Considering rabbits had not so long ago been by far the most common animal on this estate I was strangely excited by this discovery. I looked closer and could see not only fresh droppings on the sandy soil but a couple of paw marks. At last, confirmation that the humble wee rabbit was still here. I was even more pleased when I walked up the farm road and found several more active burrows under the hawthorn hedges at either side of the road. A three-quarter grown rabbit then ran from the hedgerow on my left and bolted into open woodland further up the farm road and near to where I had parked my car. I can hardly believe that the sighting of a rabbit had made my day. Let's hope that this wee colony thrives and breed like, well, rabbits.

New birds identified:
whooper swan
New mammals identified:
grey squirrel, fox, rabbit

CHAPTER 8

Wednesday 3 October 2018. Mild and calm. 11ºC.

River Earn at Aberdalgie Mains Farm

This morning got off to a bad start. I have to drive less than a mile from home via a single-track road known as the Moss Road to be on Dupplin Estate. This road is over an area of peatland known as Methven Moss. Methven Moss has no conifers anywhere near the road, only a mix of alder, birch and willow. Yet, despite the unsuitable habitat for red squirrels, I passed one lying dead on the road less than two miles from my house. We have a lot of red squirrels in the area and they are frequent and welcome visitors to our garden. This was a young red squirrel maybe looking for a territory of its own. Even though they are not uncommon it is a real pity to lose one as a road casualty, especially since few vehicles travel more than about 30 mph on the narrow Moss Road.

The next disappointment was also a road casualty, this time on part of the old A9, which has been integrated into the estate. There are few vehicles other than estate vehicles on this road and most drive very slowly, yet someone had managed to run over a young hedgehog. Hedgehogs, like red squirrels, need all the help they can get to maintain or boost their numbers. My spirits were lifted only when I drove past the estate sawmill and saw a lovely wee red squirrel busily caching a nut, and putting the final touches to its important business with a couple of pats to the ground with its front paws to ensure the nut was safely hidden.

I drove on through the centre of the estate and along the east drive. Despite having been along this drive a few times in the past weeks I'd never noticed until today that a long, narrow and in fact pretty useless field that always grew moss better than it did grass, had been planted out with native trees. This additional five acres of native woodland is a definite improvement.

I continued east and parked up in a position to continue my walk of last Friday on land between Sauchie Farm and the River Earn, then westwards towards Aberdalgie Mains Farm. I walked down a strip of trees in the

Exceptionally old alder tree in the bog below Sauchie Farm

direction of the river, disturbing a jay, which flew ahead of me – quietly for a change – and clearly showing off its white 'follow me' rump. The strip of trees led to an untidy pile of old fencing resembling a cross between a Guy Fawkes night bonfire stack and a roundabout. A wee brown dunnock flitted among the unsightly pile, which it no doubt considered a rather safe and warm piece of real estate. I walked round the pile, clockwise as I would treat a roundabout, and continued westwards along the edge of a wet, boggy area of bushes, stunted trees and rushes. The field I was in had been sown in winter wheat and the edge of the field showed lots of signs of visits from roe deer, with marks of their twin cleats and their droppings everywhere. Just now they would be having their daytime siesta among the thick cover in the bog but no doubt would be aware through their well-developed olfactory and aural senses that a human was close

by. I don't know if it was the droppings or simply the young spikes of growing wheat that was attracting them but there were also dozens of large brown slugs of a type I'd never seen before.

A heron had risen from somewhere ahead of me a few minutes earlier and I'd now passed the large white, watery splat of its faeces. I see this regularly on our drive at home, where a heron has rested for a while from the concentration of its fishing in the burn that runs through the garden. I now saw the heron watching me from the field on the top side of the strip of bog. Only its head and neck were visible, rising from the winter wheat crop like a snake under the spell of a snake charmer.

At the end of the bog I studied and photographed what was an exceptionally old alder tree. It had one very dark coloured main trunk of considerable girth and a narrower one appearing to arise from the same root system. The tree had small bunches of short purplish-coloured catkins hanging from some branches and also small bunches of grey-brown and mid-brown cones. I'm always fascinated by trees and wish that I knew a bit more about the many different species.

I cut back down towards the river, crossing a flood bank and into a field of blackfaced ewes. I spent many years on farms (East Lamberkin and Broxden, both on this estate and which I'll come to later) and I enjoyed working with sheep, but when there are a lot of sheep in a field, and when they have been there for a while, their dropping don't half stink and sour the grass. Deer realise this and almost as soon as sheep are put into a field, deer that had formerly been feeding there wisely move to another field. From the top of the flood bank I watched a cormorant flying up the river, gaining height as it saw an angler. Cormorants are not popular on fishing rivers and licences are sometimes issued on request by Scottish Natural Heritage to shoot a specified number. This is impossible to police and it is on trust to the people shooting that they stick to the quota authorised. Cormorants are clearly aware they are out of favour and most steer well clear of humans. Equally

unpopular is the carrion crow, and as I later sat on a stile beside the river a carrion crow flew over me well within shooting range. It had maybe not been paying attention to the teacher at the crow school of survival.

I had been enjoying my really comfortable seat on the stile with my sandwiches and bottle of fizzy water (from which the fizz had mostly gone due to the bottle shoogling about in my rucksack) but somewhat reluctantly set off downstream. At a bend in the river with what would be a deep, dark pool, several branches from a submerged tree that had been washed downstream were still visible above the surface, almost in the form of a drowning person waving for assistance. The submerged tree would provide a great resting place for salmon, trout and the considerable number of grayling that sometimes test anglers' skills in this river in the winter. A family of pied wagtails were flitting back and forth on the handful of branches, sometimes flying to a small area of gravel in middle of the river some twenty yards downstream, exposed temporarily because of the low water level. If they were parents and a clutch of youngsters the parents had done well, as there would be at least seven wagtails in total.

One of the pied wagtail family on the River Earn

I sat on the gravel bank and watched them for a while. Their name is most fitting as they are black and white in colour and their tails never stop flicking up and down. A chaffinch and a blue tit sat on a tree root that was growing out of the far banking, almost as spectators (as I was) to the pied wagtail show.

Further downstream still there was an interesting area of mud at the edge of a pool of water under a willow tree beside a shingle bank. I inspected the mud for footprints as I was interested in establishing the presence of beavers, otters or mink. Duck prints were all I could see but my attention was drawn to a reflection of a flock of birds in the pool of water. With such a big flock I immediately thought of fieldfares but when I looked up from this natural mirror the birds had either disappeared behind the willow tree or it had been a mirage. I came up to the riverbank but still couldn't see a flock of birds. I wondered if they had landed in the field of winter wheat at the other side of the flood bank and went to look. Indeed they had, but they were not fieldfares: they were skylarks. Around 40 skylarks rose from the field and whirled round my head, crossed the river, came back again, flew over the strip of trees at the far end of the field and landed briefly in

There were a decent number of yellowhammers on Mains of Aberdalgie Farm

the winter wheat again before finally disappearing over the river. I've no way of knowing whether they would be native birds, which flock in the winter in any case, or migrants from Scandinavia but it was a great sight as skylarks are yet another bird whose numbers are plummeting. Listening to a skylark singing high in the sky in spring and summer is most certainly one of the highlights, not just of bird watching, but simply of being aware of birds.

Immediately after the skylarks came another delight, this time skein after skein of pink-footed geese. All were quite high in the sky and heading south-west. One skein was slightly lower and I thought for a minute they might be thinking of landing but they gained height and continued after the earlier skeins. Thousands feed in the fields of this estate but normally they are those that arrive here from Greenland and Iceland a bit later. They delight in feeding in potato fields once the tatties have been harvested at the beginning of October but we are not quite at that stage yet.

As I walked further downstream a snipe rose from the point of an island in the river. This long-beaked brown bird with its white belly and white edges to the wings took off with its typical zig-zag flight. As well as confusing predators, this type of take-off also confuses shooters who have the bird in their sights as quarry since, rather surprisingly, it can still legally be shot. It is meant to be cooked and eaten still with the guts in, which I certainly don't fancy.

Looking further downstream with the binoculars I could see a small group of mallard at the far side of the river. As I came closer I could see that the group consisted of two drakes and four ducks. I went further out into the field to give them a wide berth and when I came back to the riverside further downstream I was pleased to see they were still contentedly swimming in the same place. I was hardly back to the river when up rose another snipe from a muddy area at the bottom of the riverbank. They love probing into damp places with their long beaks, which are an ideal tool to reach the invertebrates that they feed on. I was really satisfied at having seen snipe twice within half an hour.

I was not so lucky with my next identification. A small flock of birds rose from the edge of the river on the far bank. I had seen movement just before they rose, and got my binoculars up but I was too late. The birds were off, flying

A female reed bunting sat for a few minutes on an alder tree

in a loop then heading south away from the river. There were about 10 finch-sized birds and I suspect they had stopped off for a drink, possibly on an internal migration. I wondered about how the decision is made for the group to land. Is there a leader? Does one simply peel off and the rest follow or is there some way that they can communicate?

Just before I left the river I watched a single swallow busily catching flies over the water. Being so late migrating I suspect it still had chicks in a nest somewhere. The weather is still mild but it could be caught out very soon by cold weather which would drastically reduce its food supply. Even if the chicks fledged now would they be

strong enough to make it across the Sahara to the southern half of Africa? Pretty doubtful. As I watched the swallow I could hear the *prukk, prukk* of a raven behind me. I couldn't see it so it must have been in one of the trees further up the river and on the other side. It's good to see that this largest and arguably most intelligent member of the corvid family is becoming more widespread.

I now headed up the hill to the east boundary of the estate, about half a mile away. I knew from my trapping years that there were blackthorn bushes there and I hoped they had as good a crop of berries as the other trees and bushes have this year. I was not disappointed and spent half an hour filling my sandwich box and a small plastic bag with sloe berries. Sloe gin is now the next step. The blackthorn bushes were at the top of a steep permanent grass field. As I climbed the hill, much more slowly than I used to, I was reflecting on the unusual colour of some of the rabbits I caught here. Nearly all wild rabbits are white underneath, but in a decent proportion of the rabbits that I caught the white bellies were replaced by a steel grey colour, a mixture of grey and black. Though I caught wild rabbits of many colours I'd never seen this type anywhere else.

I walked back the woodland edge towards Mains of Aberdalgie Farm, then down a track through a mix of whin bushes, rowan and elder trees. There was a good variety of small birds though, with blackbirds balancing on slender branches and picking off the elderberries and rowans, less agile dunnocks seeking morsels of food under the whins and a decent number of yellowhammers. Yellowhammers seem to have made a bit of a comeback in my part of Perthshire in the last couple of years, but though I *saw* plenty this summer I never did hear them singing their song *a little bit of bread and no cheese*.

Before I went to my car I walked down the side of yet another strip of trees that leads towards the river. A jay rose from an ash tree and flew over my head, giving me a lovely view of pink, black, white and brilliant blue feathers. Small brown birds did likewise, but were mere silhouettes and I was unable to identify them. I chanced on another of Bill's owl nest boxes, this time nailed to an ash tree, but unfortunately there was no way of knowing whether or not it was in use as a roost or had been used by owls for nesting.

My last birds of the day were reed buntings. I'd disturbed them from a bird seed crop which consisted of a type of reed. Three or four flew into the conifers in the strip of trees. At least one must have been an immature bird of this year as its breast feathers were more yellow than white. One, a female, sat for a few minutes on an alder tree. It is heartening to see these lovely birds becoming more common on farmland. I'm looking forward to spring and early summer now to hear these and other small birds singing.

New birds identified: pink-footed goose, snipe
New mammals identified: hedgehog

CHAPTER 9
Wednesday 10 October 2018.
Sunny and calm. Incredible 18⁰C.

Cotton Farm, East Lamberkin Farm

Again the day began on a negative note. When I passed a layby on one of the minor public roads running through the estate and not far off the A9 a large white builder's bag full of rubbish had been dumped. Empty paint tins, plastic cartons and other rubbish had spewed out of the bag, which was lying on its side, no doubt having been pulled in haste from a vehicle. This has been a common occurrence over the past few months and the builder's bags have superseded black bin liners and other large containers holding the rubbish. It is most likely the same person; a cheat who has probably conned some vulnerable elderly person into handing over a large sum of cash for an inferior painting or gardening job. The farm road at Cotton Farm, which was my destination for today, was the scene of another flytipping incident I encountered some time ago when a lorryload of used car tyres was dumped. The culprit in this case was probably paid by an unscrupulous tyre depot for getting rid of the tyres.

Cotton Farm is worked by the tenant of Windyedge Farm and I noted on the way up the farm road an area where a large block of mature sitka spruce had been replanted with sycamore. I wanted to look round a game/bird seed crop which appeared to be about 10 acres of what looked very like millet. This will be a great draw for birds over the winter and I was hopeful that small birds would already be utilising this tremendous food source.

En route to the millet crop I walked round the edge of Cotton Wood and Coldwells Wood, both extensive woodlands of mature sitka spruce. A pair of ravens flew high over my head, deep in conversation and croaking loudly to each other; I wish I could have understood them. A hare rose as I cut over a stubble field to the gate leading into the field with the millet. It bounded effortlessly down the hill and through the open gate that I still had to reach.

The millet was amazing as a food source. I took several ears and rubbed them between my hands, finishing with enough seed that would easily have kept a budgie well fed for a couple of days. I walked along the bottom of the field then turned right up the west end of Milton Den. As I turned right a flock of birds flew from the millet and landed in bushes. As I got closer most of them, frustratingly, flew further on to other bushes, with several other flocks from the field joining them. Some then passed over my head and landed back in the bushes they had just come from. With a bit of patience I eventually managed to get the binoculars on to one which kept still long enough to be identified as a yellowhammer. Soon it was joined by more yellowhammers, and I could see a couple of dunnocks fidgeting around on the ground near to one of the feeders beside a pheasant pen. This area was a veritable banquet for small birds.

I continued round the millet crop, with still more flocks rising from its depths and landing ahead of or behind me in the bushes. In total there would be several hundred birds feeding on this crop. I gradually managed to identify some of them. Many were chaffinches and yellowhammers and a few were greenfinches. I was interested to see if the flock had been joined yet by bramblings that migrate here in late autumn from Northern Europe but I could see none. Pity I couldn't get them all to line up on the top wire of the fence, one between each pair of barbs, for inspection.

I was pleased that I had visited the game/bird seed crop and will give it a visit during colder weather to see if it attracts even more birds, but I now headed back towards the car. As I walked along the edge of a rough strip of grass bordering a field a cock pheasant suddenly jumped a few feet into the air, clearly spooked. A brown hare had been the cause and it ran from the rough grass, ears flat along its back to lessen its profile until it was at what it considered a safe distance from me, when the ears became erect again. I could hear ravens again from the direction of Coldwells Wood, three quarters of a mile away. This is where I thought I'd heard a single *prukk* of a raven on my visit to Milton Den on 29th August. If ravens are nesting anywhere on the estate this is where it will be.

Continuing my walk, I passed along the edge of a field of winter turnips. A small flock of birds rose from the field and landed in some ash trees bordering the field, but they quickly dived back down into the turnips again before I could identify them. One bird remained in the trees, a goldfinch, though I doubt that the rest of the birds were of the

What is this game/bird seed crop at Cotton Farm. Not millet

same species. My eyes still on the treetops, I spotted a buzzard's nest, a large twiggy structure high in another ash tree and many times the size of a woodpigeon's nest. A buzzard was lazily circling high above, which may well have been the occupant of the nest earlier in the year.

I moved further east to East Lamberkin Farm, where I had spent most of my youth. East Lamberkin sits between the farms of East-Mid Lamberkin and Broxden Farm, Broxden being where I worked for several months after leaving school and before joining Perth and Kinross Constabulary. At that time all were tenanted by brothers, George (East-Mid Lamberkin),

Bill (East Lamberkin), and Robert (Broxden) Robb, though the tenancy for East Lamberkin was relinquished to the estate in 2010. It had been over 50 years since I walked any of these fields and I was really looking forward to seeing what changes had taken place.

There are two main strips of trees on the farm, one at the other (north) side of the A9 which we referred to as 'Down the Strip,' and the second, which we called ''Up the Strip', running from the farm up to Lamberkin Wood, a mature larch wood. I started off ''Down the Strip' and was immediately disappointed that it was rather overgrown, probably because it had been so long since cattle or sheep had access to it. The trees, mostly oak, beech and Scots pine, were certainly showing their age. They had always provided plenty nesting places for birds, particularly starlings, tree sparrows, jackdaws and tawny owls, but they were even more suited to that purpose now. Many still had suitable holes for nesting but there were now many with cracks in the bark which would be ideal for treecreepers. Some were completely dead, almost devoid of branches and pockmarked with holes made by burrowing beetles and possibly woodpeckers. As I stepped from behind a bush I was almost hit by a buzzard that had been swooping low to the ground, giving us both a fright.

A bit further on there was a pile of droppings that I was sure were from red deer. They were much larger than those of roe deer though with nothing to compare them against I couldn't be 100% sure. I remembered a very large patch of blackthorn bushes near the bottom of the strip and was keen to see if I could add to my collection of sloe berries (you can never have enough sloe gin). Disappointingly I could only see a single berry. I could hear blackbirds in the bushes so if there had been a bigger crop birds may have

harvested them. If so their need was greater than mine.

I remembered a tree beside the blackthorns in which a pair of tawny owls always nested. Jimmy Robb, my primary school class-mate at the time and now long-time friend, along with his brothers Alex and David and I, climbed up to many nests in the strip but never to that of the owls. We were aware that the naturalist Eric Hosking had lost an eye to a tawny owl when he had gone to its nest so we always sneaked past that tree. Today the tree had deteriorated badly and I could see the remnants of a jackdaw's nest through a gap in the rotted bark. There would be plenty other choice of nest sites for the owls.

I had a look at the ditch that ran along the field at the bottom of the strip. It used to have a large colony of water voles in its banks and we frequently got a glimpse of one as it plopped into the water. There was very little water to sustain water voles now and they were long gone. There was a slight compensation in that part of the field was boggy and covered in rushes. It could be a place favoured by moorhens in the spring and is the type of place that a fox or roe deer is likely to lie up during the day. On the return journey I walked up the edge of the field of oil seed rape bordering the strip and was amazed at the number of footprints of red deer, quite remarkable considering that I was just over half a mile from the city of Perth. My assessment of the droppings seen earlier had been correct.

Next stop was 'Up the Strip'. The original oaks and beech trees had been felled some 40 years earlier and it had been replanted with young versions of the same tree species. They had grown well and, despite being fenced though not netted, there was very little ground cover. A hare rose from the strip and ran out the far side and up to the wood. I was not far behind it in reaching the wood and I sat on a log just inside the wood to have my piece. The larches had been thinned since I was last here and the wood was now quite open. This corner of the wood had always been a popular place for red squirrels, nevertheless I was quite surprised to see a red squirrel suddenly appear at the bottom of the tree next to me, not 10 yards away. I slowly put down my sandwich and reached into my pocket for the camera. I took my eyes off the squirrel for a second and when I looked back with the camera ready it had vanished. I sat for about 15 minutes sure that I would see it again

somewhere in the treetops but it really had disappeared. Somewhat disappointed I continued up through the wood, that route cutting out the climbing of two fences in the fields. I was watching the treetops for squirrels but the only thing of interest in the trees was an old buzzard nest, while at ground level I disturbed yet another brown hare.

The larch trees in the wood gradually gave way to Scots pine, with a line of beech trees on the outside edge. Further on there had been sitka spruce but they had been clear felled and replanted with what looked like fir. These had been surrounded by a brand new deer and rabbit-proof fence. By this time I'd crossed into the farm's topmost field, the moor, and was pleased to see that there was a strip of rushes running almost completely around the field. The moor had been a field that was in permanent pasture for years. It used to have a strip of whin bushes about 40 yards wide at the east end and running the length of the field. As young teenagers we thought it a good idea to reclaim this land and spent days one winter with the wee grey Fergie tractor and a chain pulling out and burning the whins. We did effectively reclaim that piece of land and in due course the whole field was put in crop, but I have always had a pang of guilt about what we did. The whins gave great nesting cover to many birds. In the years before we 'improved' the land we had found the nests of dunnock, linnet, chaffinch and yellowhammer in that area. Amazingly we had even found a woodpigeon's nest with two eggs *on the ground*, despite its proximity to woodland and adequate tree-nesting availability. The rushes round the edge of the field in no way make up for the loss of the habitat we destroyed.

I looked over the fence onto Broxden Farm fields, only two of which remain, the rest having been swallowed up by various business premises and a park and ride. They looked pretty much the same as when I used to work them and, even before that time and from about the age of ten, when we set snares for hares along the woodside fence. We caught a young capercaillie one morning, which were very common in the woods of Dupplin Estate. It was dead so I took it home and my mother cooked it and we ate it. Capercaillie are said to taste of pine but that one certainly tasted lovely, maybe somewhere between a pheasant and a duck.

On the walk back to the farm a flock of maybe 50 birds rose from the edge of a field of oil seed rape. They flew over my head and I watched them with the binoculars, hoping to get an identification. I could see they were going to land in the grass field about 100 yards from me. They did land, but out of sight just over a small crest so that I was none the wiser as to what they were. I wondered about walking closer but I could see that the north country cheviot lambs – probably bought in August at the lamb sales at Lairg in Sutherland and brought to Perthshire for fattening or even breeding – were going to run over the crest well before I got there and disturb the birds. I left well alone and had a look along at the thistles and weeds at the edge of the oil seed rape, where the flock had originated. Four sparrow-sized birds were sitting on the fence there. Through the binoculars I could see that they had forked tails, streaked sides, and of the two that I could see clearest, one had a white breast and orange chin while the other had a white breast and a more yellow chin. Most importantly for identification they had tiny bills. I was happy that they were twite, though whether they had been part of the main flock I've no idea.

I had a wander through the steading

A buzzard nest high in an ash tree

when I reached the farm. On the site of the former stackyard new corrugated metal sheds had been built, probably for the storage of grain. Their only occupants now were half a dozen feral pigeons. The old round shed, so often the centrepiece of farm steadings, had gone. With an open side it was a favourite place for swallows nesting, and easy to check their nests when hay bales were built up close to the roof. From the ground swallows' nests look pretty cold structures but with a cup well lined with layers of insulating feathers the inside of the nest must be as cosy as toast for the newly hatched young.

I walked in to the older part of the steading. Three sheds that had been used for holding straw and turnips, or sometimes sheep and very early lambs in December, had been combined into one. The old 'neep cutter' that cut the turnips into giant chips for the cattle was gone, though two or three of the wire baskets that were used to hold the

The tawny owl nest tree on East Lamberkin Farm, now taken over by jackdaws

69

The old byre at East Lamberkin Farm

chipped turnips were stored in the rafters. I'd climbed along these rafters many times checking out swallows' nests, though I only saw one nest remaining from the season just past. Looking down the passage between the neep shed and the byre, with troughs on each side for feeding the cattle, I could see that the 'reeds' or cattle courts had long been empty.

The byre was also bereft of life. I stood there awhile poignantly thinking back to very nearly sixty years earlier and I could almost hear the low, contented moaning of the Friesian cattle, the rattling of their chains as they reached up for some hay from the hayrack or down for some bruised oats or cattle cake from their trough. I could

almost hear the gurgling of the water as the cattle pressed down on the paddle which released water into their individual drinking bowls. I could almost smell their dung, which lay among some straw in the grip between the stalls and the passageway. The byre had five double stalls and a single one. The cattle that spent the winter in these cosy surroundings came in as nervous and excitable beasts. Because of their daily very close contact with humans squeezing between them to feed, bed and muck them out they left in the spring to go back to pasture as canny, confident cattle. I had a vivid image of Spot, the almost-white collie, tethered in the single stall, his tail wagging furiously as he jumped out of the trough lined with straw that was his cosy bed. Next door in the 'wee byre' there were a further couple of double stalls that held the house cow, normally a Friesian, a gentle cow which was hand-milked twice daily. Over the winter time she shared that byre with three companions.

Because farming has changed so much in the past 50 years, with huge machinery, increased grain production and the associated sprays rather than fields of weedy turnips or grass, wildlife has had to change as well. East Lamberkin, along with countless other farms, had nesting lapwings, skylarks and grey partridges in abundance; maybe even nesting corn buntings, though I don't remember seeing them. Birds that nest on the ground in fields have little success now as the eggs or

chicks are flattened by machinery or chicks are chopped up during silage-making. If they survive there is often little food for them as most insect life or weeds have been sprayed. While the production of food is important there has to be some sort of compromise with nature and the environment.

I later spoke with Stewart the keeper about the field with the crop I thought looked like millet. In fact the crop is quinoa, sown partly as a game crop but primarily for a range of finches and other seed eaters. In effect the sacrifice of 10 acres of land for a crop like this is a perfect example of compromise.

New birds identified:
feral pigeon, greenfinch, twite
New mammals identified: none

CHAPTER 10
Wednesday 17 October 2018.
Sunny with slight wind. 12⁰C.

Blairbell, Lochs, Westmuir

I started off at Blairbell Moor which lies to the north of Pitcairnie Loch, a large area of permanent pasture with patches of hawthorn, birch and a lovely area of ancient Scots pines. Blackfaced ewes had been put on to this area since I last gave it a fleeting visit and there was little in the way of wildlife save for a couple of mewing buzzards soaring over the Scots pines. A flock of birds, thrush size, flew overhead but I was looking into the sun and they were simply silhouettes. They would most likely have been fieldfares or redwing, or maybe even a mix of both on their migration from Iceland or Scandinavia. They were heading south-west and didn't look like they were putting off time in these parts.

With Blairbell Moor being rather quiet I headed for Pitcairnie Loch. I could see as I approached that there was a huge number of swans on the water. I managed to get quite close and sit with my back to a tree on the north bank near the water's edge and was treated to a delightful hour of sight and sound.

These were mute swans, well over a hundred of them, nearly all adult. They were all at the west and south-west parts of the loch and today their name was a bit of a misnomer as they were anything but mute. There was an interesting and continuous mixture of snorts and grunts as they communicated with each other. Some of the sounds were by way of a threat and accompanied by raised wings and an outstretched neck. There was something more serious going on with some of the swans on the south-west side of the loch, with a regular splashing and beating of wings. Twice a swan from the farthest away group took off and half flew, half ran across the loch to join swans nearer to me. Neither of these swans actually left the surface of the water, with their massive black paddles being in constant contact. They were in effect walking – or at least running – on water, though they could only do so with the assistance of their wings.

Mallard were constantly quacking, a loud harsh quack to start with followed

Mute swans and wigeon on Pitcairnie Loch

by several more quacks gradually reducing in volume but increasing in tempo. It is the ducks rather than the drakes which make all this noise, and it could be imagined that one had told a joke and the others were all joining in with laughter. The drakes are limited to a much quieter and higher pitched quack, as if tenor to the ducks' baritone.

A whistled *whee-ooo,* the call of a drake wigeon, alerted me to a dozen of these colourful ducks near the west bank. I paid more attention then and watched the group for a while through the binoculars. Often called the whistling duck, they are lovely looking ducks, especially the drake with his chestnut-coloured head, yellow forehead, pink breast, grey body and

black tail. Some tufted duck, both males and females, and a little grebe swam silently in the middle distance. Three black and white Canada geese, occasionally swimming among the swans, and a heron standing in the shallows made up the complement of waterfowl.

A further flock of thrush-sized birds flew over the loch in a south-west direction, but I was still unable to identify them. Frustratingly, I was also unable to see a common crossbill that from time to time gave voice to its *chip, chip, chip, chip* call in a tree somewhere above me. The sound seemed to come from either a birch tree with golden autumnal leaves through

Part of the 'band of buglers', whooper swans on Pitcairnie Loch

which the sun was shining, or a spruce tree with a thick canopy that gave little chance of seeing anything. My only hope was that I could see some movement, especially since there were likely to be several of them, but all was still.

My thoughts were taken off the crossbill (or crossbills) when I heard a band of buglers approaching. They were still some way behind me but rapidly on their way. Suddenly they were right over me. Their landing gear was down and they did a tight circle, losing height quickly until they landed on the loch, with their paddles first running along the water. The whooper

A coot and a moorhen swam just out from the reeds at the east end of Dupplin Loch

swans seemed quite at ease among so many mute swans and though they swam alongside them they never truly mingled. Their constant *hoop, hoop, hoop, oo, oo*, calls overshadowed all the other sounds from the loch as they chattered loudly to each other. Their avian conversations were a joy to listen to and I sat longer than I had intended at the base of the tree, my sandwich long since finished.

I had little time left before heading for my next stop but made a quick visit along the quarter mile or so to Dupplin Loch to see what bird life was there. It was remarkably quiet, with only four mute swans that I could see, a dozen or so mallard and a coot and a moorhen swimming just out from the reeds at the east end. For whatever reason, Pitcairnie was the place to be today. A jay screeched at me from an oak tree and a bird that looked remarkably like a goshawk flew fast over the loch; it was simply that the tail looked slightly longer than that of a buzzard. By the time I got my binoculars up the bird had disappeared behind trees so my suspicions could not be confirmed.

I returned to the car via Pitcairnie Loch but it was much quieter now. It had simply been a stopping-off point for the whooper flock and they had continued on their migration south.

I drove along the road quarter of a mile and parked at the opposite side of the public road at Westmuir, an extensive area of permanent pasture, birch woodlands and a strip of beech and Scots pine trees. I was surprised

how long the grass was compared to my regular visits there 30 years earlier. Even though there were signs of sheep and cattle having been on the moor earlier in the year, it is rabbits that keep grass well cropped. This was yet another part of the estate that had hundreds if not thousands of rabbits but there is not a trace of them remaining. Even burrows that had been quite extensive and had been in the middle of the grass field could only be recognised now by uneven ground.

I walked the three quarters of a mile to the bottom end of the moor and my list of interesting things to see comprised only of a single mewing buzzard and yet another flock of thrush-sized birds flying south-west. They were probably fieldfares since I saw a flock of several hundred feeding on hawthorn bushes laden with dark red berries just on the estate boundary on my way home later, so these winter migrants had definitely arrived from the cold north.

I had walked down the east side of the moor and as I crossed to the west side for my return journey a few hundred pink-footed geese at a time rose from a field on West Cultmalundie Farm and flew westwards over me. It looked as if they were keen to land on a stubble field just over the estate boundary on Mayfield Farm. They parachuted down towards the field but suddenly changed their collective mind and started to gain height again. I could see the reason for abandoning their intended plan was a single roe doe that determinedly stood in the middle of the stubble, despite these hundreds of wings beating almost round its head. Roe deer – 1; geese – nil.

I walked part-way up the line of mature beech and Scots pine, stopping for a while to watch a small flock of birds feeding at the top of two beech trees. They flew back and forth between the treetops, mostly landing where a branch obscured my view or straight above me so that I was at risk of falling on my backside while trying to look directly overhead. One of the trees still had a lot of leaves so I was depending on the birds perching long enough for identification on the tree that was most bare. I only managed to identify two birds of the flock: a chaffinch and a brambling. Bramblings often mix with chaffinches during their spell in the UK but I couldn't ascertain which was the predominant species in this flock.

Cutting back across the top of the field to the car I noticed that something had been scraping in the grass. It had gone down about 6 inches, scraping out sizeable chunks of turf in the process. The hole it had made finished with two smooth, wide indentations caused by the animal's muzzle. As I looked around there were about 20 identical scrapes in an area about 30 yards square. The digs

One of 20 badger scrapes on Westmuir

were fresh, no more than two days old, and I was hopeful of finding a footprint of the digger. I did find one footprint. It lacked any detail but was a broad print. Taking the size of the footprint, the size of the divots dislodged, the width of the animal's nose (as compared to that of a fox) and its propensity to dig in this manner for worms, larvae and other invertebrates it could only have been a foraging badger. I've never known of badgers in this area so this was a welcome find.

New birds identified:
pochard, crossbill, brambling, fieldfare
New mammals identified:
badger

CHAPTER 11

Wednesday 31 October 2018. Dull, slight rain but no wind. 5⁰C.

West Cultmalundie Farm, Greenhill Farm

Today I swithered whether or not to go out. The weather forecast was light rain followed in the second half of the morning by heavy rain. The forecast has been wrong in the past so I decided to chance it. The worst that could happen is that I would get wet and that wildlife with more sense than me would remain where it was dry and warm.

I parked a little over a mile from my house and walked up a farm track towards Cultmalundie Wood. I hadn't gone far before I spotted fox footprints in sand that had been washed down the track after heavy rain a couple of nights earlier. The fox had also been walking up the track – the easiest place for either of us to walk rather than in the stubble field – and I saw its tracks intermittently for over 100 yards until the sandy track was replaced by a stony surface.

At the top of the track was a large slab of concrete juxtaposed to a shed, both of which I thought were related to a water system. On top of the concrete was a freshly killed woodpigeon with white feathers scattered all around it. A raptor of some sort had killed it, partially plucked it and had eaten through its back into the heart and lungs. Very little had been eaten and I wonder if the raptor had been disturbed during its meal. I turned the pigeon over and its breast was bare of feathers. I doubted this was the work of the raptor; more likely it was a female pigeon and this was a brood patch to help convey heat from the bird to its clutch of two white, almost round, eggs, and subsequently to newly-hatched chicks. There was a good chance whatever had been feeding on the pigeon would come back for another feed. The fox, if it travels the same route two nights running, might get the remains.

I then followed a strip of ancient beech trees for about a mile up towards Cultmalundie Wood. I eventually climbed the fence into the strip as the long grass and nettles outside the fence were beginning to be hard going. I disturbed two roe deer, which appeared to join up with another three as within

A very new and posh high seat on Greenhill Farm

a few minutes two does, two bucks and a fawn were studying me from the safe distance of the centre of a field of winter barley some 200 yards away. This group ran off towards the wood but must have crossed back through the strip further up since I later saw them chasing after each other in a set-aside field adjacent to the wood.

My attention was then taken by a group of small birds that were flitting between two beech trees and the old upturned root of a long-dead tree. With damp binoculars it took a good few minutes to identify the birds as coal tits. Coal tits in my garden have been emptying the bird feeders of sunflower hearts in no time. Most of the seeds are being buried in flower pots or hidden in secret crevices in trees and I wondered if this equally-active group were also caching food for the winter.

Near the top of the strip the trees gradually changed from beech to equally-old, tattered but still beautiful Scots pine. Many had lost lower limbs to gales, with some having only a handful of branches remaining at the top. I could see that the five roe deer had crossed through the strip yet again and were running along the woodside fence. One by one, and without any panic, these graceful cervines jumped the fence into the woodland and were lost amongst the birch trees that formed that part of the wood.

Footprints of an otter in the mud in the burn

An overlapping fox print in a gap in the whin bushes

I walked along the woodland fence-side, examining any gap where the woodland creatures could exit to the field. As the crow flies I was less than a mile from where I had seen signs of badgers foraging two weeks earlier so I was particularly looking for evidence of the passage of badgers through the fence in the form of footprints or guard hairs caught on the fence. Badger hair is easily identified: it is oval in cross-section and if it is rolled between finger and thumb this can easily be felt. No luck. Despite the amount of barbed wire used on fences, that I curse regularly, there was no barbed wire where it needed to be to snag a few guard hairs from a badger. There were two very interesting runs going out from gaps in the fence and easily visible well out into the field. They may well have been made by badgers cutting through the growing grain in the summer time, but they were much more likely to have been made by roe and red deer.

At the end of the wood I turned right down a line of whin bushes edging a farm track that led into the wood. This took me to a small square wood with a pheasant release pen which didn't look as if it had been in use for years. At the edge of this wood was a very new and posh high seat from which deer could be shot. It had slats looking out towards the field, that could be closed up when the high seat was not in use. I wouldn't have been surprised if it also contained an armchair and electricity to boil a kettle.

Following a track past the high seat took me in due course along the edge of another birch wood. I had been preceded along the track by several roe deer and their dainty cleats had left plenty marks in the wetter parts. At some point a red deer had also used the track. Its huge footprints made an interesting comparison with those of its smaller cervine cousins.

At the corner of the wood I left the track and cut right-handed, now on Greenhill Farm, through a field of permanent pasture with many wetter parts filled with knee-high rushes. When I walked through one of these rushy areas I disturbed another two roe deer, that bounded off towards another birch wood on my left. The rain was coming down a bit heavier and they would be drier in the wood anyhow, rather than lying amongst damp rushes. Next to flee zig-zagging from the rushes was a snipe. This is an ideal area for snipe and had I walked through more of the rushy area rather than the easier walking on short grass I'm sure I would

have seen several more. On an open part of the field I put up a brown hare, which loped away from its form. I had a look at where the hare had been lying and it certainly looked cosy, almost justifying a 'please do not disturb' sign.

At the bottom corner of the field I noticed that a narrow burn had been flowing down just inside the march fence. I followed this burn back up the fence line for a bit as there were a number of sandy – or at least muddy – areas which might be of interest. Sure enough there were footprints of an otter at one point where it had been following the burn upstream. There were two prints, almost on top of each other though not quite. They were much broader than those of a fox though not as broad as those of a badger. Where a badger has its four – or sometimes even five – toes almost in a line, the otter's print shows the two middle toes forward of the two outside toes. Had the mud been slightly drier I may also have seen evidence of the webbing an otter has between its toes. As I cut back through a gap in whin bushes to the grass field, using a muddy path that cattle had made, I could see from footprints that a fox had used the same gap. It was an interesting and almost immediate comparison with those of an otter not ten yards away.

Gradually heading back now towards where I had parked my car, and by this time having walked the best part of five miles, I walked the edge of a loose line of birch trees. A flock of small birds had flown into the nearest tree and I approached it slowly trying to identify the birds. Since the birds wouldn't stay still long enough, and since my binoculars were damp and quickly became covered in raindrops I failed in this mission but could see another chance as the birds had now flown ahead to the next tree.

A redwing on a hawthorn bush on Methven Moss

Fieldfares were mixed in with the redwings on Methven Moss

I was more successful this time and could see, in very poor conditions, that some of the birds were dull orange and some were olive-green, so at least some of the flock were crossbills. A small part of the flock seemed quite settled high in the birch tree and were concentrating hard in obtaining seeds. I could also hear an occasional crossbill's call, *chip, chip, chip,* as the birds communicated with each other. I tried to take a photo of this small group but although a couple of birds were in the photo, against a leaden sky no colour was recorded and they were in fact in silhouette. I suddenly saw movement on the same tree, though lower down. This time it was a treecreeper, which climbed up and round the back of the trunk in its search of hidden insects.

This wee brown and white bird's stiff tail feathers are ideal to assist its climbing ability and its long downward-curving beak is the perfect tool to probe for edible morsels.

I'd one stubble field to traverse before reaching the car. As I climbed the fence into the field I disturbed yet another two roe deer, that ran down the grass strip at the edge of the field, jumped the fence and curled back over the grass field I'd just come through. Roe deer seem to be increasing everywhere and I'd certainly seen evidence of that today. Unfortunately increases in numbers means increased road casualties, usually fatal for the deer and often a real risk to road users. Another brown hare rose from the stubble just ahead of me. In a stubble field they always lie between the rows of stubble, usually picking a place where the stubble is just a bit longer and always where they have the best view around them. Despite their camouflage, when crossing a stubble field it is often possible to spot them if you look along the rows of stubble. Sometimes they can be approached to within several yards if you approach as if you would walk past them rather than directly on to them. It is sometimes also possible to circle them, getting gradually closer.

I reached the car just as the first blink of sun of the day appeared. Typical! My route home was via the Moss Road, which runs down the boundary of the estate. The flock of several hundred fieldfares was still feeding on the hawthorn bushes at the roadside. I stopped briefly in a passing place (since this is a single-track road) and could see that there were actually more redwings than fieldfares. They had almost cleared the topmost branches of the trees of berries and were beginning to work downwards. Even with the numbers in the flock they will takes weeks to clear all of the berries. Suddenly a female merlin approached low from the field on the neighbour's side of the road. Most of the birds flew to the birch trees behind me but there didn't seem to be the same panic that might be caused by a sparrowhawk. The merlin didn't seem to be in hunting mode and maybe the birds recognised this. Even after the diminutive and graceful merlin, the smallest raptor in this area, had passed over the road I could see that there were still a few redwings in the hawthorn bushes. It was a lovely conclusion to a morning which I had thought, because of the weather, would yield little of interest.

New birds identified:
coal tit, tree creeper, redwing, merlin
New mammals identified:
otter

CHAPTER 12

Friday 2 November 2018. Sunny and mild. 7°C.

East and West Cultmalundie Farms

East and West Cultmalundie farms have extensive land and incorporate the fields of adjacent Newbigging Farm. The three old farm steadings are all but empty apart from 100-plus feral pigeons, many of which were sitting on the roof basking in the morning sun as I approached. East Cultmalundie steading in particular looked as if it might be a likely place to find barn owls. I had a search through most of the buildings that would be accessible to owls but there was no trace of owl pellets. Swallows had not missed the opportunity of open buildings though and there were several nests awaiting the arrival in April next year of their former occupants.

I drove further along the farm road to West Cultmalundie where I intended to park. A buzzard was perched in an ash tree in the field on my right with an odd arboreal companion: a large blue helium-filled balloon that had got stuck on one of the topmost branches. I had read in the newspaper a few days earlier of a father about to release a batch of balloons in remembrance of his son and

thought to myself that there was surely something much more suitable and less dangerous to the environment that he could do. This very morning I had read of a farmer who had found one of his calves that was chewing on a balloon, an act that could have killed it had the farmer not chanced upon it.

Once parked, I headed for Cultmalundie Woods around half a mile away. I cut through a stubble field, a mixture of birds flying above my head at various times. The first small flock was of fieldfares, then a larger flock of skylarks. The skylarks circled above me a couple of times then landed further across the stubble. Next came skein after skein of pink-footed geese that had been disturbed about a mile away. The first lot started to tumble out of the sky quarter of a mile from me, losing height rapidly with frequent side slips, to land in a stubble field of the adjacent Windyedge Farm. The other skeins started to head in the same direction and for a while the sky was full of zig-zags and arrowheads of geese, while the autumnal air was alive with their loud

Two of the red deer that visit West Cultmalundie from the woodlands

wink wink calls. By the time they all had landed there would have been several thousand. Despite suitable weather for ploughing this autumn there seems to be many more fields left in stubble to be ploughed during the winter, or even better for wildlife, next spring.

I reached the wood and began to check along the fence line for evidence of the comings and goings of wildlife. At any suitable gap in the fence it was clear that roe deer and red deer were regular visitors to the fields, probably in the evening and during the night. The large cleat prints of red deer and the smaller prints of roe deer were in evidence everywhere, but I was particularly interested in finding signs of badgers. I still hadn't found any evidence of a badger sett from which the badger could have originated that left the foraging marks I'd found on 17th October. I'd checked the contours of the Ordnance Survey map and there was nothing that indicated a likely spot for a sett. I'd checked the west end of

Cultmalundie Wood on 31st October. The woodland surface there was damp and spongy, not really the place for a sett. The east end where I was now was much older sitka spruce woodland and, though it was flat, could have held a sett in the root of a blown tree or an earthy bank not identifiable on the OS map.

I set off walking westwards along the fenceline. The first half mile still showed lots of evidence of deer coming into the field but neither a footprint nor badger hairs to be seen. There were several places where deer hair had become snagged on low-hanging barbed wire, but unfortunately no sign of the oval hairs of badgers. At one point a roe buck in the wood must have become aware of my presence and responded with a very loud *buuuff, buuuff-buff-buff*, probably made as it ran off through the trees.

The next half mile was netted against deer and rabbits so no marks there. Though there were no clear signs of rabbits here now I remembered that the rabbits I caught here were huge; a full half pound heavier than rabbits from any other part of the estate. I doubt that the feeding was any different and assumed that it was a particular strain of *Oryctolagus cuniculus* that

A brown hare watched me for a few seconds, with a roe deer in the background

moved forward for a better view. It must have been reasonably happy that the figure it saw posed no threat and came running towards me. I had swapped the binoculars for the camera and managed a slightly fuzzy photograph of the moving hare at unbelievably close range before it turned and loped off, only slightly faster, down through the stubble. It was a lovely encounter.

Since I was near the end of the field and there were still no signs of badgers I cut back over the stubble to return to my car. I passed what had been the one-time safe retreat of a field mouse which had been dug out by a fox. The digging was not nearly as rough as the badger's foraging marks from two weeks earlier when it had been digging for worms and other invertebrates. I could picture the scene: the fox had seen the mouse run into the hole and had considered the effort to dig it out worthwhile. It had scraped and sniffed, scraped and sniffed, following the line of the mouse's burrow. The fox's nose and ears would tell it that the mouse was not far away and after digging for just over a foot in length and about eight inches deep it would have its meagre reward. I've regularly seen where foxes, and indeed badgers, have dug down to the end of one of the short nursery burrows where rabbits have their

had developed. Unfortunately the 'super rabbit' strain has now been lost.

The last half mile of the wood was also deer-fenced, though the fence was old and parts had fallen over. There was a roe buck grazing on set-aside some distance away and as I was watching it through the binoculars a three-quarters grown hare came through the fence from the wood into the field. I remained motionless and it sat and watched me for a few seconds, then

A healthy vixen on West Cultmalundie (photo: Bill McIntosh)

A mouse hole had been dug out by a fox

young. The reward in this case is much more substantial: five or six plump but unfortunate wee rabbits.

There was yet another flock of skylarks in this stubble field and they rose and flew around me in the same manner as the earlier flock had done. It was interesting to see one or two of them rising vertically into the air just as they would do in spring and summer and one even began an abbreviated version of the lovely skylark song so reminiscent of warm summer days. They landed a couple of hundred yards behind me and I left them to their feeding, hoping they would have no more disturbance.

New birds identified: none
New mammals identified: none

CHAPTER 13

The retired gamekeeper, Bill McIntosh

I have known Bill, the retired keeper, since he came to Dupplin in 1981. Bill was the keeper on the Aberdalgie and Forteviot beats, probably incorporating a third of the total area of the estate and lying to the east and the south. He is well-respected, and a landowner friend of mine once told me that if he had the choice of any keeper in Scotland to work for him it would be Bill. I called in to see him today and had a long chat with him and his wife Hilda.

As has been mentioned earlier, Bill was instrumental in the rearing and release in the 1990s of several broods of barn owls, mostly around two broods comprising eight young owlets per year. The landowner, Lord Forteviot, at that time was president of the World Owl Trust and it was he who initiated the project. The World Owl Trust, based in Cumbria, works on owl conservation, both nationally and internationally. The Trust's conservation programmes protect populations of endangered owls until their habitat has been restored. Dupplin Estate has many areas of suitable habitat for barn owls feeding and breeding, and this was enhanced by Bill making and erecting many owl boxes. Strangely they never seemed to use the boxes, preferring to nest in quiet farm buildings among stored bales. There are still some barn owls around, though they are now scarce, with the most recent of Bill's sightings being seen in daylight at the edge of woodland on Upper Cairnie Farm in late June 2019 and at night on pea stubble at Coldwells Farm in early August 2019. So they still inhabit parts of the estate.

Naturally, my burning question to Bill was about when the rabbit population crashed. Viral haemorrhagic disease came in to the estate in 1998. Because of the vast number of rabbits, Bill used to take guests out at night shooting with the use of a spotlight and a .22 rifle. There were many nights when the haul was over 100 rabbits and with a best night of 330. Between what Bill shot during his time as gamekeeper on Dupplin and what I snared and shot there the total would be at least 60,000 rabbits, a huge amount which in truth made very little difference. Many more were gassed by Bill and Gordon, and Gordon took another massive number with his drop box traps once the fences around the woods had been netted. The number shot of course is always dependent on the accuracy of the shooter and the type of weather. A dark and damp night with a breeze is perfect, whereas on a frosty moonlit night it is a waste of time as the rabbits can hear you much better and can easily see the vehicle by the light of the moon.

After the onset of VHD in 1998, suddenly, no matter where Bill looked for rabbits to shoot, they had disappeared. Very few were lying around dead, confirming the belief that most that are affected with VHD die in their burrows. I was not on the estate much at this particular time but it must have been a strange experience to look at a field with hundreds or even thousands of rabbits one night, and visit the same field a few nights later and not see a single one.

Bill had first-hand experience of the capercaillie that used to be on the estate. When he started on the estate at first capercaillie were relatively common and there used to be one capercaillie shoot per year (or maybe two if the capercaillie had a good breeding year). Like the shoot I had been on as a beater years earlier (chapter 22), no hen capercaillie were allowed to be shot and each gun on the

shoot was only allowed to shoot one cock bird. On the very last of these shoots in 1987 well over 100 capercaillie were seen, with 70 going over the guns on one particular drive. In more recent times the capercaillie was added to Schedule 1 of the Wildlife and Countryside Act 1981, which meant that they could no longer be shot.

I asked Bill why the capercaillie numbers had steadily gone downhill to the stage about fifteen or so years ago when they disappeared completely. As is often the case there was a mix of reasons. Bad weather, the felling of mature trees, and predators, such as foxes, pine martens and carrion crows, were contributory. Bad weather and predation are nothing new to capercaillie but they must have suitable habitat for shelter, food and for nesting. The reduction of suitable woodland limited their habitat but there was – and still is – sufficient suitable woodland to support a smaller population of capercaillie.

The most surprising factor given by Bill for their decline was that of bird watchers. In the breeding season of March and April cock capercaillie take part in a display called lekking. This is a flamboyant spectacle, usually in a particular part of the forest that has been used by the birds over the years, where the male capercaillie, with wings pointed down, tail flared and beard bristling, emits a series of gurgles and wheezes interspersed with cork popping sounds. He is trying to attract and impress the females, who are most likely to mate with the strongest and best male. If another male appears, a fight can result, sometimes causing serious injury to the losing bird. It is a display much sought after by photographers.

An unfortunate situation arose, partly due to advice given by an online bird club giving woodland near Bill's house as one of the best places to see lekking capercaillie. The birds were being disturbed in the early mornings by groups of bird watchers, sometimes arriving in a mini bus and with a guide who should have known better. Bill had to get up at 5.00 a.m. each day during the lekking period to try to keep well-meaning bird watchers, who were ignorant of the possible negative outcomes for the capercaillie, away from lek sites. The resultant disturbance from these birders was yet another nail in the coffin of these magnificent turkey-sized birds on this estate. In 2004 new legislation made it an offence 'to intentionally or recklessly disturb

any bird on Schedule 1 of the Wildlife and Countryside Act 1981 which leks, while it is doing so'.

While we were discussing the felling of some of the mature conifers in one of the principal woods that used to hold capercaillie, Bill told me that this substantial wood was planted out in the 1930s when the previous Lord Forteviot decided to give employment to a number of local people during the years of the depression. Formerly the area had been a grouse moor which yielded around 25 brace of grouse on shooting days.

Bill, in his 'retirement' and after 37 years on the estate, is now self-employed and hired by Dupplin estate to take clients out deer stalking, and also to control the grey squirrel population under the red squirrel protection scheme funded by the Scottish Rural Development Programme (SRDP). As part of the scheme, 56 live-catch traps are used on the estate, with Bill operating 22 of them. The scheme dictates that the traps are used for at least 5x10 day trapping periods throughout the year. I have only seen three live and one dead grey squirrel on the estate, but plenty of red squirrels, so the culling programme is certainly paying dividends in reducing the non-native grey to the benefit of our native red squirrel, which is at risk of contracting squirrel pox virus. This is a disease with similar symptoms to myxomatosis, which can be carried by grey squirrels but is fatal to red squirrels.

Bill is also responsible for the culling of red deer on the estate, having shot 31 during 2018. Red deer do considerable damage to crops when they are on arable farms, eating and trampling cereal crops, trekking over tattie drills where they partly knock the earth off the drills and expose the crop underneath, and munching turnips in winter, which then become frosted. Red deer are fabulous animals but when they leave the open hill and transgress on to farmland they can become a nuisance.

Orange tip butterfly at Milton Den

Small tortoiseshell butterfly at Bankhead Farm
Painted lady butterfly at Sauchie Farm

Peacock butterfly at Wester Cairnie Farm

CHAPTER 14
Wednesday 7 November 2018.
Dull, mild, stiff breeze. 11°C.

Lochs

Another dull day with heavy rain forecast but I took the decision to go for it. I wanted to visit the lochs again before we get a cold spell and they freeze over. Since my last visit here an ancient beech tree and a huge, ramrod-straight conifer had been blown over. The foresters had trimmed the branches off the conifer and no doubt it will be carted off to the estate sawmill. The beech will either finish up as firewood or be left to rot down where it fell.

Dupplin Loch's attraction to wildfowl has waned, with the birds now favouring Pitcairnie. There were three mute swans on the loch today plus ten or so tufted ducks. Newcomers though were a small flock of about 25 greylag geese tight in to the rushes on the east shore. The loch – in fact this whole estate – is much more popular with pink-footed geese so these slightly larger geese are less-common winter visitors. In the distance, a herring gull overflew the loch. As it came over the trees on the far side it somehow looked like an osprey, with its long narrow wings.

Also new to the area today were two cormorants sitting on a partly-sunken branch at the far side of the loch, plus three more sitting in a tree to their left, their white breasts briefly shining in a blink of rare sunshine. The two on the sunken branch were drying their wings which, spread out, made the birds look like miniature Angels of the North. I watched for a while and the three on the tree flew closer to me and started to fish. They look strange birds when they are in the water, with almost all of their body submerged and their neck and head sticking out like a periscope or a sea serpent. I wondered if they sometimes hunt as a pack since most of the underwater forays were carried out in unison. I'm always hoping for a sighting of an otter but though I watched for nearly half an hour none of these large mustelids put in an appearance.

I walked along the forest track to Pitcairnie Loch. It had its usual complement of mute swans, most of which were at the east end today. The wind was from the south-east and the waterfowl were taking advantage of a bit of shelter. A single male tufted duck was busy at the north-east corner. I took a couple of photos through one of the wire squares in the deer fence. When I looked at it later one photo summed up my photographic skills: I'd captured a black spider hanging on a silk thread in the centre of the square.

I began to take a bit more notice of a small flock of swans feeding in the reeds on the far shore. It's difficult to define why but I just thought they looked a bit different. Sure enough when I studied the members of this group through the binoculars they had yellow and black bills, wedge-shaped heads and, though I was mostly seeing their raised bums, their necks were straighter than those of their mute cousins. There were half a dozen youngsters among this group of whooper swans, plus one away on its own half-way up the loch.

I continued up the north shore of the loch, noting a dozen or so tufted ducks resting on the far shore along with the same number of mallard. Further up, a raft of eight wigeon relaxed just out from the far shore. As I watched they were joined by another four which had flown down the loch. When the two groups merged they seemed to celebrate the meeting with much whistling. Their lovely musical calls *whee-ooo, whee-ooo, whee-ooo* floated across the surface of the loch.

As I continued up the lochside the numbers of waterfowl decreased, which was the complete opposite of my last visit. It demonstrates the influence the wind has on where waterfowl feed. One of the last birds on the loch was a heron, which rose at the edge of the loch ahead of me, circled over my head and landed somewhere behind me. I sat on the bank near the west end of the loch enjoying the view – albeit without waterfowl – enjoying my sandwiches and, most of all, enjoying the fact the rain had stayed away.

Having exhausted the lochs I had a look over the gate into Blairbell Moor. Two croaking ravens flew over at a distance and a flock of what appeared to be fieldfares were landing on the loose clump of berry-laden hawthorn trees on the moor. As I got closer to them I was able to confirm that all the birds I could see were indeed fieldfares. A jay landed momentarily among them but quickly spotted me and made a hasty departure. A buzzard flew over at that point and it was interesting to note that the fieldfares were not in the least threatened; they continued gulping down hawthorn berries though no doubt still keeping one eye on the buzzard.

I sat down at the base of one of the trees and though the birds had flown to the furthest-away trees at my presence I knew their pattern and was satisfied that they would be back within a short time. Within ten minutes the flock was starting to return to the hawthorn trees beside me. Suddenly they rose in a cloud and fled towards taller trees in the wood. The cause of their panic was a male sparrowhawk that flew straight

Flock of pink-footed geese on stubble on Windyedge Farm

at them at tree height. It certainly meant business but was possibly confused by the sudden volume of birds and veered away. Amazingly, it was then mobbed by a single fieldfare which almost made contact with the raptor. Do birds know that they may be safer from a sparrowhawk if not taken by surprise? Could it have been that because the sparrowhawk was now high in the air the fieldfare could have risen higher above it to safety if required? I once watched a merlin trying to catch a meadow pipit, which climbed higher and higher and eventually outflew the merlin, which gave up and looked for an easier meal. It seems that raptors have difficulty in catching prey species of birds which are above them rather than by their normal means of capture: surprising them or outflying them in level flight.

I walked back to the car but on the way home I spotted a large flock of pink-footed geese in the same Windyedge Farm stubble field as they had been on my previous walk. They were in a position that I could stalk them with a reasonable chance of getting within seventy-five yards or so. I succeeded in getting behind a drystane dyke just as several more skeins with maybe forty geese in each were gliding in to join the feeding flock. Luckily I had my back to the wind, which meant the geese would land into the wind and not have to overfly my position and spot me. I'm always fascinated by geese landing; the way that they bank and twist and wiffle the air from under their wings. I'd watched this at a distance on my previous walk and here it was happening right in front of me. I managed to creep away from the much-enlarged flock without disturbing it. It was a great end to my morning. And a bonus that it had stayed dry.

New birds identified:
herring gull
New mammals identified: none

93

CHAPTER 15

Friday 16 November 2018. Dull, calm, 12°C.

River Earn at Forteviot

Today was my first visit for many years to the part of the estate on the south side of the River Earn. I intended to park at Milton of Forteviot Farm and was delighted that as I drove down the farm road it was clear that there were rabbits here. There was evidence that burrows on the banking on my right were in use and the flattened grass confirmed that rabbits were going through the fence on my left into the grass field. A virtual network of runs in the field meant that there were plenty of rabbits. I was pleased in fact that the first animal of interest that I saw, less than a hundred yards down the farm road, was a rabbit sitting at a burrow entrance on the Forteviot Haughs. Initially it seemed that the vile disease VHD had not crossed the river but speaking to the former keeper, Bill McIntosh, later, he stated that the rabbits on that side of the river had indeed been affected but somehow had made a much quicker recovery than those on most of the rest of the estate.

As I walked down the side of the May Burn, a heron rose silently and its ponderous wingbeats guided it left to go upstream on the River Earn to find another suitable place where it might be able to catch a fish or two.

The May Burn runs into the River Earn and I stood at the confluence for ten enjoyable minutes. Salmon run the burn about this time of year and some spawn further up. I'm particularly attracted to the May as I used to cycle the six or seven miles out from Perth in my early teens and fish up the burn towards the Ochil Hills, often catching half a dozen small trout to take home, and one day also filling my haversack with hazelnuts. I also have a vivid memory of another day fishing there when I was lucky enough to see a ring ouzel, at a time when they were considerably more common than they are today. As I stood reminiscing, a chocolate brown dipper, with typical rapid wingbeats, flew downstream just above the surface of the water. It landed on the branch of a tree jutting out from my side of the bank and just inches from the water. It was a perfect place from which to launch an underwater search for caddis fly larvae and other invertebrates. I spotted the white bib of

Rabbits at burrow entrance at the Forteviot Haughs

another dipper on the far bank sitting in a similar spot just above the water level. It remained there almost all the time I stood observing and I wondered if it was singing. Unfortunately I now need to be very close to a dipper to hear its song as the pitch is rather high for my ageing ears, and of course the gurgling of the May water meeting the Earn water did not help.

Two anglers were fishing just downstream of where I had stopped. I had a chat with them as I passed. Both had fished the River Earn for years, salmon and trout being their target in the summer and grayling at this time of year. They were complaining that grayling were far less common now, putting the apparent scarcity of the fish down to increasing numbers of cormorants. One of the anglers told me that one day he counted 52 cormorants on one of the pools. There is no doubt that if each of these sawbills caught a fish that day it would significantly deplete stocks of small fish. The angler told me that he sees goosanders, kingfishers, otters, beavers and an occasional seal on the river. As I chatted, one of the men hooked a fish that turned out to be a brown trout of about quarter of a pound with lovely markings, and which he carefully returned to the river.

As I walked further down the riverbank I saw signs of very fresh digging. Something had recently dug down about six inches and when I pressed with my walking stick it suddenly went down as if into a chamber. I then saw what appeared to be an entrance to a tunnel just above the waterline and wondered if it was an entrance to a beaver tunnel or an otter

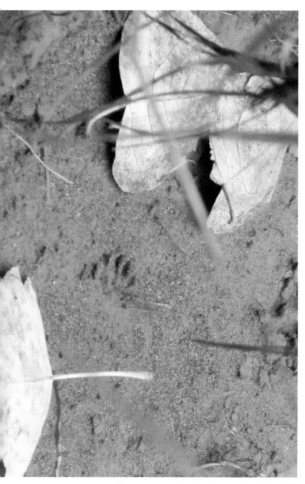

Otter paw print in the sand at the side
of the River Earn

think that an otter was using the 'slipway' to the river and maybe where the digging had taken place was an otter holt and the terriers had reacted to the smell of the inhabitant.

Further down the river I stopped for a wee while at the fishermen's hut. As well as the shelter that the anglers can use if the weather turns nasty, the picnic table and the rack for fishing rods there is a bench facing out to the river. I sat there and had my sandwich and half of my bottle of water, looking across the river to an old carrion crow's nest at the top of an oak tree that had a massive chunk out of its lower trunk and may not survive many more storms. Two buzzards mewed from the treetops near the carrion crow's nest then flew across to my side of the river over my head. Two mute swans flew down the river and shortly after, three whooper swans flew in the opposite direction. The whoopers were two adults and a youngster of this year and were surprisingly silent. Maybe, as families sometimes do, they'd simply run out of conversation.

Having had some sustenance, I continued down the riverbank, spotting a small brown bird flitting about in a willow tree. I got a flash of very bright yellow and immediately thought

holt. I had earlier met a lady walking a Jack Russell and a border terrier off the lead and wondered if they had been the diggers. The lady was pleased to tell me that she often sees otters on the river. A few yards further on there was a steep but narrow gap in the bank that was clearly used by some water creature. There was an otter paw print in the sand at the bottom of the steep slope that I couldn't access to put a scale to a photograph. I checked around for gnawed trees but there were none, so I think that eliminated beaver. I can only

Shiny, tarry, inky-black goo –
otter spraint on the river bank

'goldcrest'. Sure enough, once the bird stayed still long enough for me to fix my binoculars on it my initial identification had been correct. It was a lovely wee bird, with its bright yellow patch on its crown bordered on both sides with black. We've had one of these tiny birds from time to time in the garden but so far it never seems to have found a mate. As I was looking at the goldcrest a great tit appeared in the next willow tree and a few trees further down three or four blue tits hopped around the branches.

Suddenly the peace was shattered by a blackbird chattering loudly in alarm. I looked towards the noise to see a male blackbird flying straight towards me and a sparrowhawk close on its tail.

When it was as close as I could have touched it, the blackbird suddenly veered to its right, round and into a willow tree growing over the river. It is not often that the close proximity of a human will make a sparrowhawk abort a hunt when it is so focussed on catching its prey; they seem not to see the human. In this case, luckily for the blackbird, it did abort and turned sharply to its left, gaining height and sailing effortlessly over the top of yet another willow tree and out of sight. The blackbird had missed death by seconds.

A few yards further on I found that I could make no further progress through the ever-thickening willows and retraced my steps to go around this riverside jungle. It was quite lucky that I had to go back along the river's edge a bit as I had missed an otter spraint (droppings) on a rock that I must have stepped over on my first journey. This shiny, tarry, inky-black goo had recently been left by an otter to mark its territory and would be smelt by any passing otters as a sign of the occupier. Any passing otters (or even people) may also have been surprised (and slightly amused) to see me kneeling down to smell the spraint. Otter spraint has a sweet smell which is not unpleasant and is sometimes described as a cross between lavender and fresh fish. I don't know if I got either of these elements but, considering its origins, it wasn't a disagreeable smell.

I had to leave the riverside and go on to a track down the side of a field of winter wheat. The winter cereal was on my right with willows on my left stretching about 40 yards to the river. A heron rose from the edge of the willows ahead of me. When I got to the spot where it had been resting before I disturbed it there was a large patch of whitewash dropping, the complete opposite in colour and texture to that of the otter, considering that on many occasions they will eat similar food in the form of fish. A robin was singing somewhere in the centre of the willow trees, which made a pleasant walk even more so. There was also a ribbon of water just inside the willow thicket which got wider as I walked down the track. A single mute swan was feeding in this wider part. I doubt if the area of

water was large enough to support a pair and a nest of cygnets in springtime and I wondered if this was a swan which had lost its mate and was settling here at least in the meantime.

At the end of the ribbon of water three birds were feeding at the top of a willow. At first glance they looked like house sparrows but house sparrows were out of context in these surroundings. Closer inspection through the binoculars showed that they were a male and two female reed buntings. They allowed me quite close and I managed to take about 40 photographs but, like photos I had taken of other birds on a dull day, they lacked colour and the birds were little more than silhouettes.

I had decided when I got to this point to return to my car and leave the next stretch of the River Earn for another day. I marched back towards the car on a farm track, deviating to the river's edge to see how the two anglers were faring. Their day had improved and they were quite happy with their catch, which comprised a mix of small grayling, brown trout and even a small sea trout. They had returned all the fish to the river (the season for taking brown trout and sea trout had ended in any case) and were now surprisingly upbeat about the number of small grayling, optimistic that they would grow into larger grayling that they could catch in the future. Their day had been as good as mine.

New birds identified: dipper, goldcrest, great tit
New mammals identified: none

CHAPTER 16

**Saturday 1 December 2018.
Drizzle and sunny spells, 4⁰C.**

Milton Den, Cotton Farm, Coldwells Farm

Today I was keen to see if flocks of finches were still feeding on the quinoa at the west end of Milton Den. As I walked over the field from Cotton Farm there was a lovely line-up of wee birds on the telephone wires just above the crop. I was looking into the sun so I couldn't make out what species they were but as I got closer they flew to the trees and bushes at the west end of Milton Den. This was quite handy as when I came round the quinoa crop, hopefully I would be much nearer to them. Unfortunately, approaching north to south, the sun would still be in my eyes. But with having had so many wet days in the past two weeks I shouldn't complain about a bit of sunshine.

As I walked up the edge of the field towards the birds I could hear the *cha-ka, cha-ka* call of a magpie. I spied round with the binoculars, especially searching the tops of the trees and bushes since that's where they mostly call from. They don't stay still for long and I was sure I would see it flying between trees at some stage.

I was disappointed that there was no sign of this iridescent member of the crow family, usually described as black and white. I was even more disappointed that the flock of finches had left Milton Den *en masse* and were flying over the quinoa to where they had earlier been perched on the telephone wires. Getting a decent view of birds is not always straightforward.

I left the uncooperative finches to it and climbed a gate and a fence to continue round and down the other side of Milton Den. I could see the pond in the Den with a dozen or so mallards quietly resting on its bank and, from time to time, I could still hear the magpie. I could also see a face peering over the fence between the track I was on and a field of rape. Closely watching my approach, it was a strange round, grey face with yellow hair, white eyes wide open, a black dot of a nose and black teeth gaping from a vivid red mouth. Under the face was a grey ribbed jersey, in remarkably good condition considering the recent weather and with khaki shoulder

Scarecrow watching my approach

patches. Lower down was a pair of faded pink trousers which were hardly a match for the top. I don't know whether the scarecrow was on duty but there were certainly no woodpigeons feeding on the luscious-looking (to sheep, deer and some birds) rape.

I sat on a stile near my new-found pal and hoped to see the coy corvid. After 20 minutes there was still no sign of the magpie and all had gone quiet. None of the birds were playing ball today at all. Even a large flock of fieldfares that had been feeding on a variety of berries in the Den kept well out of reach, though three female and one male blackbird were gorging greedily on hawthorn berries just over the fence inside the Den

I retraced my steps, crossing the stile and gave the scarecrow a wave as I headed up between a game/bird seed crop and a hawthorn hedge. I rose a group of twenty or so red-legged partridges which fluttered close to the ground up the slope ahead of me then gained another few feet in height, enough to let them glide over a fence into the wood ahead of me.

When I came to the point that the partridges entered the wood I could see the carcass of a woodpigeon

surrounded by white feathers some thirty yards into the wood. I climbed the fence to examine the scene of the kill. There was little left of the woodpigeon and it had been freshly eaten, probably earlier in the morning. The woodpigeon had been plucked so the predator was most certainly a bird rather than a mammal. I'd love to know which bird it had been but most likely it was a sparrowhawk, buzzard or even a goshawk. In woodland like this a peregrine would be a less likely contender.

From here I walked a further mile until I passed the North Lodge, tenanted by a friend of mine, David Henderson. Suddenly blue tits and great tits appeared on bushes just beside me. I could see the reason: there were plenty signs of the birds having been fed, with empty feeders hanging on branches and mud underneath the

Male blackbird in Milton Den

long, had been planted since I was last there nearly 40 years earlier. It runs at right angle from Coldwells Wood and is a nice mix of oak, birch, some conifers and a variety of bushes, including some lovely snowberry bushes laden with shiny white fruits. A strip of game/bird seed crop had been sown down the west side of this new plantation and as I walked down the edge of the wood a flock of finches flew off the crop into the trees. Looking through the binoculars at the birds perched atop birch trees I could see that most were chaffinches, next in numbers were yellowhammers, then greenfinches and a solitary – so far as I could see – male brambling. There is no doubt that these crops provide a great source of food for a variety of wild birds in winter. With the considerable acreage of game/bird seed crops on this estate, hawthorn hedges, berry-laden bushes and grain distributed for pheasants and partridges, wild birds should thrive.

feeders where probably pheasants had been paddling about cleaning up any dropped seed. The point was that the feeders were empty, and maybe the birds thought I was there to re-fill them. It would be the birds' turn to think I was being uncooperative.

I walked a further mile, eventually along the top edge of a field on Coldwells Farm. This field has a strip of whin bushes about 40 yards wide and several hundred yards long between Coldwells Wood, which is mainly mature conifers, and the cultivated part of the field. A new strip of woodland, maybe 100 yards wide and 300 yards

Further along a farm track from this new plantation and secured to an oak tree was yet another barn owl nest box made by Bill, whose beat before retiring was this end of the estate. Unfortunately, it didn't look as if it was in use and it would be a real pity if all the work he did in rearing and releasing barn owls into perfect habitat has left no legacy.

Near where I had parked my car I noticed a woodpigeon sitting on the top of a newly-trimmed hawthorn hedge. It remained there as I got closer, and closer and closer still. I eventually managed to photograph the bird from a couple of yards away. It didn't look ill or injured but I most certainly couldn't approach a healthy and extremely wary wild bird to within such a short distance. I suspect it would fall victim to a predator before too long.

I finished the day by driving the short distance to The Parsonage in the centre of the estate. I wanted to look more closely at the wide hawthorn hedge that had been planted between The Parsonage Wood and the sawmill. I walked down one side of the hedge and back up the other. It is a magnificent hedge, now about 8 feet in height and 5 feet wide. It is uncut this year and if it bore a crop of berries none remained. If there is a chance of either red-legged or grey partridges nesting under the hedge, gaps may need to be made to allow any chicks to enter and exit, though I am informed that the netting enclosing all of the mature hedges will be removed shortly.

I was surprised at the number of nests in the hedge. Most – rather surprisingly considering the number of mature conifers close by – were wood pigeon nests, though some looked blackbird or song thrush size and a couple would have been smaller finch-sized birds. The hedges are certainly a great wildlife-friendly addition to the estate.

When I had returned to the top end of the hedge I noticed an industrious treecreeper busily searching for insects on an oak tree in the wood. I climbed the gate and sat at the bottom of a tree, hoping for a photograph. Predictably the uncooperative wee bird decided to continue its search for micro-morsels on the far side of the tree. It flew to the next oak tree but immediately disappeared round the back again. My patience was rewarded by a red squirrel that appeared slightly higher up the tree and, in an upside-down position, studied me for a few minutes before scampering further up the tree and out of sight. Red squirrels are fascinating wee acrobats.

As I climbed back over the gate I noticed that there were two clumps of ladybirds on some rotting wood forming the side of the gate. The biggest group would number at least

One of several clumps of hibernating ladybirds on gate at The Parsonage

twenty, which seemed to be the 7-spot variety. Smaller clumps held about ten in each, plus there were odd ladybirds on their own tucked into small crevices in the wood. I wondered how they knew to congregate here; can they release pheromones that attract others? Might they have more chance of surviving the winter in a group? Though these ones were bathed in sunshine when I saw them there will be many perishingly-cold winter days before they eventually emerge around April. It has been a bumper year for ladybirds; I've probably seen more of them during 2018 than I've seen for several decades. Let's hope these lovely wee red and black buttons make it through the winter.

New birds identified:
magpie
New mammals identified: none

CHAPTER 17
Wednesday 5 December 2018.
Calm, with frost. -1ºC.

Back Hill, East Drive

It was time to have a look through the centre of the estate again, but this time in winter weather. At the west end of Back Hill there was a lovely winter scene with white frost on the grass and a large rhododendron bush with frosted leaves looking as big as saucers. A cock pheasant emerged from under the bush and came strutting towards me. Even when I came out of the car he kept coming and studied me as if he was waiting for food. I suspected he was a wise (and lucky) pheasant from at least last season who knew the system: accept handfuls of wheat scattered by humans but clear out quickly when noisy humans with dogs appear or at the first sounds of shooting.

I walked along Back Hill, managing to stalk and photograph two roe deer that were sitting relaxing inside the wood. This is a great area for roe deer and before long I could see another grazing in the wheat stubble. I managed to stalk in a bit closer and took one or two photos, then stalked closer still. I was happy there was not enough wind for the doe to scent me, but a second doe closer to me that had been unseen because of a rise in the ground must have heard me. The deer, both does and in lovely dark winter coats, trotted down to near to the fence bordering the wood at the bottom of the field and watched me from there. I remained still and managed a few more photos but once I started to walk they jumped the fence into the wood.

About half way along Back Hill I noticed a huge structure at the top of a larch tree. It was about the size of an osprey nest but it was an unlikely location. If it was a buzzard nest, it was one of the biggest I've seen. It blended well to the golden colour of the now bare birch tree, but something just didn't seem right about it. It was right in the centre of the rather spindly tree top and may have been some sort of growth. A visit in springtime was on the cards to see if there was any buzzard activity.

I could see a third deer well along the field and the stalk towards it was quite easy since I was hidden by the same rise in the field. I was now about

Two roe deer sitting relaxing at Back Hill

Looks like a buzzard nest at the top of a larch tree but probably a growth

40 yards from the deer, a buck this time that had cast his antlers but was easily identifiable by the smaller rosette on his bum and the absence of the short tail-like tush of the doe. Unfortunately he must have heard my footsteps crunching on the frosted grass and suddenly appeared on the track ahead of me, briefly, before clearing the fence with ease and making off into the wood.

At the end of Back Hill I turned right and made my way up the track where earlier in the year forest operations had been carried out. There were still huge piles of cut timber at the sides of the track but with the recent timber extraction most of the wildlife will have moved temporarily from that part of the estate to somewhere a bit quieter. One roe buck, again minus antlers, ran across the track ahead of me but that was the extent of the wildlife in that part of the walk.

As I was about to leave the wood for more open fields and tracks I could see a huge flock of woodpigeons ahead of me feeding on the track that runs

between East and West Munday. I guessed it was spilt grain, or more likely grain scattered by the keeper, Stewart, that had attracted them, and they were sharing their spoils with a cock pheasant. As I got closer the woodpigeons exploded from the track, as did an equally large flock from the field of rape to the right. As I came out of the wood more flocks of woodpigeons rose from further across the rape field. Woodpigeons will gorge themselves on rape, the same as they do with clover in summertime. I was sure their crops would be filled to bursting point with the greens. These portly pigeons and their pals will be delighted with the supply of winter fodder meant to sustain the estate's sheep until springtime.

The recently-cut hawthorn hedge on my left was now neat and tidy. Tidiness is not so good for wildlife but many of the other hedges on the estate are uncut and I suspect they may be trimmed on a two or a three-year rotation, which is good practice. I noticed a used nest near the top of the hedge, of which the former occupant may have been a dunnock. Dunnocks' eggs are the most exquisite turquoise blue and to see a clutch of four or five in a cosy nest is indeed a treat.

Amazingly we have young dunnocks in the garden every year yet I have never found an active nest, only a nest after the birds have finished with it for the season.

I walked along the East Drive on my return journey to the car and was taken by the lower trunk of one of the several mature monkey puzzle trees bordering the drive since it looked exactly like a giant elephant's foot. It reminded me of an elephant's foot that had been made into a stool and was on display in the UK National Wildlife Crime Unit office where I worked. It was one of several parts of various endangered species that had been confiscated. Most likely its original owner had been poached for its ivory; what a waste of a magnificent and intelligent animal.

I spotted a squirrel's drey high in a conifer, then another close to the trunk in a mature beech tree. There was no way of knowing whether they had been built by a red squirrel or a grey squirrel, though maybe the one in the beech tree was more likely to have been built by a grey. I was thinking that I had only seen one grey squirrel on the estate when I spotted a slight movement on the ground to the left of the drive. With experience you can develop an instinctive knowledge of the subject of a fleeting glimpse like this. I was sure the colour was grey. This probably meant either a rabbit, a rat or a grey squirrel. There are no rabbits here, rats are primarily nocturnal and anyway would be much less likely among mature trees. This leaves the grey squirrel as the most likely possibility. I moved forward slowly and indeed it was a grey squirrel, which saw me and scurried up the gnarled reddish-brown trunk of a massive red cedar. This was a grey squirrel that Gordon the rabbit trapper still has to capture

I watched for a few minutes to see if the squirrel would reappear. Amazingly two red squirrels appeared from behind the cedar tree and started chasing each other round the giant trunk. The noise made by their claws on the bark was incredible, typical of the scratchy, tinny sound normally made by squirrels on bark but at several times the volume. After a couple of circuits they also disappeared into the canopy of the tree and though I waited ten minutes for them to reappear there was no further sign. When I walked on I could see a red squirrel high in the branches of a tree 20 yards away from the cedar but I'd no way of knowing if this was one of the original two or a completely different squirrel. There is nothing new

in grey and red squirrels living alongside each other but the risk remains that the red squirrels could catch squirrel pox from their North American non-native relatives. While the grey can remain unaffected yet a carrier of the virus, this virus causes lesions around a red squirrel's eyes, nose, mouth, hands and genitals. It leads to breathing problems, blindness and usually death.

Birds smaller than a blackbird had been noticeably absent today so I was pleased to see a large flock of coal tits feeding below one of the trees, probably a hazel tree, near the estate office. There were hundreds of large yellow catkins lying on the ground underneath it and I suspect those are what attracted the coal tits. There were over 50 in the flock. They flew to a tree in the field but after I passed I saw them flying back to their feast on the ground.

I continued on past Stewart's house and kennels to my car. My day had begun with a pheasant looking as if it were waiting for food. It ended with a robin sitting on a fence post beside my car. All that was missing from this picture postcard scene was some snow.

New birds identified: none
New mammals identified: none

CHAPTER 18
Wednesday 12 December 2018. Calm, dull. 6⁰C.

Broombarns Farm

The day started well. I was barely on to the lands of Dupplin Estate, driving along the single-track Moss road, when a female kestrel glided off a telephone pole bordering Greenhill Farm. Kestrels used to be so common and could be regularly seen at roadsides, especially motorways, where they had a good supply of mice and voles in the rough grass bordering the road. It's really sad that their numbers have crashed. A snowy winter can affect them badly through starvation and they now have to compete for food with buzzards coming back to the level they should always have been at were it not for persecution. I wonder in springtime if kestrels will nest in any of the barn owl nest boxes on the south-east part of the estate?

My destination today was Broombarns Farm on the south side of the River Earn between Forgandenny and Forteviot. As I turned into the farm road a roe doe ran across in front of my car, jumping the fence on my right with ease. It cantered over the winter barley stopping, as deer sometimes do, for a look back when they think they are at a safe distance. Further down the farm road, I passed through lands of the former Newton of Condie House. This formerly magnificent mansion was owned by the Oliphant family from 1601 but was gutted by fire in 1866. Only part of the shell of the great house still remains. I was really impressed by a great example of wildlife-friendly farming here. The grass field I drove through, which would have been part of the one-time Condie Estate parklands, was dotted with very ancient oak trees and huge specimen conifers. Half of them, about twenty, had bird nest boxes on their trunks. One really old tree had a newish owl nest box, which looked more like the design sold by RSPB rather than Bill's home-made ones. On my right, on slightly younger oak trees down the edge of the field, there were a dozen or so bat boxes.

I parked at Broombarns Farm steading and crossed the Perth to Gleneagles railway line via the underpass. Turning right, to go between a small strip of trees and the railway line I disturbed yet another two roe deer, this time only seeing their white rumps disappearing into the distance. I followed the boundary of the

Parklands of the former Newton of Condie Estate

estate down to the edge of the River Earn, seeing another disappearing white rump in the wood on my right.

The ruins of Newton of Condie House

My walk upstream was surprisingly uneventful apart from a wary cormorant that flew downstream, flying back upstream again a few minutes later. I noticed a tree on the far bank of the river that had white splashes on a branch. A look through the binoculars confirmed this as a popular resting and toileting place of a large bird, maybe even the cormorant I had just seen. For all my walks up and down the River Earn this autumn I have never seen an angler hook a salmon and never seen one jump or

Brown hare resting in a form in a stubble field of Broombarns Farm

even break the surface. Salmon angling is in a precarious position throughout Scotland and, according the annual report of the Tay District Salmon Fisheries Board, 2018 on the Tay catchment fishing has been extremely poor. To quote the chairman, 'It is clear that there has been a significant increase in mortality at sea in recent times. The return rates of smolts leaving the Tay currently are most likely the lowest ever known. The rate of decline, particularly of grilse, is unprecedented.' Not good news and most likely the principal factor in the lack of salmon activity.

Another look through the binoculars, this time into the stubble field I was walking through, confirmed a brown hare resting in a form about 75 yards away. I wondered how close I could get to the hare and started to walk in its direction. Rather than walk straight towards it, which would alarm it and probably make it run off, I walked as if to pass it by maybe ten or fifteen yards. Apart from flattening itself to the ground as much as possible, the hare sat still as I got closer and I eventually managed a photograph from about eight yards away. The stubble was just the perfect height to allow me to have spotted the hare in the first place yet give the hare sufficient confidence that lying still would be the best form of defence. It is fantastic to get so close to one of my favourite mammals.

I cut back to the river down the side of a long strip of rushes and a couple of willow trees growing in a damp part of the field. It was a lovely wet bit for snipe feeding and four rose, one after the other, from the watery edge of the strip. Rather surprisingly two skylarks (or maybe meadow pipits) also flushed. Both birds are similar and each has a white feather on either side of their tail, making identification difficult when they are out of context or when only a fleeting glimpse is obtained. I could imagine this area being an ideal place for these birds to roost, but I'm not sure what food they would have found here.

Nearer the river I disturbed a heron, resting at the edge of the field. It flew upstream but, like the cormorant earlier, it flew back downstream again. I had a new camera with me and was keen to try it out on a wide range of subjects. A rather tame (or naïve) hen pheasant was walking through the bushes at the riverbank. I was just about to photograph it at the time the heron was on its return journey, this time screeching quite loudly. I was distracted from the hen pheasant in trying to see the heron behind the riverbank scrub. In fact I didn't manage to see the heron and also missed spotting a brown hare that had been sitting in the rough grass almost at my feet and which now scarpered over the field. Too many subjects at the same time and I finished up with no photos!

Ahead of me I admired a carrion crow's nest in a tree overhanging the river. It was a safe place for any chicks hatching provided they didn't fall out of the nest. A buzzard also landed on the very tip of a conifer in the strip of wood ahead of me, appropriately enough at this time of year looking like an ornament on a Christmas tree.

I walked up the side of the wood to where it met the railway line, cut through the wood and was confronted by a very deep ditch that stood between me and the field at the other side of the wood. I walked up and down the ditch looking for a place to cross where I was least likely to fall into the water. With some difficulty, and with only wet knees from crawling up the far bank, I managed across but I resolved to find an easier way to cross on my return journey.

I walked down the other side of the wood and continued up the riverbank. I was keen to explore an area of willow further up the river where Bill had showed me a beaver lodge in 2009. Unfortunately when I reached this area the willow was now so thick and the ground underneath so wet that I was unable to proceed to see whether or not beavers were still there. The area suited snipe, and yet another one rose at my feet, as did another brown hare.

As well as conditions, time was also beating me and I began to make back towards my car. I had that dreaded ditch in the wood to cross again and I was not looking forward to it. I had a look at the river end of the wood and there was an open but narrow route past the bottom of the wood to the other side. The difficulty was that I would be walking (or crawling) right on the edge of a high crumbling banking overhanging the river. The danger of it giving way was too great so I went up the wood a few yards and managed to half walk and half crawl through between the trees, which were unbrashed and with branches in places almost to ground level. The ditch loomed ahead, however I could see a bridge in the form of an old railway sleeper across it. Great!

When I got to the 'bridge' I could see that the ten feet long sleeper was very old, with a significant hole in the centre. It was covered in wet moss and very slippery. Even worse, the ditch was more than twice as deep here, with at least eight feet between me and the water at the bottom. Referring to the ditch as a crevasse would be too strong, but not by much. Thankfully my stick gave me some balance and I started to edge across. I gained some confidence that the sleeper was still quite strong

The rotten and slippery ten feet long sleeper 'bridge' over the deep ditch

and wouldn't break in half at my weight but the slippery surface was the real danger. I kept edging across as if on a tightrope and eventually reached *terra firma* at the other side. At 71 years of age that is now a wood to avoid on any future visit.

New birds identified:
kestrel
New mammals identified: none

CHAPTER 19
Friday 14 December 2018. Calm, sunny. -2⁰C.

Lochs, West Mid Lamberkin Farm, West Lamberkin Farm

I've been lucky with most of my visits so far in that the weather has been reasonably mild. There was a forecast for colder weather coming in so I thought I'd give the lochs another visit, which may well be the last visit of the winter. I parked beside a grass field that had two trees in the centre, one of which hosted a huge osprey nest right on the top, though it was not occupied in 2018.

I meandered up towards Dupplin Loch, yet again admiring the ancient conifers, oaks and birch trees in the woodland. A red squirrel was flat against the trunk of one of the conifers, legs sticking out at all corners in an imitation of a flying squirrel. It began to play a game with me, being stationary only until I locked on to it and was about to take a photograph, then scurrying further up the trunk onto a branch. The mischievous squirrel won the game, with me giving up after about five minutes when it moved to another tree. There were three dreys high in the trees within a forty-yard radius, one in an oak tree looking particularly new

Red squirrel drey in an oak tree looking particularly new and fresh

and fresh. It was a really tidy and spherical drey, made of thin branches, moss and oak leaves and with a very clear entrance hole on the side facing me.

There had recently been vehicles up the track, most likely the foresters dealing with a fallen beech tree and a fallen conifer, and red deer footprints showed well in the mud of the vehicle tracks. I see roe deer on nearly every visit yet red deer, these much larger ungulates, manage to remain out of sight, leaving only evidence of their passing.

I was disappointed to see that, even with a comparatively mild temperature

Preening male goldeneye on Dupplin Loch

Three whooper swans resting on Pitcairnie Loch

of minus two degrees, Dupplin Loch had a covering of ice. Half a dozen mute swans, a similar amount of mallard and one small white duck had found an area at the far (north east) side that was not frozen. When I put the binoculars on the 'white duck' it was a male goldeneye. It was actually standing on ice and busy with ablutions, preening as if it was about to undergo a plumage inspection. The distinctive white spot on its cheek really stood out in the morning sun, especially against the background of its bottle-green head. We're slightly further south of its normal breeding range in Scotland but I wonder if tree nest boxes were erected could it be encouraged to breed here?

I continued on to Pitcairnie Loch and I was not surprised to see that it was frozen as well, though the north east edge nearest to me was still free of ice. The main body of mute swans had moved on, possibly to the coast, and no more than half a dozen remained. Most of the duck species were tight into the tree-lined north banking and impossible to see until I was almost upon them. There was a good mix, with tufted duck,

mallard, wigeon and another single male goldeneye. They were not keen to leave the loch and when they rose they wheeled round the loch and landed behind me. I love the sound of the wigeon and I could have followed their course round the loch by their whistling alone.

Three different herons rose and sailed over my head; ungainly looking birds in flight, with their huge wingspan, long necks folded into their bodies and lanky legs trailing behind. Furthest up the unfrozen part of the loch was a small flock of about twenty whooper swans. For whoopers they were particularly quiet. I suspect they had not long arrived on the loch after a lengthy journey as they seemed determined to catch up on sleep, with most curling their necks back and resting their heads between their wings. I sat for a while, leaning my back against the fence round the sylvan burial area of an earlier laird of the estate and his wife. This is one of the few places along the lochside with a clear view over the wate and I can appreciate why it was favoured as a last resting place. The whoopers seemed as relaxed as I was and at one point the whole group were dozing, heads between their wings and gently bobbing on their giant water mattress.

On my return journey I tried unsuccessfully to photograph a coal tit and a wren that were feeding on and in some whin bushes. They'd had lessons from the red squirrel in frustrating humans with a camera; they'd been good pupils and had clearly paid attention in class.

My intention was to stop off at West Mid Lamberkin on my way home. This farm now incorporates most of the former 150 acres of East Mid Lamberkin, a farm with which I was well acquainted in my youth. My abiding memory of the place was the day that the farmer, George Robb, asked the then gamekeeper for that area of Dupplin Estate, Adam Dickson, if he would look into the farm to shoot some cats as there had been an explosion in their numbers and they needed thinned out. George had shut the cats in the stable and when Adam was ready with his shotgun outside in the close George went in to the stable to chase the cats out one at a time. We, as boys, stood behind the 'tooled-up' Adam awaiting the outcome. The scene from *The Good,*

the Bad and the Ugly where there was duel in the street between Clint Eastwood and Lee Van Cleef was maybe even based on this dramatic spectacle.

The first cat bolted from the stable, but George shouted loudly, 'Leave that one Adam, that's a good cat'. The second one followed shortly after. Adam raised his gun, but just as quickly lowered it again when George shouted, 'Leave it'. The third cat bolted, and again the shout went up, 'Leave it Adam'. When the fourth cat bolted George bellowed from the depths of the stable, 'Shoot that one Adam'. Adam raised the gun quickly. . . and missed the cat with both barrels! The stable was now devoid of felines, good or bad, and the 'cat thinning' exercise was never repeated.

As I turned in to the West Mid Lamberkin Farm road the small woodland on the left used to be a quarry with a really deep pool in the centre, now completely filled in and levelled. As boys we were well warned about the dangers of this water and of going too near the cliff that formed a vertical face at one end of the pool. The main pool had a smaller pond leading off it and one day when we looked down from the top of the cliff to the pond there was a huge fish swimming near the surface. We'd no idea what species the fish was, though I suspect now it was either a brown trout or a pike. We tried fishing in the pool to see if we could catch it but during these expeditions there was no indication at all that these deep waters held any piscine treasures.

What the quarry did hold was an immense quantity of rabbits. They always fed on the field on the west side of the quarry and several hundred could be seen munching away in the evenings at whatever crop was in the field. One night when I was in my mid to late teens Jim Ogg – a gentle giant of a man then the tractorman at East Lamberkin, and seldom seen without his bunnet – and I had a go at the rabbits with a couple of long nets. We were able to cover 200 yards of the field with the nets and set them just out from the fence. We walked quietly out into the field beyond where the net ended then noisily tried to chase any rabbits in the field towards the wood where the net lay in ambush. It was an amateurish attempt yet we still managed to bag about 30 rabbits.

I parked my car at West Mid Lamberkin Farm steading and walked along the track to the farm cottage that lies between West Mid and East Mid Lamberkin. I hadn't been in this cottage since I was about 12 years old, probably about 1959. On that occasion the then tractorman from East Mid Lamberkin, Jake McLaren, a jovial red-cheeked man, proudly invited us in to see a new fire grate he had installed in the sitting room. We trouped from East Mid Lamberkin along to Jake and his wife's cottage keen to see this new fitment. Boys at that time must have had different interests and levels of excitement compared to 12-year-old boys today.

I walked down the strip of beech trees leading from the cottage down to the estate boundary. There were some whin and broom bushes interspersed between the trees and these held a decent number of wee birds: blackbirds, blue tits, coal tits, a dunnock, a robin and a pair of bullfinches. Further down the strip a hundred or so jackdaws that had congregated on a tree flew off with a noisy chorus of *chak, chak, chak*, the call that gives them their name.

I walked along the march fence with Blackruthven Farm, a neighbouring farm to Dupplin, disturbing a snipe which had been feeding on the marshy ground at the edge of the field. I'd a lovely view of this wee dark brown and

The sylvan burial area of an earlier Baron of Forteviot overlooking Pitcairnie Loch

white wader as it flew off almost from my feet, showing off the straw-coloured streaks along its back. A mistle thrush sat proudly in these birds' favourite position: right at the top of a tree. In a few weeks it may well be singing from the same spot.

I walked up past West Lamberkin Farm steading and up to the wood above the farm. I'd seen very few marks of deer until this point but as I walked along the wood edge in the direction of my car there were roe deer and red deer footprints coming out into the field of winter barley at any gap in the old deer fence. There were high seats at regular intervals along the wood, all the way from West Mid Lamberkin , past West Lamberkin and further westwards on to where the Peel Farm meets the public road, a distance of nearly a mile,

which would allow anyone controlling the deer ample time to identify the most suitable beasts to cull as they come out from the wood to feed.

Before completing today's walk I had a quick check down through another beech strip on East Mid Lamberkin. All of these trees are ancient and many have missing limbs. There were numerous holes in the trees, of different sizes that would accommodate nesting tawny owls, jackdaws, starlings, tree sparrows and tits. There were also splits in the bark that will be perfect for nesting treecreepers. It was a ready-made bird housing estate awaiting occupants.

New birds identified:
goldeneye, bullfinch
New mammals identified: none

CHAPTER 20
Wednesday 2 January. Calm, sunny. -4°C.

River Earn at Forteviot. Milton of Forteviot, Kildinny Farm, Sauchie Farm

After a somewhat sedentary period at Christmas and New Year it was time to blow the cobwebs away. I decided on a river walk down the south bank of the River Earn starting at Forteviot. It was a fantastic day weather-wise and the river was running as clear as crystal. Stewart, the keeper, had earlier told me there would be people shooting geese a field width from the river on Kildinny Farm and I could hear odd shots, some of which would no doubt have resulted in a goose for the pot. I did some goose shooting nearly half a century ago and was really partial to goose breast cut thinly and fried like minute steak but I have not had that delicacy for many years. As I have aged I am much happier now shooting with a camera than for the pot. I haven't used a gun since 2011 and in fact sold the last of my guns in 2014.

As I walked down the riverbank a cormorant with a breast that seemed whiter than usual – or was it just the sun glinting off it? – flew up the river high above me. A good deal further downstream a dozen or so mallard rose from my side of the river then split up, with some flying down the river and some curling back over my head.

I had now to cut out into the field to pass a thick stand of willow and was surprised to see three roe deer in the field. The goose shooters were less than a quarter of a mile from where the deer were grazing and I was amazed that they were tolerating shots so close by. I had my back to the willow trees but the deer still spotted me and began to walk off across the field, crossing a five-yard-wide beetle bank that ran quarter of a mile from the river to the railway line. They made towards the riverbank ahead of me where there was a large jungle of willow and marsh. Since there was no wind I wondered, since I was looking into the sun, if my face would be shining like a beacon or if the deer may have seen the sun glinting off the binoculars or camera round my neck. Wild animals live much longer the more they are aware of and act on potential danger.

Further down the river there was an oval-shaped patch of grass on top of the bank where the frost had melted. An animal of some sort had been lying there resting. There was no other clue as to what the animal might have been but possibilities are roe deer, fox or otter. Some mysteries in nature can be solved easily; others require experience or even guesswork. A short distance further on I passed the rock on the path where on my previous visit I had seen fresh otter spraint. There did not appear to be any new spraint today, though with a covering of frost I couldn't be sure.

I cut through part of the jungle of willow, which took me out to an area of shingle on a bend in the river. There were lots of areas of sand with a mix of footprints of pheasant, waterfowl and deer. I searched for prints of otter, fox or beaver but it seems they had not visited the area recently. In the middle of the shingle was a dead sheep, having fallen into the water further upstream since there were no sheep kept here. As I contemplated the sheep's demise a dipper shot upstream just above the surface of the water, a whirr of brown wings and snowy white breast. The mild winter we've had so far will be suiting birds that are dependent on water that is not frozen.

I had to backtrack for a bit to bypass a pool of deep water and when I emerged on to the field again the three deer were still there. They quickly spotted me again and trotted into yet another watery willow jungle. A ribbon of water 100 yards or so in length ran just inside this area of willows. On my last visit this pool held a single mute swan. This time there were two so they may well nest here in the spring. As one of our biggest birds, they dwarfed a dumpy wee wren that was exploring the undergrowth beside me. As I watched the wren I wondered why, unlike with most other birds, its tail was carried at almost right angles to its body. Wrens have a particularly hard time finding food and keeping warm in a bad winter but can make up losses quite quickly by producing a large number of chicks, sometimes two broods of six or seven in a year.

Several skeins of pink-footed geese were approaching the place where the goose shooters had been operating. I'd not heard any shots for half an hour and wondered if they had packed up for the day. As the geese came over several shots rang out and I saw a couple of geese fall out of the sky. The shooters were clearly still there.

I started to head back towards the

car, following the track up the side of the field rather than the riverbank this time. The two swans I'd seen earlier flew a circuit over me. It seemed as if they were checking to see if I'd gone, though more likely they were just exercising their wings and they soon glided gracefully back into their home stretch of water.

Nearer the car I watched three siskins feeding on small brown cones on an alder tree. The tree had a great supply of these cones, which are full of small seeds that sustain a variety of seed-eating birds in winter. It was also covered in small purple catkins, giving the tree a distinct purple hue. The three siskins were all female, tiny brown birds streaked with yellow, and appeared to be having a great feast, often hanging upside down to get the best access to the cones.

When I reached the car there was a huge flock of birds perched right at the top of a clump of ash trees growing near the river. They flew from the treetops, allowing me to estimate that there were several hundred birds in the flock. When they completed their fly-past they landed back in the ash trees and I was able to confirm that they were yellowhammers. I checked, so far as I could, the perched birds and could see

no species other than yellowhammer. I was amazed at the number of birds. In the spring and summer I've certainly seen better yellowhammer numbers locally in recent years and wonder if they are having – at least in this area – a bit of a recovery.

I drove a little further down the river, on the north bank this time, as I still had a couple of hours to spare. I had a look at a couple of marshy areas close to the river on Sauchie Farm as they often hold wildfowl, but the ponds in the centre of these areas were frozen. That gave me some hope that the river would be full of wildfowl, but the first few hundred yards was devoid of birds apart from a heron which flew downstream ahead of me. The main point of interest was a straight line of fox tracks, hind paw landing almost on top of the front paw mark, in wet sand on a sand and shingle bed on a bend in the river. This is the same place as I had seen fox tracks on my earlier visit and must be a favourite part of this fox's nightly patrol.

On a bend in the river where I had seen four whooper swans on my last visit I could see the head and neck of a swan. A look through the binoculars identified this as a mute swan. I did a detour away from the bank to be able to

Two members of a large flock of yellowhammers on an ash tree beside the River Earn

come back unseen to the part of the river beside the swan. This must be a favourite spot for wildfowl as, in addition to the swan there were several mallard and five teal. All the ducks saw me at the same time and rose in unison, the teal springing into the air in their typical style. Many clay pigeon shooting areas simulate 'springing teal' by launching the clay targets almost vertically into the air. I can vouch for these clay targets being extremely difficult to hit. The teal continued downstream and the ducks made off across the fields on the far bank. The swan slowly paddled out to the middle of the river and drifted gently downstream with the current. Ducks

that have been shot for food and sport clear out at the first opportunity while the swan, protected from being shot for years, simply keeps its distance.

I caught up with the heron again, and it flew further downstream. The swan still coasted slightly ahead of me, unperturbed by my presence. When it was 500 yards from its starting point it had gone far enough and wanted home. It turned and swam against the current for a few minutes then took off upstream, wings noisily flapping and paddles running along the surface for about 10 yards. It flew with noisy wingbeats just above the water level

A substantial tree for a beaver to have felled

and I watched its water ski-type touch down at the bend where I had seen it at first.

I had now caught up with the five teal again. They were in an eddy at the far side of the river and when they sprang into the air they curled over my head, making their rapid wingbeats and pointed wings even more obvious as factors in identification. They made for the biggest of the ponds I'd passed earlier. I thought this pond was frozen but there must have been part of it without ice. They knew exactly where they were going and dropped into the pond in the centre of the wood without any circuit to check that it was clear of danger.

I passed another drowned sheep, this time tangled in a tree on my side of the river and a few feet above the water level. Sheep (and farmers) have a hard time when riverside fields flood.

There was a much more interesting piece of former flotsam a few yards further on. A tree trunk 40 feet long and with a diameter of around 2 feet at the base had been washed up onto the bank. It lay there resembling a colossal caber that a giant had tossed. It was well above the present water level so the flood that abandoned it must have been considerable. I thought little of it – apart from the fact that it had appeared since my last visit – until I looked at the base. There was evidence of gnawing right round the base, leaving a core about six inches in diameter. The gnawing had the clear trademark of beavers. This was a substantial tree for them to tackle and probably took several nights to get to the core. The wind probably finished the job for them. The branches had been stripped and all that remained was the trunk. There are beavers now all the way up the River Earn so this tree could have originated on this estate or could have floated for many miles. It may have been felled several years ago or quite recently, its presence here all depended on flooding – and busy beavers!

New birds identified: siskin, teal
New mammals identified: none

CHAPTER 21
Wednesday 9 January. Calm, sunny. -3°C.

Wester Cairnie Farm, Nether Keir, Upper Cairnie Farm, Blairbell

I drove into the Wester Cairnie Farm road, passed through the steading and then west along one of the farm tracks. A flock of birds erupted from a hawthorn hedge on my right landing further along the hedge. This was a substantial flock of yellowhammers, at least a hundred strong. As they gradually flitted ahead of me I searched for any birds that were not yellowhammers but could see nothing but wee yellow heads. It was great to see on Dupplin Estate such a flock of birds, red-listed with numbers documented as falling.

Reaching the top of Cairnie Den I proceeded on foot down the east side. The field I was walking in has now been merged with the one below it since I was last here. That was one fence less to climb. Half way down, two roe deer fled from the very bottom of the den, not too far from where the logs would have landed that years ago my friend Gerry and I rolled down. The deer scrambled up the far bank and out over the field at the far side, white bums flashing in the

sun. Despite bucks being less identifiable by having shed their antlers in the winter I could see by the white tail-like tushes at their back end that both were does. With one of their favourite snacks, oil seed rape, in the fields on either side of the den they will have plenty food.

At the bottom of the den I turned right and walked up the bank of the River Earn for half a mile or so. It is frustrating not to get right to the water's edge because of invasive Japanese knotweed and Himalyan balsam. I came to the part of the river just downstream of where Dunning Burn flows in from the far side. My thoughts went back to one winter's night when Gerry and I, as young teenagers, walked in the pitch dark for about a mile from Gerry's house down to this exact spot on the river. We had trailed about the fields in that area so often that navigating in the dark was easy. Our reason for going to the river was that we had read or heard somewhere that salmon come to a light

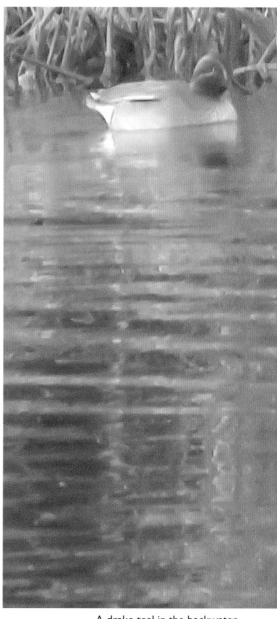

shining into the water. We wanted to try this out and shone our powerful torch into a deep pool at the edge of the river. We waited, with as much patience as teenagers can muster, anticipating a shoal of silvery salmon to come swimming towards us. We felt incredibly let down when not even a small brown trout or grayling appeared.

I turned about and followed the river downstream to a big sweeping bend. I was surprised to flush a snipe off the field, since the ground was frozen. I doubt if it could have been feeding there; maybe just having a rest. At the point of the bend there is a backwater at the far side that held eleven mute swans, about a dozen mallard and a pair of teal. None of the species seemed to be too bothered about my presence about 150 yards from them. I was surprised and pleased that the flighty teal hadn't taken off and managed a reasonable photograph of each of them. The drake was a lovely silvery-grey bird with a chestnut head and a dark green patch running from the back of its neck and over its eye. It was interesting to see the female teal for comparison alongside a female mallard. It was a lighter brown colour than its larger cousin and much more dainty.

A drake teal in the backwater of the River Earn below Wester Cairnie Farm

Further round the bend there were more mute swans in the centre of the river. They were joined by four wigeon that swam out from my side of the river, followed by four little grebes. The wigeon and grebes were just over the

Female teal and a mallard, showing the difference in size

flood bank separating the river from two flooded areas in the field that had unfortunately frozen during the night. I've no doubt that these pools would be favoured by them if they hadn't been frozen. I was pleased to see that at least the pools had filled up; on my last visit they were dry and I'd had doubts that they would ever fill with water again. The pools are surrounded by reeds and long rushy grass, which had appeared since I was in this part of the estate 30 years earlier. At that time the area around the pools had been covered in short grass. Quite a change of habitat over 30 years and one which is little use to farming but absolutely perfect for a great variety of wildlife.

There were a good few herons around today, and they were more vociferous than usual, making loud *kaark* sounds as they flew up or down the river. With them being more vocal I wondered if they may have been starting to pair up. Herons are early

nesters, starting to build up their nest in late February or early March. Generally they nest in trees, often several pairs nesting together in heronries and not necessarily beside water. There used to be a small heronry in Cairnie Wood, where I intend to go later today, but the mature conifer wood has been clear-felled and replanted. I know of no other heronry on this estate, but the springtime might throw up a surprise.

I headed uphill, away from the river and in the direction of my car, following the edge of a game/wild bird crop I had mistaken on my last visit for sunflowers. It was a crop of quinoa, though when I checked an earlier photo there were lots of sunflowers amongst the quinoa. Most of the seeds from the crop had fallen or been eaten but a couple of dozen chaffinches were still visiting for a feed and flew to a nearby tree as I passed.

The roe deer came slowly walking towards me

At the top of the game crop I cut across to a pond surrounded by trees, hawthorn hedges, rushy grass and reeds. Another flock of birds was feeding there. I looked through the binoculars and most seemed to be yellowhammers though I did see some chaffinches. There was also a greenfinch that would have blended in nicely with the yellowhammers had it not been a chunkier bird. I took a few photos of yellowhammers on the top of one of the trees. It was only when I looked more closely at the photos later that one was a decent photo of a male reed bunting.

I collected my car and continued along the farm track to what used to be the next farm, Nether Keir, though no farm steading remains. I parked up and walked along a narrow strip of woodland that bounds the A9. There

was a roe deer about 150 yards ahead so I stood, motionless. Luckily the west wind was in my favour and the deer came walking slowly towards me. It stopped every so often for a better look but then continued on, gradually getting closer until it was less than 40 yards from me. At that point it stopped again, studied me for a few seconds, then jumped the fence into the strip of woodland.

There was a strip of woodland running at right angles from the roadside wood almost bisecting the large field of winter rape. A roe deer jumped the fence from the far end of this wood into the field. It was followed by another, and another, and another until there were twelve roe deer running across the field as if in a race. They made for a small wood near to where I had parked my car but I suspected this area would be too small for them to take refuge. They passed the wood on the bottom side and continued on towards the next strip of woodland, which was larger and denser and would provide plenty cover. As they ran I studied the backsides of the deer to see what sex they were (remember bucks have no antlers at this time). Almost all of them were does. There was only one mature buck and one young buck. Even if I had missed a couple the ratio was still at least 8 does to four bucks. I followed the deer back in the direction of my car as, apart from deer, Nether Keir was quiet. The interesting part of nature-watching is that one day an area is quiet and on the next visit it can be brim-full of a wide variety of wildlife.

As I drove out of Wester Cairnie Farm I passed yet another game/wild bird crop of sunflowers beside the farm road. This time the flock of birds that crossed in front of me to land in a hawthorn hedge was of chaffinches. There would have been nearly a hundred birds and when they settled on the sunny side of the hedge it gave me a good chance to look for any birds other than chaffinches. This time chaffinches seemed to comprise the whole of the flock and they seemed to be enjoying basking in the sun. It is significant that most of the flocks of small birds I have seen have been near game or bird seed crops or hawthorn hedges, clearly great sources of food and shelter in winter.

I drove to Cairnie Toll Cottage to have a look around part of Upper Cairnie Farm and I walked up the farm track to Cairnie Wood, following the track right and then left again through the wood to the fields of Blairbell. I could see through the trees to Pitcairnie Loch but today it seemed to hold only a couple of dozen mute swans and a few mallard. I suspect that many of the wildfowl have moved temporarily to rivers such as the Earn since lochs freeze much more readily than running water.

The cottage at Blairbell looked magnificent in the sun. It has possibly the best situation of any of the houses on the estate, looking south over fields and woodland and down towards Pitcairnie Loch. In the 1970s it was the home for a short time of the most incompetent and unpleasant gamekeeper that the estate has ever had the misfortune to employ. The headkeeper at the time related the story to me of Mr Nasty looking out of his upstairs bedroom window at Blairbell one morning in May and seeing what he thought was a sparrowhawk sitting on the garden fence. He quickly got his shotgun, slowly opened the window. . . and shot a cuckoo that had newly arrived from Africa.

Nowadays in Scotland, though not in the rest of the UK, an employee committing a crime such as this puts his employer, in this case a landowner, and possibly even his manager, in this case a headkeeper, at real risk of being charged and convicted under vicarious liability. Conviction could result in a substantial fine, imprisonment and having a single farm payment worth many thousands of pounds withdrawn by the Scottish Government.

This vile man lasted only a few weeks in employment, and just before he moved out of Blairbell, I, as a police constable at the time, arrested him for giving his wife a terrible beating at the side of a public road on the estate, causing her serious injury. At that point his wife, and the estate, were well rid of him.

I retraced my steps back to Upper Cairnie and headed round the edge of a field of winter barley towards the pond. I have always loved this pond but on my last visit in September I was disappointed to see that the pond was completely dry. I was keen to see if it had filled with water since then. The route took me past a new high seat from which deer are shot. There had earlier been a lot of damage to an Upper Cairnie tattie field by red deer and I could see that some turnips had been scattered along the edge of the barley crop, starting about 100 yards from the hide and extending for a further 100 yards. This would bring the deer into a perfect range for whoever was shooting to select the most suitable ones to be culled. Many of the turnips were well-eaten by the deer and there were red deer prints everywhere.

When I reached the pond I was delighted to see it had filled with water, though it still had a bit to go – maybe two feet – to reach the height of the overflow. There were no ducks on the pond though several mallard feathers floated on the surface, suggesting recent occupation. As I stood by the pond I could hear a croaking noise that was repeated irregularly. *Croak*, then a short gap, then *croak*, then a longer gap, *croak* again. Since I was beside a pond I wondered if it could be a frog. The weather has been unseasonably mild and I wondered if they might be mating and spawning earlier than usual. *Croak* again. The noise was coming

Pond at Upper Cairnie Farm,
now re-filled with water

from behind me so less likely to be a frog away from the pond. Could it be a mute swan? I looked to the sky for the answer. There was no swan but there was a raven flying in the distance. It went *croak* again and solved the mystery. Ravens have a large repertoire of sounds, with the most usual being *pruuk, pruuk*. The *croak* threw me and I might still have been mystified had I not seen the bird.

As I left the pond, crossing a deep ditch to return to the field, I passed a slightly muddy area with a single paw print. Initially I thought it had been a fox but when I looked more closely there were no claw marks. It had been a cat, and a pretty large cat given the size of the print. This field had formerly been in tatties and on my last visit I found a single cat print at the opposite end of the field. Two single cat prints. Surely there is not a one-legged cat on the estate!

New birds identified: none
New mammals identified: none

CHAPTER 22
Wednesday 23 January. Calm, sunny. -5⁰C.

River Earn at Aberdalgie Mains Farm

A cold one today but a lovely sunny winter day to be out. The countryside is white, with a mix of frost and, in some places, light snow. I am heading for the River Earn at Mains of Aberdalgie Farm but am barely on to the estate when there is a lovely sight of five roe deer in a winter barley field of Windyedge Farm. They are no distance from the public road and right on the skyline, framed against the background of cobalt blue sky. They would make a great photograph but there is nowhere safe to quickly park the car. Further around the corner are another three roe, this time two of them bucks, looking fantastic in their partly-grown antlers in velvet. I suspect all eight have earlier been disturbed and were hoping to gain the sanctuary of the large conifer wood on the other side of the road.

The wood on the other side of the road is surrounded by a deer fence but it is old so no doubt the deer would know an access point where the fence is damaged. The woodland here is the western end of the much larger West Lamberkin Wood. The conifers in this part must be around 40 years old but when I knew the wood first, about 50 years ago, it held the original mature conifers which were a great food source for capercaillie but eventually had to be clear-felled. They had been thinned years before that and the canopy was fairly open. I was one of half a dozen beaters on the one and only capercaillie shoot in which I ever took part. The late Lord Forteviot and several others were the guns and the instruction the laird gave to the guns was to only shoot cock capercaillie. There were about three drives in the wood and, although plenty capercaillie were seen, only five males fell to the guns. They were remarkable birds and there were high numbers on the estate, probably many hundreds. It is a real pity that, despite the best efforts of the estate to maintain their numbers, there were fewer each year and they are now completely gone from this part of Perthshire.

I park at Aberdalgie Mains and head for the river. It is probably a good day to have a walk beside the river as any still water will be frozen and waterfowl will congregate on ice-free water. Before I reach the river I have to jump across a ditch and in doing so disturb a snipe. Their feeding places will be limited because of the frost but there are plenty marshy areas available which take a few days of hard frost to freeze over.

A large pack of about 40 mallard rise from slightly further upstream. They fly round in a circle and come back over my head. I see then that there are several wigeon in the group. They are keen to land back in the river at the same place they'd come from. They glide down as if to land but for some reason gain height again, make a further circle round me and land half a mile further upstream. I've already climbed four fences to get to this point and don't fancy the next obstacle, which is a slippery tubular steel gate covered in frost. I decide to turn around and head downstream.

A few hundred yards downstream another 40 or so mallard rise, again coming high over my head and continuing upstream. It is likely that these groups of birds have been shot at during the shooting season and were rightly skittish when they become aware of the presence of a human. I never really get anywhere near them when they are on the river but with the shooting season for wildfowl above the high-water mark ending on 31st January they may settle down after that and be more approachable. Just beyond where the mallard rose there is a group of oystercatchers sitting on a grassy bank, their long orange bills glistening in the low morning sun. There will be little food for them in this frosty weather and most will already have headed for the coast. These ones must have missed the bus.

I have a bit of a shock when I see what I initially thought was a dead crocodile washed up at the side of the river. It has extremely rough skin, a massive head and it looked as if the

'Crocodile' at the side of the River Earn

Some of the woodpigeon flock landed on the tops of conifers in the wood

crows had picked out the eye that had been looking skywards. In fact it is a large limb off a tree but the rough bark and the shape of the limb could almost have passed as a crocodile. As I teenager, if I'd seen this at night by torchlight I would have suffered a real fright!

As I head away from the river I can see a flock of birds flitting between the ground and a line of hawthorn trees. A look with the binoculars confirms them as fieldfares. Their main feeding interest is on the ground and I wonder if the last of the berries have fallen off the hawthorn trees. Just ahead of the line of trees is an area of marsh about 70 yards long and 20 yards wide. A snipe jumps from the rushes as I reach them and makes off with its erratic flight and a single *chip* of alarm. It is closely followed by another three snipe and a couple of hen pheasants. I walk around the rushes but I suspect if I had walked

through them I would put up many more snipe. The length and density of the rushes have protected some of the wetter parts against being frozen and make a great dining area for waders such as snipe. There will also be food here that would suit the hungry oystercatchers, though they don't usually feed in thick cover, preferring open areas.

I continue up a farm track that runs from the public road up towards the estate march. The track is bounded on each side by whin bushes and I could see from occasional footprints in small patches of snow that bunnies have not been completely wiped out. It would have been nice to have seen even one rabbit sitting basking in the winter sun. A cloud of many hundreds of woodpigeons come over my head, with some landing on the tops of conifers in

A delightful male siskin feeding on seeds from the cones on an alder tree

the wood I am about to reach. With this massive flock needing to be fed I'm not surprised that almost all of the fields of oil seed rape are dotted with flapping white scarecrows. Many of the fields of winter cereal also have their contingent of scarecrows, though this is to try to limit damage from geese.

When I reach the wood there is a further exodus of woodpigeons and as I walked along the wood edge back towards my car I can hear the scolding *cha cha cha* of a great tit. I look in to the wood and can see the wee yellow and black fellow on a low branch of an ash tree, still chattering at me. I am a bit taken aback as this call is normally used if someone is near their nest or if a predator is about. It clearly sees me as a source of danger.

I'd parked my car beside a line of alder trees and the antics of half a dozen delightful wee siskins feeding on seeds from the cones on the trees is a lovely end to that part of my walk. Siskins are a relaxing species to watch as, once they have found a food source, they get on with the job in hand: feeding. Goldfinches feed in the same relaxed manner but the tit family, especially coal tits, usually grab a morsel and fly off elsewhere to eat it. Long-tailed tits are the most frustrating of the tit family. They arrive *en masse* but, even if there is plenty of food to keep them going for half an hour, they usually fly off in search of another food source within a few minutes. But the siskins feed heartily and when I leave them after about fifteen minutes they are still making the most of the seeds available.

New birds identified: none
New mammals identified: none

CHAPTER 23

Wednesday 30 January. Calm, sunny. -2°C.

Milton Den, Harlaypoint Wood, Back Hill

Today is another glorious day for January, with my only complaint that I can see absolutely nothing when walking into the sun. I deal with that by planning my route so that where I am most likely to see wildlife of interest I will be walking with the sun at my back. I park at Munday House and have a quick look at a small field situated between two conifer woods that still has some remains of a game/wild bird crop. There is a pheasant feeder at the far side of the field and a cloud of birds rise from the ground around the feeder and land in the trees above it. They are mostly yellowhammers with a sprinkling of chaffinches and at least one linnet. As the sun shines on the finches perched on the fir trees they look like gaudy pink and yellow Christmas decorations. The decorations don't last long on the trees and as I leave the field they quickly drop off to have another fill of wheat around the feeder.

I head down the edge of another former game/wild bird crop to Milton Den, preceded by the shepherd with his brown and white collie balanced on a box at the back of his quad bike. Sheepdogs soon learn this energy-saving trick and have a great sense of balance. A jay screeches and a buzzard mews as I reach the den. Since the pheasant shooting is all but finished for the season I walk up the track in the middle of the den, whereas my former walks have always been round the edge of woodlands. This is fantastic habitat for wildlife with a lovely mix of mature ash and alder trees, hawthorn and whin bushes, a small pond, a burn and open grassy spaces. I watch a pair of dunnocks hopping about under a hawthorn bush and a friendly wee robin perched in front of me on a whin bush. A couple of hundred woodpigeons rise from the tops of ash trees at the far end of the den and a male bullfinch flies from an alder tree. The deep rosy pink of the bullfinch's breast, its jet-black head and its glossy white rear end all seem even more dazzling than usual as it flies across the cloudless blue sky. They really are one of our smartest-looking birds but it is quite unusual to

Mallard on the frozen pond in Milton Den

see one without either its mate or as part of a winter flock.

Near the far end of the den I stand for a while overlooking the quinoa game/wild bird crop in the field beyond. It seems quiet bird-wise and I think that the last of the seed from the crop has been eaten, but after a few minutes a huge flock of several hundred finches rises from the crop and flies into the den ahead of me. Most of the birds are chaffinches though I've no doubt there will be a mix of a few other species. The wild bird seed crops on this estate would be ideal for the now-rare corn bunting. If they are not here already I'm sure they will be before long. As the crow flies it is not that far from their main strongholds in Angus and Fife. In my early days as a teenager and later in my 30s there were no game crops or bird seed plots on the estate. What a huge benefit they are to small birds in winter, supplying a steady source of seed.

When I entered the den I heard the quacking of mallard and wondered about that as I was sure that the pond would be frozen. Sure enough when I reach it ice covers most of the surface but there is a very small area at the edge where fifteen or so mallard have managed through their constant paddling to keep the ice at bay. They leave the water and slowly waddle over the ice towards the centre as I pass but they are relatively unfazed at my presence. There is a strong possibility that they will be the survivors of the 100 young mallard that Stewart released on to the pond away back in August. Some will have been taken by predators, some will have been shot and some will have moved to other wetlands. With only one more day of the wildfowl shooting season to go there is every chance that these surviving mallard will now go on to breed, starting even in the next couple of weeks. Mallard nest early in the season, though their first attempt is often doomed to failure due to minimal cover for nesting and lack of food for the ducklings if the eggs are successful.

135

The earliest I had mallard ducklings come to the burn running through my garden one year was 14 February, when there was a very cold spell with snow on the ground. The duck disappeared with two ducklings, leaving four huddled in the snow and almost frozen. I heated them and hand-reared them and they were fat and healthy wee ducks when their mother appeared in the garden almost two months later with a new brood.

As I walk up the track through the den I notice a few places where rabbits have made small scrapes in the grass. A bit further on there is a rabbit burrow with some fresh rabbit droppings at the entrance. So some still remain. Despite all that the humble rabbit has suffered over the years with predation, gin traps, snares, ferrets, nets, shooting, road traffic, myxomatosis and VHD, they (thankfully) refuse to be exterminated. My next stop further demonstrates their resilience. I walk through a small strip of coniferous wood that runs from Munday House down to the public road. There are several active burrows (and more fresh droppings) within the wood and amongst brambles on the western edge of the wood. I look forward to seeing pairs of rabbits sunning themselves at the wood edge in March and young rabbits scurrying about there come April.

I move on to the east drive of the estate to do a circuit of Harlaypoint Wood, a mixed wood of conifers, beech and birch. This wood is bounded on the north side by Back Hill. As I make my way along the east drive a buzzard crosses from right to left. It seems to have come off the ground, flies low across the drive and lands in a tree 50 yards from me. It is probably a male as it is small, in fact I mistake it at first for a female sparrowhawk. I can see nothing on the ground that might have attracted it but a short distance further on a small flock of blue tits, great tits and coal tits lift in small groups off the ground where they have been feeding and land in bushes ahead of me, some crossing the drive to the left-hand side. As I pass a large rhododendron bush I can hear, almost imperceptibly, a quiet *pic, pic, pic*. Though I can see nothing, the scene is absolutely clear in my mind. One of the tits has flown into the bush with a seed, is holding it with a foot against a branch, and is hammering at the seed with its beak to expose the edible morsel inside.

I cut up through the lawn park to the scenic grassy ride that separates Harlaypoint Wood from Pond Wood. At

Harlaypoint Wood I stand admiring some of the ancient conifers, beech and even an odd monkey puzzle tree. It is also great to see that large areas of the wood where trees have either been felled or blown over have been replanted with beech and sweet chestnut, though I wouldn't have known the chestnut and had to ask Robin, an employee involved in the management of the trees on the estate.

At the end of the wood I approach the gate slowly, knowing that there are likely to be roe deer in the field. Sure enough there is a buck and a doe about 200 yards off to my right. I am standing beside a thick straining post and am barely visible to the deer. There is only a very light west wind, which will be blowing from me towards the deer. By whatever means the buck becomes aware of me and walks smartly back into the wood, followed by the doe. I can see another three deer further along the field and I manage to walk up the field to the track at the top and then head towards the deer.

These three deer, all does in magnificent condition, are not quite as smart as the buck. They have a far greater chance of seeing me than the buck but since I am above them and not in line with them they don't pick up my scent. I manage to get to within about 100 yards before I have to completely show myself, which convinces me that the wily buck must have got my scent rather than having spotted me. It is a good lesson on how little wind is required for wildlife to recognise potential danger.

When I reach what on my last visit I had thought may have been a buzzard nest high in a larch tree on the wood at Back Hill, I go into the wood to have a closer look. I am distracted by a red squirrel that is near the top of another tall but spindly larch tree. It is busily feeding on the seeds within larch cones and takes little notice of me, giving me a great chance for some photographs as it sits on a branch with a cone in its front paws. I am impressed by how far out on some of the thin branches it ventures and how little effect its tiny body has on the branches, barely bending them.

Coming back to the possible buzzard nest a few trees from the squirrel, I have another look through the binoculars and take a few photographs to try to decide whether it is indeed a nest and not some sort of growth on the tree. It is huge, at least three quarters way up the tree, tight into the trunk and appears to be

Red squirrel busily feeding on the seeds within cones at the top of a larch tree

constructed completely of larch branches. I'm still not convinced it is a nest but will have another look later in the year. Sometimes when the weather is warmer some greenery can be seen growing from an old nest, fed by the droppings in the nest from the young birds and from remains of prey. It is certainly an interesting structure. As I walk round the larch trees I am aware of more signs of rabbit runs in the frosty grass, which is a really satisfying conclusion to my visit into this wood.

As I finish for the day and pack my rucksack into the car I look up to see five buzzards interacting in the sky just west of me, swooping and diving on each other. With the recent sunshine and the open winter weather they are maybe thinking ahead to the forthcoming spring and this interaction could be a prelude to choosing a mate and claiming a territory.

My last treat, as I drive through the centre of the estate, is a red squirrel feeding at the side of the estate road. It poses several times for a photograph, but always runs off just a bit further before I can get my camera in action. There is a good population of red squirrels on the estate, but young red squirrels don't have a high survival rate and some strategically placed squirrel feeders may just help one or two more to survive the winter.

New birds identified: none
New mammals identified: none

CHAPTER 24
Wednesday 6 February. Calm, sunny. 5⁰C.

Beech Alley, Factor's Strip, The Parsonage, Garden Bank, Methven Moss

I can hardly believe the weather we are having this winter. We're near the end of the first week in February and really have had no bad weather in this part of Perthshire. I had hoped for some snowy days for tracking but no snowfall as yet.

I parked in the centre of the estate and walked down towards Beech Alley, which is a long narrow wood of mostly conifers but with some birch interspersed. On the way down to Beech Alley, in the gardens of Dupplin Castle, I photographed a three-foot high conifer growing out of a part of a beech tree where the trunk split into three. It was about 10 feet from the ground and I suppose would have a good supply of water in what was effectively a basin in the tree. Around the corner on a mature conifer, possibly a giant fir laden on the top half with cones, there was a large round viral canker growth about 18 inches in diameter hanging from a branch. The bottom half of the globe shape was brown and seemed to consist of dead needles. The top half was green and was fresh needle growth. I'd seen nothing like it before and yet again had to seek the counsel of the tree expert, Robin.

I walked along the ride running the length of Beech Alley, maybe quarter of a mile. It was disappointingly quiet, with no birds other than pheasants for the first half. In the second half a buzzard rose from a tree from where it may have been watching half a dozen pheasants feeding on the ride ahead of me. I've never seen a buzzard take a full-grown pheasant but I've no doubt the larger female would manage to tackle a hen pheasant. Buzzards are similar in size to goshawks, which can take even a large cock pheasant with ease; but then goshawks are much more aggressive predators.

The west end of Beech Alley has been planted with a type of extra-large rhododendron which was starting to show the beginnings of flowers. It is certainly not the wild *Rhododendron ponticum* with purple heads which tends to take over woodlands, smothering every other plant in its path. It would be nice to see it in flower. I was also pleased to see that there were one or two active rabbit burrows in the south-west corner of the wood.

I climbed the fence into the grass field beyond the wood and noticed there was a small flock of birds feeding under one of the old oak trees that dot the field. A look through the binoculars revealed the birds to be a mix of fieldfares, redwings and, surprisingly, starlings. A line of oaks at the far end of the grass field and leading up to the bottom end of the Factor's Strip held an even better surprise. A bird was half way up the first oak on top of a thick branch and not far from the trunk. The bird then climbed down the side of the branch, climbed under the branch and from there on to the trunk, where it proceeded to climb head first down the trunk. This certainly got my attention and the binoculars came into use.

Bird enthusiasts will know already what this bird is and it only the second one I have seen in Scotland, the first being in 2016 at Killiecrankie Visitor Centre. Nuthatches have been breeding at Killiecrankie for several years and come regularly to the bird feeders there. These great tit-sized birds are slowly spreading from England up through certain parts of Scotland and it is fantastic that they are now on this estate. This wee bird is blue-grey on top, buff underneath and with bright chestnut on its flanks. The most noticeable features in identifying this bird – apart from it climbing head-first down a tree – are the chestnut flanks, short tail and sharp pointed beak with a black stripe running lengthways across its cheek.

The nuthatch tormented me by refusing to stay for more than a few seconds in a position I could photograph. It flew to the next oak tree, where I was distracted initially in trying to photograph a treecreeper. This effort was also unsuccessful and I turned my attention back to the nuthatch, which promptly flew back to the first oak tree. The good news was that there was a second nuthatch still in the oak tree, but the bad news was that it was no more cooperative than the first one. Even without a photograph I was delighted with the sightings.

I continued on up the line of oaks, then crossed a fence to walk up the east side of the Factor's Strip. It has been doubled in width and this is the first time I have really seen the recently-planted trees, a lovely mix of conifers and broadleaf trees. A pair of yellowhammers sat as bright as a couple of canaries on a branch of one of the young trees. I'm certainly impressed with the number of yellowhammers about.

Another two fences to climb and I walked across another grass field to the south-east corner of The Parsonage, where I wanted to see how the ladybirds hibernating on an old gate and gatepost were doing. The original groups were still there but they had been joined by more than double the original number. Ladybirds were packed into each gap in the gatepost and in each join in the gate as well as behind a chain securing the gate shut. I wonder what it is that attracted them to the gate in such numbers, or might ladybirds give off pheromones when they are about to hibernate so that they can do so in a colony? It's the first time I've seen so many hibernating and I'll check them again at the beginning of spring.

I went into The Parsonage woodland behind the ladybird gate as the last time I was there I watched a red squirrel and a treecreeper. No luck with these two today but a bird flew ahead that looked suspiciously like another nuthatch. I'd difficulty finding it with the binoculars on the tree where it settled and just as I did so it flew to another tree. I could make no positive identification but in any case the two I'd seen earlier had made my day.

I continued clockwise around The Parsonage noting lovely little clumps of snowdrops in the woodland not too far from the Factor's House. At the north-west corner a bird flew right to left along a line of beech trees just outside the wood. Its size – just a bit bigger than a blackbird – and its flight made it easy to identify, even at 100 yards. Great-spotted woodpeckers have an undulating flight, with a few flaps of their wings on the upward part of the cycle, then they close their wings and lose some height on the downward part. It is the time of year when great-spotted woodpeckers will be looking for mates and setting up a territory, which is accompanied by them drumming on a tree or even a telephone pole. I was disappointed not to have heard this during my walk today. I stood and watched for a while hoping this woodpecker might drum. In due course it flew silently back along the line of beeches and then into The Parsonage without even the usual *tick tick* call that they make.

From The Parsonage I made for Garden Bank. This is a fantastic piece of woodland with some ancient trees and running between the East Drive and the public road to the south. I walked along the East Drive first of all, hearing the song of a mistle thrush in the distance. In my book *A Wealth of Wildlife: a year on a Highland Perthshire estate* I had written down, as best I could, the notes of the songs of a couple of mistle thrushes. I sat at the base of a tree hoping to do the same with this one, the first I had heard this year, but I'd no success; it was a bit too far away and I was missing too many of the notes.

As I stood up I flushed a woodcock from amongst leaves under an oak tree. It must have been sitting watching me, depending on its amazing camouflage since they are almost invisible when sitting amongst fallen leaves. It flew off, landing 100 yards away under another oak tree in the lawn park. It is the first I have seen this winter, but until now, because of the shooting season, I had been avoiding going into woodland and doing my observations from tracks and clearings. Many years ago I trained gundogs and learned that some gundogs are reluctant to pick up woodcock as they have a smell that appears to be unpleasant to the dog. I could never smell anything but then a dog's nose is much more finely tuned than mine.

I stopped soon after to photograph an ancient cedar tree, then after that an equally old Douglas fir. It would be really interesting to know the age of these trees, which must be measured in centuries. As I left the Douglas fir a red squirrel that had been feeding on the ground ran up a beech tree. It paused, still facing up the trunk, about 10 feet from the ground, wagged its tail violently from side to side and chattered at me in annoyance at interrupting its important business of finding food. I had a further experience with a busy squirrel some 50 yards further on as I cut through the woodland to the track that runs back to my starting point. On a lovely sunny day it is not surprising to see industrious squirrels.

The highlights of the route back included a giant sequoia tree, still with the metal sign depicting its Latin name at its base. It was absolutely enormous and is another tree of which I'd love to know the history. Towards the end of Garden Bank buzzards were mewing overhead. I looked up to see two distinct pairs, a smaller male and larger female in each pair, circling overhead. One pair gradually circled left over the castle while the other pair rose higher and higher into the sky until they were mere specks in a lovely blue sky. What

Evidence of a beaver on one of the ditches running through Methven Moss

an amazing view they must get from that height, and even that is nothing like the height that golden eagles regularly achieve. Lastly, just before I reached the car, I encountered a small flock – eight or so – of one of the loveliest birds in the countryside: long-tailed tits. They look like wee pink and grey lollipops with their fluffy body stuck on to their long tail. The unfortunate trait of long-tailed tits is that they seldom stay long in one place and are always keen to move on. Between this frustrating habit and the fact that I was looking into the sun I failed to get a photograph.

On the way home I stopped off at Methven Moss. One of the residents on the estate had told me that she had seen evidence of a beaver on one of the ditches running through the Moss. I easily found the recently felled saplings she had mentioned, which were just a few yards from the public road. One of the trees, yet to fall, was chewed part-way through and there was a pile of fresh chippings on the ground. The beaver had begun to build a dam between the gabion baskets that lead the ditch under the road. It is a perfect place to build a dam and if completed it will create a pool maybe four or five feet deep but contained by the high bank on the field side and the bank on the road side, but extending partly in to the woodland. It should cause no problems, it will increase biodiversity and it will slow the water flowing down the burn, reducing a flood risk. Human engineers would charge a considerable fee to achieve the same result.

Methven Moss is designated as a Special Area of Conservation (SAC). It is described as a raised bog which is capable of regeneration and although it has been damaged by past drainage activity it retains a significant area of intact surface and continues to support typical bog vegetation and species. It seems logical that a beaver or beavers reducing the flow of water from the bog will raise the water table slightly and help to repair this damage. The restoration of the bog is certainly not helped by the regular deepening and widening of the ditches that I see being carried out by a neighbouring farmer to Dupplin Estate. The ditches also appear

The bog area below Wester Cairnie Farm

to be a perfect habitat for the almost-extinct water vole and, if they are present, neither will they be helped by the operation of a JCB.

As I drove the two miles or so home from the beaver activity I reflected that where I expected to see evidence of beavers was on the River Earn, where I have seen plenty evidence in past years. There are no beavers presently on the Dupplin part of the river that I can see but it is good to know that they are colonising out-of-the-way places where beavers maybe even have lived prior to our thoughtless and selfish ancestors exterminating them in the sixteenth century.

New birds identified:
starling, nuthatch, woodcock, long-tailed tit.
New mammals identified:
beaver

CHAPTER 25
Friday 22 February. Calm, cloudy with sunny intervals. 15⁰C.

Wester Cairnie Farm, River Earn

Yet another amazing day weather-wise for February. I'd initially thought of visiting the lochs to see if the waterfowl had returned after the lochs had been frozen over for a few days and had now thawed but decided against it. Belgian visitors had been shooting roe deer there earlier in the morning. Though they would be gone by the time I was at the lochs, if they had fired rifle shots the disturbance would limit what I might see. I decided instead to have a walk along part of the River Earn.

I passed an old caravan that some parasitic individual had dumped at the roadside near to Upper Cairnie, in the knowledge that someone else would have to see to its disposal, but as I drove in the Wester Cairnie road I was pleased to see a pair of buzzards circling over Cairnie Strip. No doubt that will be their chosen nesting site for this year. As I passed through the farm steading I met Stewart, who had been chasing swans off a field of oil seed rape. He told me that a fox had killed a hare in the south-west corner of the field, and gave me the location of a possible den site that he asked me to avoid. Though it is an unpleasant job, it

is perfectly legal to kill young fox cubs with a terrier in a den. My many years of policing have taught me to make a distinction between what may be wrong in the opinion of some and what is legal. Human presence at a den just before cubs are born may make a vixen change her mind and cub elsewhere. Human presence at a den with cubs will almost certainly cause a vixen to move the cubs to another den. Stewart had shot just over 200 foxes since he came to the estate a year earlier; that's nearly four a week. As with many predators, if one dies or is killed another will quickly take its place so long as the habitat and food source remain suitable. Rabbit numbers are well down but pheasant numbers remain the same. Of the other principal food sources of foxes, mice, voles and rats are probably stable, as will be earthworms and beetles. I can't quite work out why there is now such a high incidence of foxes.

I parked my car midway between Wester Cairnie Farm and the river, heading off on foot eastwards along the north side of a wet, reedy area with two large ponds (which had been dry in the summer time). Three reed buntings

One of the reed buntings, a male, sat on top of one of the bushes

Pair of oystercatchers on an island of gravel in the centre of the River Earn

flew from some bushes ahead of me, as did a pair of red-legged partridges and a hen pheasant. One of the reed buntings, a male, came back and sat on top of one of the bushes giving me a chance of a photo. He was a smart-looking sparrow-sized chap, with his jet-black head, white collar and streaked white breast. One of the other two buntings also came back and circled above the male, giving off a metallic *ching, ching, ching* call. Unfortunately I couldn't make out whether this second bird was a female or another male.

Fifty yards further on I came upon a sandy bank on my left. There were three large holes into the bank, possibly originally made by rabbits and enlarged by several generations of foxes. At the third hole some fresh sand had been scraped out a few days earlier so this looked very like another place that a vixen would be giving consideration as a den in which to have her cubs. I moved on quickly to leave minimal scent behind.

As I neared the river a great black-backed gull flew upstream. Its size is impressive, considerably larger than a buzzard. This one was an adult, with jet-black wing tops and back contrasting with its snowy-white underparts and tail and with a bright yellow beak ending in a red tip. It is a really majestic and powerful bird and can out-compete most other predatory or scavenging birds if it feeds from a carcass.

As I followed the flight of the gull I spotted another white bird on the river. This time it was a male goosander. I stalked closer behind the cover of the flood bank until I was opposite the goosander. They are wary birds as they are regularly shot if a licence has been granted by Scottish Natural Heritage because of their predation on young fish. I had barely put my head above the flood bank when the goosander and a female that had been with him saw me and took off up the river.

I could see small groups of swans further upstream. Some were taking off and flying to the field of oil seed rape that Stewart had earlier chased them off. There were now about fifty grazing on the field and a quick look through the binoculars showed that roughly half were mute swans and the other half whooper swans. I reached a bend in the river where there were at least another hundred swans, mostly mute but with a fair proportion of whoopers. They were slightly more obliging than the goosanders and I managed a few decent photos of the whoopers. Thinking back to the 1970s I can't think of any whoopers on the river and I wonder if their numbers have increased and their

winter distribution is expanding or if they have simply found a new place that they like. This was a corner where, on my last visit, there were good numbers of mallard, wigeon and teal. At that time lochs and ponds were frozen but their absence now suggests that they have moved back, preferring still, shallow water to deep, running water.

I had heard the sound of oyster-catchers as I approached the bend in the river and had seen them flying off the edge of the field. They had landed on a long narrow island of gravel in the river where they clearly felt safe, in fact most were now sitting with their blood-red eyes closed or carrying out a bit of feather preening. Lovely birds, and the emblem of the Scottish Police College, below which is the Gaelic term '*Bi Glic, Bi Glic*', which mimics the call of the oystercatcher with the translation '*Be wise, be circumspect*'. I could never understand how two identical Gaelic terms could translate to two different terms in English.

As I had come up the river I had noticed a dead swan on the far bank. I now saw a further two dead swans in the field behind me and saw that all three were below power lines. The two in the field were only a few yards apart. One was a whooper which looked as if it had been dead for four or five days

Dead whooper swan and mute swan below power lines at Cairnie Haugh

and was beginning to be predated, maybe even by the great black-backed gull. Its eyes had been pecked out and there was a small area of its breast where the feathers had been pecked out and crows, gulls or maybe even a buzzard had begun to eat at the breast meat. The mute swan lying almost next to it looked as if it had been killed in the last 24 hours. It was also on its back but with no predation having taken place. Both birds looked as if they had been killed instantly. I'd be surprised if hitting a power line would always kill rather than injure a big bird like this. A broken wing might be more likely. These swans, though, might have been electrocuted if their wings came into contact simultaneously with two of the three power lines.

I climbed the fence into the field of oil seed rape and saw the hare that Stewart had mentioned. It was an adult hare and its head was missing, often a trade mark of a fox kill. I could feel that some of its ribs were broken, another indication of a kill by a fox or dog

rather than by a large avian predator since it would be killed by being crushed and violently shaken. The top of its rump was slightly eaten. Though this looked more like predation by a bird it was strange that there was no fur lying around as avian predators or scavengers usually pull out fur or feathers before dining on a carcass. It seemed that the fox had just killed the hare, taken its head and left the rest. It must have been a well-fed fox and if it comes back to the area there are also two swans for lunch over the fence. A healthy adult hare would take a bit of catching even for the fittest fox, though the fact it was lying near to a fence may mean that the fox gained a few valuable seconds while the hare tried to get through the fence.

I continued up the field side of the flood bank, meaning that the swans were yet again deprived of their feed of oil seed rape. They had caused a fair bit of damage to the crop and I'm surprised that no measures such as scarecrows or a banger had been deployed to try to keep them off. As they flew off the whoopers curled back to the bend in the river while the mute swans headed further west and I later saw that they had landed in a field at the other side of the river and about a mile distant.

I crossed a burn flowing from Cairnie Den into the river and was now in a field of winter barley. When I looked down at the river again I could see that my pair of goosanders were again busy trying to find small fish. This time I waited until both of them had dived then ran a bit closer to the river, managing to switch on my camera while I ran. I achieved one half-decent photo before they saw me and yet again set off upstream.

As I walked up the field edge I rose half a dozen hares either from the rough ground between the field and the river or from the bottom end of the field. Unusually I had seen none of these hares before they rose. On my return trip I walked back half-way up the field. The winter barley was barely three inches high so I scanned the field with binoculars looking for any hares that I might get close enough to photograph. Nothing. Not a sign of a hare, though I appreciate it is only the top few inches of their body that I would see. By the time I was three quarters through the return trip I'd risen another five hares, some right in front of me. The last one that rose had been lying beside a partially buried stone about twelve inches by five. It had given the hare great cover.

Part of the reason that I hadn't seen this latest recumbent hare was because

I had disturbed five or six skylarks that flew around but were determined to land in near enough the same place as they had just left. Photos were impossible once they landed as they simply disappeared, but I managed one photo in the air though the subject looked about moth-sized. One of the skylarks had been thinking about spring time and rose higher and higher in the air, singing its heart out. Their song is a bit high pitched for me but I managed to hear this one. It immediately took me back to my youth and lying on my back in a grassy field on a spring or summer day and listening to one or more skylarks singing high in the sky. It is one of the best countryside sounds of spring, matched only by the lapwing, the curlew and the grey partridge, all four species sadly depleted now.

Then a snipe flew past from behind me and landed at the edge of the reeds near to the car. It was making its *chip-er chip-er chip-er* call that a snipe often makes in flight and I wondered if it was trying to elicit a response from another snipe in the reeds. The walk finished with a song from another mistle thrush, again at a distance and coming from the bottom end of the Cairnie Den. What a pity it hadn't started to sing as I passed the den.

New birds identified:
great black-backed gull
New mammals identified: none

A dipper came from the water and sat on a stone at the water's edge

CHAPTER 26
Wednesday 27 February. Calm and sunny. 13⁰C.

River Earn, Forteviot, Kildinny Farm, Broombarns Farm, Newton of Condie

On yet another spring-like morning I made for the south side of the River Earn intending to start out from May Burn. The gates on the railway line closed at the Forteviot level crossing as I approached and I sat in my car looking at the old grey stone building on my right. In my (much) younger day this was the Forteviot Hotel, a small hostelry that would have to be described as unique. Looking from the outside at what had been the public bar the window was still the same. It wasn't even a window, it was just a square painted black with white-painted cross sections to mimic the window frames. A South African, Jack Davidson, ran the hotel, though I never did find out if he owned it. He worked during the day in Perth and only seemed to be in the hotel in the evenings and at weekends. A young woman, probably in her early twenties, helped in the hotel. She was always referred to as Cinders, and I doubt if many folks knew her real name.

Inside the bar the floor was of old dark wood, which wouldn't even have looked posh in a farm hayloft. The highlight in the bar was an ostrich egg which was suspended on string and had probably been brought by Jack from South Africa many years earlier. Jack was a moaner. Anything that was done in Scotland that was done differently (or not done at all) in South Africa was wrong. He would have won competitions for complaining, yet was a likeable old soul. Strangely there were issues that could have justifiably sent him into a rage and he remained calm. An example was when, during one of my infrequent visits to the bar, Fraser, a man who I knew well and who operated a cattle and sheep transport business, looked in for a quick pint on the way home after delivering his last load of sheep locally. It had been a day of torrential rain and Fraser was still wearing his waterproofs. As he stood drinking his pint, the rainwater, gradually gathering sheep shit off his coat and leggings as it meandered its way south, began to form a green pool around his boots. This was clearly accepted practice in the Forteviot Hotel and Jack, the moaner, never batted an eyelid.

The Perth to Glasgow train clattered through the level crossing, the gates lifted and I was suddenly back to the present.

I parked beside the River Earn and wandered slowly downstream. Birds were beginning to pair off and three separate pairs of mallard swam from my side of the river and sailed gradually downsteam with the current. A pair of carrion crows perched high in an ash tree on the far bank as if they might have been eyeing up a suitable place to nest, though it would be some time before they are ready to do that. Carrion crows build their nests a week or two after rooks, and rooks, though they are now gathering at rookeries, are only reserving their preferred nesting spot in the colony and have not yet started to build. The chances are, though, that this year many birds will nest earlier than usual.

I continued on to the fishing hut and sat in the sun on the bench at the riverside. A song thrush in a tree just behind me sang a beautiful song, repeating each line two or three times.

They are fantastic birds to listen to and I'm surprised this is the first I have seen or heard on the estate. At the other side of the river, on a line of oak trees, two great-spotted woodpeckers drummed on trees. The timbre of their drumming was different and as they drummed in turn it sounded a bit like a version of a police two-tone horn but further down the scale. Completing the orchestra a chaffinch sang from a bush on my right and not far from it a great tit gave me a rendition of its *tea-cher tea-cher tea-cher* song. Bliss!

I checked the stone on the riverbank where I had seen otter spraint on an earlier visit. Nothing new there but on a stone on the path twenty yards further on there was a spraint, though this time a few days old. Thirty yards beyond that there was also a small patch of grass on the banking burnt by otter spraint. This otter is definitely keen for other otters to know they are trespassing if they venture on to this stretch of river.

Another resident of the river popped up a few yards further on. A dipper came from the water and sat on a stone at the water's edge. It bobbed few times, as if curtseying, then dived back into the water again in search of caddis fly larvae or other aquatic food.

I eventually reached a ditch that flows from near Kildinny Farm to the river. The ditch had a single sleeper forming a bridge. The sleeper looked a bit safer than the one I had foolishly ventured over at Broombarns in December and the bottom of the ditch, in the case of a fall, was not so distant. This time the sleeper had wire netting nailed to the first three feet at either end, giving anyone crossing some grip. In competition for danger with the Broombarns sleeper which had a hole in the centre this one had no netting in the centre. The tightrope walker is lulled into a false sense of safety by the netting giving good grip to start with then safety is withdrawn half way across. I immediately thought of a line by William McIlvanney in one of his Inspector Jack Laidlaw novels when he is describing a man he is referring to as a real bastard, the type of man who helps an old lady half-way across a busy road. Anyway, despite this ditch not being quite as deep as the Broombarns one I thought it was a suitable time to turn back.

On my route back to the car I spotted a pair of bullfinches feeding on willow buds. I watched them for about ten minutes, trying unsuccessfully for a photo without branches in the way. The birds were never more than a couple of feet apart, sometimes feeding right beside each other. Bullfinches have an amazing bond and these two were a real couple of lovebirds. Further on and just before I reached the car several birds flew from the edge of the field to trees beside the river. Some were chaffinches, some were yellowhammers but one I photographed thinking it was either a female yellowhammer or a female linnet turned out to be a female reed bunting. It was a decent photo taken at a distance and I'd never have managed to make an accurate identification of the species without it.

I moved on to Broombarns Farm where I met the tenant, Donald Mackie, busy ploughing. I had thought that it was Donald – since he farms Newton of Condie Farm as well – who had put up all the bird nesting boxes I had seen on an earlier visit on the trees at Newton of Condie parklands. He told me it was a woman who was interested in birds who did so and that she hopes to encourage tree sparrows to nest in them. I would see them again on my way back out of the farm. He also told me that he regularly sees barn owls around the old ruin of Newton of Condie House.

Leaving Donald, I cut along a ditch

Two great-black-backed gulls sat as if on guard
on top of a huge pile of gravel

line heading gradually for the River Earn. Two separate pairs of mallard rose from the ditch. They'll be nesting soon if they are not already doing so and this boggy ditch area is an ideal spot. Early mornings are the best time to discover where a mallard is nesting. While she is on the nest laying the drake hangs around close by. He continues this devotion until she has laid the whole clutch, normally eight to ten eggs, then leaves her to hatch the eggs and raise the brood herself, then he, the scoundrel, takes a new mate if one is available.

There were several hundred gulls sitting on the grass field at the far side of the river. They were mostly common gulls, though part of one end of the group had a fair scattering of black-headed gulls, many now beginning to take on their chocolate-brown coloured head. One of these gulls immediately took my attention as it had a jet black rather than a chocolate-brown head, with a much larger proportion of the head being black than that of its near black-headed gull neighbours. It was also slightly bigger than the black-headed gulls. It was in fact a Mediterranean gull, which are apparently not too uncommon though I can't remember ever having seen one before.

I continued up the river, noting several dozen oystercatchers on the far bank and in the field behind, and the pack of resting gulls taking off in the direction of Donald's tractor as he continued to plough. Further on and on top of a huge pile of gravel scraped from the riverbed two great-black-backed gulls sat as if on guard. They eyed me up as I photographed them but they obviously felt safe with the river being between us. I sat for a while and watched them, also looking out for signs of a kingfisher as the bank at this part of the river seemed ideal for these delightful birds to burrow into and nest. After fifteen minutes no sign of kingfishers, and after a couple of gruff *ug ug ug* barks from the gulls telling me to move on I did so.

I returned across the field towards my car, watching three skylarks rising and landing again in front of me. It's great to see skylarks so regularly. I was telling Donald about the value of leaving skylark plots and he sounds just the kind of farmer who might try that.

I drove uphill the short distance to Newton of Condie and had a walk around the parklands. There are so few places where trees are allowed to flourish in permanent grasslands and the summer wildlife in these ancient trees will be interesting to see. The winter/spring wildlife seemed scarce and unfortunately there was not a sign of a tree sparrow. The volume of nest boxes might encourage them as they prefer to nest in colonies so let's wait and see. The old ruin of Newton of Condie House may also hold a few surprises. It is too dangerous to enter but I did notice a reasonably fresh owl pellet at one of the empty windows. Right above it was a place that an owl could easily perch or roost and there was a white splash of droppings running down the wall just below it. My one worry was the presence of bait boxes for rats or mice round the buildings. There are many owls, kestrels, red kites and buzzards that carry a residual amount of rat poison from eating rats and mice that have partaken of the baits. It can build up to a point where it can be fatal.

On my homeward journey a female kestrel crossed the quiet country road just at Mains of Cultmalundie Farm, still on the estate. I'm always pleased to see a kestrel, especially when I had just read on social media earlier in the day of a kestrel that had been shot in North Yorkshire. I knew a gamekeeper in the 1960s who was adamant that a kestrel would take a proportion of the grey partridge chicks on the estate and that they should be got rid of the same as any other bird of prey. Thankfully few modern-day gamekeepers would consider a kestrel as any threat to their game bird charges.

Since I was passing, I stopped off to see how the beaver was doing at Methven Moss. I'd had a very quick look from the car a few days earlier and the part-built dam had been removed. Today it had been rebuilt, though there will be some engineering yet to be done before it starts to hold water. I had my suspicions about who removed the dam, and the suspicions were proved correct when the dam was again removed on 2 March. It is not appropriate in this book to name the person but he has no responsibility whatsoever on Dupplin Estate.

Around 2005, unregulated releases of beavers were made in Tayside, where

Beaver dam at Methven Moss had been rebuilt

the population in 2019 now stands at around 500. Some farmers have been unhappy about the presence of beavers and since, at the time of writing this chapter, they are still not protected by law, many, numbering in the hundreds, have been shot, dams have been wrecked and lodges set on fire. There rightly has been a public outcry about female beavers nursing kits being shot and the kits starving to death.

Research has shown that beavers, which were native to Scotland before being hunted to extinction, provide important biodiversity benefits.

However, the animals can also cause significant difficulties for farmers and land managers in vital agricultural areas.

The call for urgent legislation came to a head in February 2019 when yet another female beaver was shot, this time on a nature reserve. Legislation has been in preparation for some time but as a result of that latest shooting Roseanna Cunningham, Secretary for Environment, Land Reform and Climate Change, immediately announced that from 1st May 2019 the shooting of beavers will be allowed only under licence, which will be managed by Scottish Natural Heritage. All licences will be issued in accordance with the law on European Protected Species (EPS). As with other European Protected Species the beavers' breeding site or resting place, which will include lodges and some dams (guidance by Scottish Natural Heritage indicates dams that have been in position for more than two weeks) will also be protected.

It will sometimes be necessary to minimise or prevent beavers' impacts on farming, and other interests. In readiness for beavers' protected species status, SNH has been consulting a range of partners, including Scottish Government and farming and conservation bodies, to produce a strategy for beavers' sustainable future. Beavers will be allowed to expand their range

naturally but, where justified and under licence, can be actively managed to minimise adverse impacts on farmers and other land users.

So the interference with this dam was (unfortunately) legal. If it is interfered with again after 1 May it is likely to be illegal, likely to be a strict liability offence and punishable by a fine of up to £5,000 and/or 6 months imprisonment, unless the action is taken under licence. I doubt very much, however, that the culprit will get a licence to carry out this activity on someone else's land and hopefully in due course a pond and its associated wildlife benefits will be created on Methven Moss.

New birds identified:
song thrush, Mediterranean gull, Black-headed gull
New mammals identified: none

CHAPTER 27

Monday 18 March. Calm. Cloud but with sunny intervals. 10⁰C.

Milton Den, Lawn Park, Pond Wood, Harlaypoint Wood

After snowy and windy weather which caused me to miss a couple of week's walking it was great to get back to Dupplin again. I parked at Munday House and made down through a grass field with yearling lambs towards Milton Den. Gulls were gathered around the area where the sheep had been fed. They were mostly common gulls but when they lifted into the air I could see that there was single black-headed gull and a single lesser black-backed gull.

The largest gull in the group didn't seem to be part of the coalition and while the main group settled further along the field the lesser black-back flew off eastwards.

Milton Den, normally a part of the estate with a great variety of birds, was surprisingly quiet, with only blackbirds in the trees and bushes ahead of me. As I approached the pond the silence was broken by the sound of much splashing

Milton Den pond

157

and a mallard duck suddenly rose into the air pursued by two mallard drakes. The drakes chased the duck around the sky, no doubt hoping it would land so that they could mate. They are determined suitors and can be quite hard on the poor female. When we had mallard at home my wife was often out with a brush trying to rescue a duck from almost being drowned in the burn by three or even more amorous drakes.

The trio of ducks disappeared over the distant wood and as I walked in closer to the pond no less than six herons rose from its edges and flew in almost slow motion flight over the adjacent ploughed field. I wondered what had attracted such a large group to the pond and suspected it would be frogs spawning. Despite a search round most of the perimeter of the pond I could see neither frogs nor frog spawn so the reason for the congregation of herons remains a mystery.

At the west end of Milton Den I surveyed the field of quinoa, the heads now looking rather dead and empty, for a feeding frenzy of finches. There was a small flock at the far end of the quinoa, flitting between the crop and the electric wires that provide an aerial bisection the field. They were just out of my binocular range and unfortunately remained unidentified.

I moved my car further along and parked near to the estate office. In a nearby field a tractor was ploughing with a six-furrow reversible plough. This immediately took me back about 40 years. The field had been in grass and a large number of rabbits came from The Parsonage wood on to the field to feed. I had set snares for the rabbits about 30 or 40 yards from the wood. In the morning when I came to check the snares and gather up what I hoped to be a decent harvest of rabbits the field had been ploughed. All the snares, maybe between 70 and 100, had been ploughed in. In anthropomorphic terms I could just imagine the rabbits sitting in a row at the edge of the wood rubbing their paws together with glee.

I was brought back to the present when a red squirrel ran across the grass near my car. It stopped at the base of a monkey puzzle tree and began digging. It seemed to be unearthing nuts or cones and alternated between digging and munching. While it was digging it was distracted and I managed to inch closer until I was less than 20 yards from the busy wee squirrel. It continued its brunch for a good ten minutes before making for higher ground and a well-earned rest up the conifer next to the monkey puzzle.

I walked up through Lawn Park and

The young roe buck was stuck between the metal gate and the straining post

crossed the fence towards Pond Wood. A roe doe crept quietly away from where it had been resting behind a fallen tree trunk on my left. Simultaneously a really dark-coloured buzzard mewed from somewhere above the deer and glided across the clearing just ahead of me. The shepherd with his brown and white collie on the back of his quadbike then glided – much more noisily and with far less elegance – from right to left across the clearing.

Ahead of me the high metal gate on the deer fence surrounding Pond Wood was closed. I could see a movement to the left of the gate, which turned out to be a young roe buck, antlers in velvet. It had tried to squeeze through the gap between the metal gate and the straining post, managed most of its body through but the gap was just too narrow for its haunches. It was well and truly stuck. It kept straining forward but in fact needed a reverse gear. The buck squealed like a baby as I approached but seemed to settle a bit while I stood beside it, trying to work out how best to extricate it from its plight. I was also making sure it had no broken legs, which would have resulted in a far less satisfactory outcome. Mercifully the legs were fine and I gripped both back legs and gently pulled. There was neither sound nor resistance from the deer. I moved it slowly backwards through the gap and it was free. I let go the legs and it bounded away apparently none the worse for its potentially fatal adventure.

I hadn't noticed there was a head of a second hare when I took the photo

Surprisingly, after about 50 yards, the buck stopped and looked back, then continued out of sight round the back of a fallen tree. There were relatively few marks indicating the deer had been stuck for a long period and I suspect it had only been there overnight.

Further up the track there was a stridency of sound coming from both left and right. To the left, in Pond Wood, a group of jays had spotted me and were sounding their alarm call. Jays are lovely birds, brightly coloured and intelligent. There is no doubt they take the eggs and chicks of some other birds but they have all co-existed happily for thousands of years and it really is a pity that in some circumstances they can still legally be shot or trapped as 'pests'. On my right, in Harlaypoint Wood, a green woodpecker yelled out its mocking *kew kew kew kew*. I was tempted to go through the trees and look for it but they are incredibly elusive birds and I've always found that the best way to see them is to come across them accidentally. It's great that green woodpeckers are on the estate. During my many years here in the 1970s and 1980s I neither heard nor saw one.

I cut left through Pond Wood and when I came out at the far side I could see a hare sitting on a cultivated field. I managed to get quite close to it and took several photos before backtracking and exiting the wood further up to avoid disturbing the hare. It was only when I got home and put the photographs on the laptop that I saw that there was a head of a second hare in some of the photos. Two hares had been sitting almost together and I had only spotted one.

Two fields further on and another hare was sitting clapped down in the grass. I got quite close to and took several more photos and I could see the hare visibly relaxing and becoming far less flat against the ground than at first. Again I continued without disturbing the hare, which is not always possible. I was nearly back at the car now and the day was complete with a sighting of a lovely melanistic cock pheasant, almost jet black with a bright red head. It strutted about as if in the knowledge that the shooting season had ended and it was relatively safe (apart from motor vehicles and predators) until October and the start of the next shooting season.

New birds identified:
lesser black-backed gull, green woodpecker
New mammals identified: none

CHAPTER 28

Monday 25 March. Slight wind. Cloud but with sunny intervals. 6⁰C.

The Parsonage, Garden Bank

Yet again I encountered flytipping in field gateways on one of quiet public roads through the estate. One field gateway was strewn with large conifer branches, rubble and blue plastic sheeting. In a gateway on the opposite side of the road was a pile of branches that may have come from a different source. As if this was not bad enough, further along the road in another gateway was a white builder's bag full of broken glass, much of which had spilled on to the ground, clear plastic bags filled with rubbish and a yellow and a green bucket. This third lot was the most infuriating as it was well inside the gateway and no doubt the council would leave it to the unfortunate tenant farmer to clear. In each case a van or a small truck would be required to transport this junk to the countryside. Whatever the folks involved saved in fees from taking their rubbish to a council refuse site they probably used in fuel to bring it here. There is nothing I'd like more than somebody to be caught at this anti-social and environmental blighting practice and receive a substantial fine in the court.

I'd had an earlier start than usual today, though not quite early enough to catch the dawn chorus. The centre of the estate looked extremely peaceful and I was amazed at how the pheasants had put the terrors of the shooting season behind them. On a large grassy triangle near the sawmill a dozen colourful cock pheasants scratched and pecked contentedly, completely disregarding my presence only a few yards from them.

I walked through the east side of The Parsonage, noticing a brown hare loping along just outside the fence. Song thrushes were singing lovely repetitive arias from the tops of some of the trees. They are really woodland birds, much more at home in these surroundings than in gardens. Blackbirds, on the other hand, seem equally happy in urban surroundings. I've been disappointed so far at the lack of mistle thrushes. Considering the large flock of at least 60 mistle thrushes I saw not 100 yards from this point on 27th August I'm surprised I'm not surrounded by their song. They relish singing into the teeth of a gale on wet, windy days, but of course these are the very conditions I try to avoid.

The drumming of great-spotted

woodpeckers seemed to be late this year but they were making up for lost time this morning. At least three were busily hammering the trees round about me and I occasionally caught a fleeting glimpse of one as it flitted from one tree to another.

At the ladybird gate at the corner of the wood the number of ladybirds had reduced and those that remained were much more scattered on the wooden spars of the old gate. It certainly looks like most have survived the winter and have begun to disperse with the warmer weather.

A buzzard that had been mewing and circling above The Parsonage landed right at the top of an oak tree ahead of me. It perched on a branch eyeing me up and I took a few photos but a blink of sun on the bird would have improved the pictures. I watched the buzzard watching me for a few minutes but as soon as I moved forward it was off.

I came out of the wood to have a look at a line of old beech trees nearby. Many had missing limbs and provided ideal nesting places for owls and jackdaws. The most suitable trees had pairs of jackdaws in position to claim a nest hole. One tree with the whole top blown off had at least six pairs sitting on its remaining branches. They are happy to nest colonially, like rooks, so

Buzzard in The Parsonage perched on a branch eyeing me up

this tree would be prime residence.

Further along I climbed the fence back into The Parsonage again. On an open piece of woodland I encountered a fresh 'couch' made by a roe deer. Rather like a dog, if a deer is settling down for a rest it scrapes in a circle and removes leaves, stones or any other obstruction so that it can lie comfortably. Very often several deer lie together but when I checked the area near to this 'couch' this deer seemed to have been on its own. Another tell-tale sign of the wood's inhabitants was fresh hedgehog poo on the grass verge as I exited the wood, jet black and glistening with the wings and body casings of beetles. Hedgehogs should all be out of hibernation now and

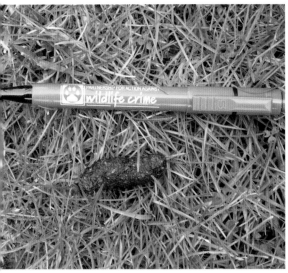

Hedgehog poo, jet black and glistening
with the wings and body casings of beetles

hopefully a good breeding season will
swell the numbers of this rapidly
declining mammal.

I walked along to Garden Bank and
did a quick circuit there, walking
outwards on the East Drive and back on
a track running parallel but 100 yards
below the East Drive. I have seen very
few grey squirrels on the estate, I think
just three so far. I got a short glimpse of
number four as I walked along the East
Drive. It had been sitting at the base of
a tree and ran quickly through some
rough grass and out of sight. The
unusual aspect of this particular North
American interloper was that it had a
white tip to its tail, just like a fox. I'd
never seen that before.

On the return journey a small light-
brown bird with pale yellow underparts
and black legs landed on some
undergrowth in front of me. It was a
chiffchaff. They are difficult to tell from
willow warblers though the black legs
as opposed to pale legs and duller
yellow underparts are the main factors
used to tell the birds apart. Further,
chiffchaffs arrive in Scotland from Africa
in March, whereas most willow warblers
arrive in April. The chiffchaff hopped on
to the ground and I moved forward
hoping to get a photo. I stood for fully
ten minutes looking for this wee brown
bird but it had disappeared. I started to
walk back in the direction of my car.
The bird was tormenting me now; as
soon as I was 20 yards away it started to
sing, *chiff-chaff, chiff-chaff, chiff-chaff.*
Still no sign of the songster but it had
confirmed my identification.

I wanted to have a look up to the
lochs to complete the day and drove to
the old A9 to park. A grass field that
held sheep and lambs had a flooded
patch and several dozen common and
black-headed gulls were taking
advantage of the clean water to bathe,
much to the amusement of some of the
lambs. Looking at the sheep and lambs
reminded me of the son of a former
headkeeper on Dupplin. Wee Peter was
about four at the time and loved going

out and helping Geordie the shepherd. I often saw him awaiting Geordie's arrival outside his house. Peter never waved like any other four-year old might do, he wore a cap – a wee bunnet – and nodded his head at the passer-by much more like an old farmhand. He started primary school at Forteviot and one his class exercises was to make up a sentence using the words 'I can'. Peter immediately and proudly stated, 'I can fling a dead sheep o'er a dyke'.

As I headed towards the lochs there was a very fresh fox scat on the left-hand track. It was still wet, very shiny and with plenty fur and small bones showing as evidence of the fox's recent meal. Foxes in this area will be missing rabbits as much as I am, though for a different reason. They are true omnivores and will manage to survive on smaller and less substantial items such as voles, mice, moles, berries and earthworms. That they can manage to catch larger prey was demonstrated on a recent walk when an adult brown hare had been the victim. May is the season when roe fawns are born and some of those will no doubt also fall prey to foxes.

Both lochs were surprisingly quiet bird-wise. Dupplin Loch held about 10 mute swans, some of them youngsters from the previous year, two Canada geese, two herons that were busy

chasing each other at the far side, some mallard and a single male goldeneye. Pitcairnie Loch had only a pair of adult swans, about 25 tufted ducks, two female goldeneye, some mallard and two herons, one of which was perched on a branch overhanging the loch and kindly posed for a photograph.

On my return walk to the car I spotted a roe deer in an extensive deer-fenced area that had just been planted with new trees. I moved to a different position to get a better view and saw that there were three deer: two does and buck with a lovely head still in velvet. They'll not be popular if they start to nibble the tops off the young trees or in July, the rutting time for roe deer, if the buck starts to thrash the young trees with his new antlers. I suspect their days might be numbered.

New birds identified: chiffchaff
New mammals identified: none

There was a very fresh fox scat on the left-hand track

Tree sparrows, with the chestnut crown to their head, at Sauchie Farm

CHAPTER 29

Friday 29 March. Stiff breeze. Cloud but with sunny intervals. 12°C.

Sauchie Pond, River Earn at Sauchie Farm

Since I began walking Dupplin Estate I had skirted the wood holding Sauchie Pond but had never gone inside for fear of disturbing the ducks before and during the shooting season. I was keen therefore to have a look to see what wildlife the pond and its environs might behold. I knew that it held a decent amount of mallard as I had heard them from outside the wood and had seen teal and mallard flying in towards the pond. So, the pond was to be the main focus of today's visit to the estate.

I parked at Sauchie Farm steading and was pleased at my first bird sighting of the day, which was a female kestrel. It must have been perched on one of a group of trees that grew half-way up a steep field behind the farm and it flew towards the Garden Bank. There are plenty nesting options for a kestrel in the Garden Bank as there are many old trees with suitable nesting holes. There are also possibilities in the old steading at Sauchie Farm. It would be lovely if a pair managed to rear a brood of chicks in this area, and even better if I managed to find their nesting place.

I walked towards the gate into the grass field between the farm steading and Sauchie Wood and noticed a small group of five or six birds flying from just beside the gate, down the hawthorn hedge, where three of them perched on top of the hedge. I hadn't been able to identify them up to that point, and even through the binoculars was a struggle as they were a good distance away. I took one or two photos and enlarged them later. The birds were tree sparrows, quite similar in size and plumage to a house sparrow but with a chestnut crown to their head, a pale collar around the back of the head and a dark, comma-shaped, patch on their cheek. Sauchie is on the other side of the River Earn from Broombarns Farm and only a mile and a half as the tree sparrow flies from the dozens of nest boxes there that are intended to host tree sparrows, so there are certainly potential occupants in the area for the nest boxes.

After a walk of a few minutes I reached the wood and walked along Stewart's vehicle track to near the side

Sauchie pond is banana shaped and with an island just off-centre

of the pond. The pond is banana shaped and with an island just off-centre, ideal for some of the waterfowl nesting. The downside of the pond for nesting waterfowl is that it contains pike, some of them quite large. Bill related a story to me that he had visited the pond one day when he was gamekeeper for that area and saw a number of adult mallard swimming on it. All except one swam away from him. The remaining duck gradually disappeared under the water never to reappear. For a pike to accomplish that it must have been a decent size.

The spell of mild weather had encouraged hawthorn leaves on the trees at the fence side to begin to show some green, and white blossom was on the blackthorn bushes. Both species formed a strong boundary between the wood and the grass field. Chaffinches were flying between willow bushes growing at the edge of the pond. They were acting rather like spotted flycatchers, darting out after a fly (or as if they were after a fly) and returning to a pond-side perch after their attempt. They are primarily seed eaters though they do take insects when they are available.

I sat for a while on the banking and watched the antics of the chaffinches. It was also an opportunity to listen. A heron croaked from the furthest reaches of the pond, which is a small offshoot of shallow water little more than a marsh. Two Canada geese flew overhead, not intending to come into the pond but making their way either up the nearby River Earn or to some larger pond or loch. A male chaffinch sang in a tree behind me, and in the distance, again towards the river, I could hear the shrill piping *keep kleep* call of oystercatchers. A frog, unseen, croaked from somewhere on the other side of the willow bush and there seemed to be movement in the water among the willow stalks. I thought it might just have been the wind but when I moved to go a bit closer the movement in the water stopped. It may have been frogs but there was no frog spawn visible to make it more likely that this amphibian had been the cause of the water disturbance.

I walked clockwise round the pond, seeing several reed buntings, some of which crossed to the other side of the pond at my approach. I sat on a fallen tree for a while to see if one of the smart male reed buntings might land close enough for a photograph, but no luck. It was only when I got up off the tree did I notice I had sat down within five or six paces from a brown hare, which had remained still all the time I'd been there. Resuming my movement had been too much for the hare and it

loped off towards the field. About the same time as the hare rose so did the heron that I had heard earlier. It rose squawking from the shallow, marshy end of the pond. The heron's departure also alarmed a single teal, which rose vertically until clear of the trees, then levelled out and headed towards the river.

I was unable to continue my exploration of the pond clockwise because of the marsh so I about-turned and headed anti-clockwise. This took me back over some of the ground I'd already covered but I could now see four mallard drakes swimming near a small island in the pond. No doubt they would have partners sitting on eggs somewhere within the wood and I now had to be aware when I was walking that I didn't put a duck off her nest; many wild ducks simply desert the nest and eggs if they are disturbed.

As I passed where the drakes had been I noticed a pair of long-tailed tits on a willow bush. I was keen to get a decent photograph of a long-tailed tit as they are such lovely birds but they wouldn't stay still and, with their background of willow, were damnably difficult to capture in the viewfinder. They flew off after a few minutes and I consoled myself by realising that in any

'Glory of the Snow' growing on the far bank of the River Earn

case I was looking into the sun and this would have produced a pretty poor picture.

To get further round the pond I'd to cross a marshy area, but I'd also to sprachle through some wispy trees, which wasn't too pleasant and resulted in several stinging whacks across the face with thin branches. This was a popular area for hares and I put up three, all of which were reluctant to leave the wood, continuing either anti-clockwise ahead of me or clockwise behind me. When I came to a drier part I sat down again near the water's edge, again hoping for a chance to photograph a reed bunting, now with the sun behind me. Reed buntings appeared, but either were in unsuitable positions or only stayed for seconds. I diverted my attention to a treecreeper climbing up the trunk of a young ash tree. On a smooth-barked tree like that

it found nothing to eat, hopped round to try its luck on the far side and never re-appeared. Sauchie Pond has great potential but maybe I was just a couple of weeks too early.

I was lucky to have finished my circuit of the pond at a stile and clambered over into the field. I walked across the grass field and climbed a fence and the flood bank to the River Earn. I stopped again at the 40 feet long tree trunk that I had discovered on 2nd January and which had been washed up on the riverbank after being chopped down by beavers further up the river. It was a mature ash tree and I was in awe that a beaver or beavers had managed to fell it. Their teeth are amazing.

I was directly opposite Broombarns Farm and when I looked across the river I was surprised to see a substantial

Male goosander on the River Earn

clump of low-growing blue flowers on the river banking. Through the binoculars (and later from a long-range photograph) I could see that the flowers had six petals which became lighter in colour towards the centre, which in turn was pale yellow. The leaves had the appearance of stalks of grass, though wider. Later investigation identified the flowers as 'Glory of the Snow'. This flower grows from a bulb which most likely had been washed down the river and over time formed this lovely clump of early springtime flowers.

A lone blackfaced ewe was ahead of me on a narrow strip of land which was my route downstream. This narrow strip was bounded by the river on one side and a fence on the other. I hoped that she would have enough room to pass me but, as lone sheep usually are, she was extremely nervous and jumpy. I

certainly didn't want her panicking and jumping into the river so climbed the fence into the ploughed field at the other side giving her a wide berth. I continued down the riverside once the sheep had safely passed me, noting a mixed flock of oystercatchers, herring gulls, common gulls and a pair of great black-backed gulls on a wide shingle bank. They flew off as I got nearer and I thought it could have been an ideal place for the oystercatchers nesting, though not with egg-guzzling gulls about.

A pair of goosanders swam in the river ahead of me and flew upstream as I got closer to them. With the sun shining on the resplendent, almost pinkish, feathers of the male he was a really beautiful bird. Such a pity that they come into conflict with anglers about the fish that they eat, after all they were here before anglers. Slightly further downstream I saw the heads of two female goosanders poking above the banking. If I saw their heads they could see me, and they were off on the same route as the earlier pair almost as soon as I spotted them. Three pied wagtails, birds with little reason to fear humans, that had been feeding on the banking near the goosanders, were all that now remained.

I cut out from the river to have a look at a narrow area of water surrounded by a necklace of reeds in the field. Two mallard drakes exploded from the water – we were unaware of the other's presence – and they flew off, quacking very quietly as mallard drakes do. At the far end of the pool of water frogs had laid their spawn, but some of it had been laid too close to the edge and as the level of water dropped giant globules of spawn, still with the thousands of wee black eyes visible, had unfortunately been left stranded and had perished.

I headed back to the car along a ditch side and up the edge of a long narrow wood. My day finished with a roe doe running from the top of this wood across the farm track and into the continuation of the wood above the track. So far the roe deer have retained their grey winter coats. Soon they'll look scruffy for a few weeks as they shed the grey coats and grow into their lovely foxy-red summer coats.

I'd now reached Sauchie Farm steading and my car, which I'd parked beside an old car which I suspect is destined for scrap. As I got in I happened to notice that a bird, species unknown but one with initiative, had been roosting on top of the front tyre of the old car on the leeward side, leaving only its white droppings to alert the casual passer-by as to its bedtime accommodation. Clever and cosy.

New birds identified: tree sparrow
New mammals identified: none

CHAPTER 30

Friday 5 April. Sunny but with stiff breeze. 10°C.

River Earn at Aberdalgie Mains Farm

I spoke with Stewart early this morning and asked him if he had seen any lapwings. It's an extensive estate and I'd neither seen nor heard any so far. Stewart couldn't think of anywhere he'd seen lapwings, which is a terrible indictment of farming practices Scotland-wide. Lapwings love to nest in arable fields but the fields are cultivated so regularly that there is little chance of eggs or chicks surviving. I've even seen grass fields for silage or hay being rolled at the end of May or the beginning of June. Any chicks still unable to fly will perish under the rollers. Lapwings are also attracted to fields that are left ploughed after the grain fields are sown. These fields are also deadly as most often they are cultivated for peas or beans later in the season and at a time when any eggs have just hatched. If lapwings are lucky enough to hatch a brood of chicks, depending on the type of crop in the field there may be insufficient food for the chicks due to the spraying of insecticides. The same set of circumstances has also caused numbers of another of my favourite birds, the grey partridge, to crash.

All was not bad news from Stewart, and he told me that the day before he had seen the first of the season's sand martins near a sandy riverbank on the Earn. That area, then, would be my destination this morning.

I parked at Aberdalgie Mains Farm and walked up a farm track through a large bank of whin bushes. The whins were in full flower and the smell coming off this sea of yellow was delightful; it was a real smell of spring. Whins are horrible jaggy bushes to walk through but their potential for safe nesting places for birds and their perfume makes up for the nastiness of their thorns. A roe buck had been resting amongst the whins and it made off up the hill as I passed. This is the first buck I have seen with its antlers clear of velvet. It didn't have a great set of antlers; fairly narrow and with one slightly shorter than the other, but otherwise it was a lovely buck.

Reminiscent of Jack and Jill or the Grand Old Duke of York, once I was at the top of the hill I walked back down again, this time through a permanent pasture. As I approached a large rabbit burrow, an area near one of the burrow entrances caught my attention. The grass was cropped extremely short over an area of a few feet from the entrance. This is often caused by young rabbits of four or five weeks old taking their first foray outside and beginning to munch at grass. Sure enough there were tiny rabbit droppings in this area confirming my suspicions. No doubt the doe rabbit will be pregnant again and will have another litter soon after the present one is weaned and fending for themselves in a couple of weeks.

I crossed the quiet country road at the bottom of the field and made my way down to the river, walking upstream. I was paying attention to sandy banks on both sides. In one or two of the sandy banks I could see the elliptical nest holes of sand martins from previous years. The birds burrow into the sand for two or three feet and make a rudimentary nest of straw and feathers in a nest chamber at the end. Sand martins are fussy about the composition of the sand into which they burrow and often there is an almost straight line of nest holes when they find the correct strata of sand. Sand martins are the earliest of the hirundines to arrive here from sub-Saharan Africa, with the first arriving towards the end of March and the main influx around mid-April. I was expecting to see one or two sand martins flying over the river in search of flies but so far there was nothing.

As I was looking into the water I pondered the fact that I had not seen a single salmon move in the river since I began these walks on the estate in August. Going back 50 or even 30 years any walk up this riverside was accompanied by splashes of salmon jumping, especially around September and October. In the winter months I always saw dead salmon, completely spent after the exhausting process of swimming hundreds of miles and spawning, lying dead in shallower parts of the river. Many were also washed up on shingle banks and provided a meal for gulls and carrion crows. Not a single salmon this season, live or dead. Seals, cormorants, goosanders and mergansers get blamed for depleting salmon stocks but they have co-existed with salmon for centuries. Whatever the real reason, I've little doubt it rests with us.

Despite the limiting effects of a moderately strong east wind I could hear a skylark singing. I stopped to look for the skylark but despite searching the

Ahead of me on a finger of grass leading out to the river was a pair of greylag geese

The wigeon remained while the mallard flew off

sky I couldn't see it. What I did see, though, flying towards me in line abreast were three sand martins. It was a lucky sighting as these were the only ones that I saw. Their numbers will swell and they will be much more plentiful around their chosen nesting sites in a couple of weeks.

Ahead of me on a finger of grass leading out to the river was a pair of greylag geese. The gander spotted me first and rose to his full height in a threatening pose. They will be a pair that will breed here rather than going with the flocks that are returning now to Iceland. I don't know if they join up with a flock here over the winter but I suspect not. There are plenty greylag geese that breed in the north of Scotland and on the Western Isles but more and more are now breeding much further south. They were much less wary than those as part of a flock would be and the gander, with his larger and more brightly coloured bill, honked a few times at me, just like farmyard geese would do if an intruder appeared. They finally took flight and flew off down the river.

Slightly further upriver I'd a tubular steel gate to cross (the one I'd baulked at the last time I was here) and from there I could see the white of a male goosander at the edge of the river. As I got closer I could see there was a pair of goosanders plus another female sitting 20 yards from them on a shingle bank; obviously three's a crowd! The pair flew off first, along with a mallard drake that had been hidden from my view, then the female goosander followed shortly after, taking the same route.

Further upstream still a group of mallard took off with much quacking from behind a riverbank tree which had gathered a variety of detritus washed down by various floods. As I reached the tree four wigeon flew from the same place as the mallard had been. Wigeon are quite wary ducks and I thought it unusual that they had remained while the mallard flew off. Among the rubbish against the tree was a large quantity of straw. On the straw was a mallard egg that had been taken and eaten by a predator, probably a carrion crow. The egg had the crow trademark hole in it where the contents had been sucked out, completely different to an egg that has hatched naturally. Hatched eggs are

The female of the pair of shelduck

split neatly almost round the centre by the chick making its entry into the world and usually show veins of blood in the inside of the shell. Many of the mallard I had seen so far were females, most of which will have lost an earlier nest of eggs, either to predators or because of the weather. Most will lay a further clutch, though the proportion of successfully hatching eggs or surviving ducklings for wild mallard is quite low.

It makes my day when I get a surprise and this was such a day. In the distance, on temporary flooding in the grass field beside the river, I could see two ducks that looked almost white. A look through the binoculars identified them as a pair of shelducks. I've never before seen shelducks on this estate and it would great if they stayed to breed. I got closer and managed a few photographs as the ducks waddled slowly from the flooded pond they were in to another flooded area further across the field. I gave them a wide berth to allow them to settle but

unfortunately the shepherd on his quadbike, brown and white collie as passenger as usual, came over the field to check on the sheep and the shelduck made off up the river.

Shelduck are considerably larger than a mallard, mostly white but with a bottle-green (almost black) head, a chestnut breast band and a broad black stripe along the shoulders. The bill is blood red and the male has a distinctive knob at the base of his bill. They are incredibly attentive parents, with both male and female rearing the ducklings. I've often seen shelduck with a brood of ducklings on the Western Isles and it would be a real treat to witness that on this estate.

I made my way up the side of a ditch that ran from the fields to the river, disturbing a hare (which I am sure ran from the same place the last time I walked up this ditch). The hare ran off behind me after I had passed. It ran low

A mass of lovely yellow celandine flowers with their round glossy green leaves

and with its ears down, almost out of sight along the side of some reeds, then turned left behind a knoll. It certainly knew the topography of the area and used it to advantage.

A field ahead of me that had recently been sown held several thousand woodpigeons, heads bobbing up and down as they searched for grain. They flew off as I climbed the fence to cross the field and it was interesting to see all the newly-turned earth where they had been pecking, almost in the manner of turnstones, to unearth any seed near the surface.

Another ditch to jump, three fences to cross and I was on the narrow public road heading to my car. The ditch on my left was a mass of lovely yellow celandine flowers with their background of round glossy green leaves. They looked like miniature versions of the sun with their eight petals radiating the sunshine; yet another treat to end this part of the day.

I drove through the centre of the estate and was surprised to see a small group of up to ten fieldfares fly across the estate road. They will be stragglers as many of the fieldfares and redwings wintering in the UK from Scandinavia will have left for home. There are always stragglers, and in fact later in the day there was still a male brambling feeding with chaffinches in my garden. I wonder if the brambling will still find a group of bramblings to accompany it on its journey home to north-eastern Europe or will it make its way back alone, a risky option.

New birds identified: sand martin, shelduck.
New mammals identified: none

Nursery rabbit burrow with entrance blocked by doe

CHAPTER 31
Wednesday 10 April. Sunny and calm. 14°C.

Greenhill Farm, Methven Moss

A lovely spring morning and, for a welcome change, no wind. My last visit to the estate had been to the extreme east end. Today I was going to the extreme north-west. I parked at Greenhill Farm steading and was delighted to see the number of house sparrows at different parts of the steading. There would be at least 60, a number that is much more in keeping with numbers at East Lamberkin Farm when I was young.

I walked up the farm road to a prairie-sized field that had been sown with spring cereal just a few days earlier and I was pleased to see the work on the field was completed, with the last task being rolling the field with Cambridge rollers. These are the ridged type as opposed to the flat rollers. There's nothing I hate to see more than a field sown, but not being rolled until a couple of weeks later. The eggs of any nesting bird are then destroyed.

There was a grassy end rig round the field that made both for easy walking and gave an added chance for birds such as partridge, skylarks, curlew and mallard duck to nest. I could see three or four rabbits on the grass

further up the end rig. There was a ditch and a line of whin bushes on the other side of the fence; ideal places for rabbits to take refuge and dig their burrows. A roe buck, antlers cleaned of velvet, broke cover ahead of me, jumped the fence, and joined up with a doe on the other side.

The rabbits scurried for cover at my approach but I could see from the runs going through or under the fence that there was a decent colony in that area. There were lots of scrapes in the recently cultivated soil, and further up the field was a burrow that would have new-born young rabbits inside. Most doe rabbits dig a shallow, short burrow, maybe two or three feet in length, away from the main burrow or warren. The chamber at the end of the burrow is lined with dry grass and fur which the doe pulls from her belly to make a cosy nest for the young. This particular burrow would contain four to seven naked and blind pink and black rabbits that at that stage resemble mole rats. The burrow was barely noticeable, since for about the first week the doe pushes earth into the entrance to prevent stoats and weasels entering and killing the

The burrow two days later with entrance partly-opened

young. At night she removes the earth blocking the entrance to enter and feed the young, and pushes it back when she leaves. If the burrow has been blocked on a wet night it is slightly more easily spotted as much of the earth pushed forward by the doe goes into small balls about half the size of rabbit droppings.

Nearer the top of the field my attention was drawn to a scattering of dried grass near some disturbed earth. I walked over and my suspicions were confirmed. A rabbit nesting burrow had been dug out, with the suspect being either fox or badger. The burrow had been about two feet long and little more than six inches below the surface. The nest chamber at the end of the burrow had been lined with grass but there was no rabbit fur present. An absence of fur means that the likelihood is that the young had not yet been born. However a fox or badger would smell the doe rabbit in the chamber of the burrow. It is unlikely to dig out an empty burrow so the chances are that the predator would have dined well.

I crossed from the cereal field into a large area of permanent pasture and whin bushes, ideal habitat for many species of animals. A far higher

proportion of the estate was in permanent grass 50 and even 30 years ago than now. Farming is always evolving but modern farming methods are not necessarily better for wildlife. In these not-so-distant times this permanent pasture had a good number of nesting waders, particularly lapwings. Apart maybe from one or two snipe and maybe an occasional curlew, I doubt that many waders nest here now.

Ahead of me two hares were chasing each other and boxing. As they boxed and kicked at each other I could see tufts of their fur flying. They were much more intent on their sparring than watching for danger and, had they not continued their springtime boxing match into and through a large patch of rushes I could probably have got much closer to them.

At the top of this field I crossed into a rougher area of grass, rushes and a mix of birch, alder and willow. I stopped for a while to listen to a song thrush on top of one of the birch trees. My attention was also taken by a large bird at some distance and flying away from me. First thoughts were options of peregrine, common gull or curlew. Various factors in the bird's flight quickly eliminated gull and peregrine and I was left with curlew. Because of the same changes in agriculture that are adversely affecting the lapwing and grey partridge the curlew is not doing well and its numbers have crashed. The habitat here is ideal for nesting curlew so let's hope it has a mate and nests successfully.

The field now on my left was yet another newly-sown cereal field and at the top was a flock of at least 500 pink-footed geese. They were mostly resting and I suspected they had flown some distance on their route back to Iceland or Greenland and were recovering before the next lap. The heads of these ever-alert birds rose in unison as they saw me and they walked rapidly away. I turned about and walked in the opposite direction but they had been spooked and took flight. They were keen to come back though and after flying in a wide circle and giving me time to walk further away from their favoured field, they returned.

I was still in permanent pasture with patches of rushes. A hare rose from rushes ahead of me, and I was surprised when it was closely followed by a young hare of maybe three or four months. Brown hares and rabbits can be born in any month of the year but it is far less common for leverets to be born, as this

one had, around the turn of the year. The exceptionally mild winter was no doubt a factor in its survival. The leveret cleared the patch of rushes just as a snipe rose from a wet patch in the centre; great habitat for snipe nesting.

I checked the ditch area at the march fence for footprints of otter or fox but the only prints in the mud there were those of roe deer and red deer. A brown bird with white outer tail feathers flew from a dead tree, rose in the sky like a skylark and parachuted down to earth among the rushes. I only got a quick glimpse of the bird, which lacked the crest of a skylark and was probably too small. The mystery bird was most likely a meadow pipit or a tree pipit. Unhelpfully the skylark and both pipits have white outer tail feathers. Very shortly after, when I crossed the fence into an area with many more birch trees a bird rose from one of the trees, flew up into the air then parachuted down again onto a nearby tree. Meadow pipit or tree pipit? Its parachuting onto a tree rather than the ground, and having much whiter underparts than a meadow pipit, made identification easier. Tree pipit this time!

I'd now to pass through an area of thick whins and rushy grass, peppered with birch and willow. I'd to retrace my

Overlapping back foot on top of front foot of a badger at Greenhill

steps a few times as it was a bit of a maze. A ladybird on a whin bush caught my eye, leading me then to spot a clump of half a dozen apparently snoozing ladybirds a few inches away. There was an incredible number of ladybirds last summer and it looks like this year might be similar. Even when I was weeding in the garden a few days ago there was a ladybird on many of the weeds.

Summer migrants are beginning to appear and I recognised the beginnings of a willow warbler's song in this jungle. The bird was only singing part of the song, as if practising, which I've also heard blackbirds doing in January. I spotted it on – appropriately enough – a willow tree, where it shared the branches with a blue tit. I waited to see if it would burst into full song but it seemed to be needing a few day's practice yet. The maze continued and I followed a couple of further blind ends before I managed to get to the fence, at the other side of which was more open permanent pasture.

A buzzard mewed, then flew from a large beech tree near the march fence and soared across the grassland. I noticed that there was a large nest in the tree, probably that of a buzzard, but I doubt that a buzzard will be nesting yet, though they'll be thinking about it

shortly. I was surprised to see a rabbit run from almost under my feet into the bushes at the edge of the field. I had startled it as it was digging a burrow, probably similar in length to the burrow I had seen earlier. The earth it had scraped out was red and almost as fine as sand. I doubted though that this was a burrow for a nest of young rabbits as the rabbit was a big bruiser with a wide head and almost certainly a buck.

My last part of the walk was down the side of a wet gulley in the field with whin bushes on the banking on either side. My first find, at a muddy gateway, was a badger pawprint. The smaller hind foot had landed almost on top of the larger front foot. The five long claws on the front foot, so necessary for the badger in its daily excavations, could clearly be seen in the mud, plus its unusually broad pad. This is the second clear sign of a badger at this end of the estate (the first being scrapes in the grass for worms on 17th October at Westmuir, less than a mile away). Stewart has never seen one during his regular patrols at night with the spotlamp for foxes, though he did say that on the previous estate where he worked there were a lot of badgers yet

The burrow 19 days later with entrance completely open

he seldom saw one at night. I have also spoken with the previous tenant farmer of Greenhill, Peter Allan, who had farmed the land with his brother Jock for many years. He had not seen a badger in all that time either.

Further down the gulley there were several pairs of yellowhammers, which I am pleased to say seem very common on this estate. There were also several pairs of linnets, which are a lot less common. The male has a grey head, a chestnut back and has crimson patches on either side of its breast, with white in the centre. The female has no crimson and has a streaked breast. They sat in pairs on the top of whin bushes or in bushes still bare of leaves, but were shy birds and quite difficult to approach closely.

On the way home I stopped off at Methven Moss to see if there was any progress on the beaver dam. The dam had been partially rebuilt, confirming that the beaver is still in the area. The date when beavers have the full protection of the law, 1st May 2019, is drawing close. The suspect who is interfering with the dam could be hit by the full force of the law after that date, however I now notice there are two field drains running into the burn just yards upstream of the dam under construction. Raising the level of the burn above these drains might cause water to build back in the drains and lessen the draining effect on the field. Even though he has no business to interfere on the estate, rather than destroy the dam he may be better employed before 1st May to move the dam upstream by 10 or 15 yards beyond these field drains and encourage the beaver to build there.

New birds identified: tree pipit.
New mammals identified: none

Update: I checked on the rabbit burrows in the recently sown field two days later, since earlier that day this and the adjacent newly-sown cereal fields had been sprayed. The burrow with the young rabbits was fortunate since the tractor tracks of the sprayer straddled the burrow. Had it gone over the burrow the young rabbits would have been killed. The burrow had again been filled in by the doe but, since the young were getting bigger, this time she had left a small gap for air. This gap will become bigger up to the point, when the young are about two weeks old, the doe leaves the entrance completely open.

CHAPTER 32

Wednesday 17 April. Sunny spells with moderate wind. 12°C.

River Earn at Forteviot and May burn

Lapwings at last, but I'll come to that in due course.

I wanted to keep abreast of activity on the lochs so started today's visit to the estate with a walk up through the ancient woodland to Dupplin Loch. It was disappointingly quiet, with a dozen mute swans dotted along the northern half of the loch and possibly one sitting on a nest half-way up the north shore. There are extensive reed beds round the east, west and north shores so it's possible there may have been more swans nesting out of sight. A few mallard, a cormorant that took off as soon as it saw me and a couple of smaller white dots, just out of binocular range, that may either have been goosanders or goldeneye, made up the remainder of the sparse complement of waterfowl.

As I had been making my way down to the loch shore I could hear an osprey alarm-calling. As I came back from the lochside to the woodland track I'm reasonably sure I identified the tree from which the sound was emanating.

Right at the top of a tall conifer I could see a nest. It was not the usual huge structure associated with ospreys but was more akin in scale to that of a buzzard. I doubt that a buzzard would build right at the top of a tree; that is the place normally favoured by ospreys but because the tree didn't have a flat top this maybe limited the size of the nest. I moved on quickly so as to limit disturbance, but if that indeed is the nest the bird will have to get used to disturbance as the tree is right next to the forest track which I'm sure has someone passing along it at least once a week. Most birds, including ospreys, become accustomed to a certain amount of disturbance. An osprey nest in north Perthshire is in a tree right beside a track used several times on most days by walkers. The bird has been regularly seen to fly off the nest as a hillwalker approaches then quickly return to the nest as soon as the person has passed.

Pitcairnie Loch was equally quiet, hosting just a raft of around 40 tufted ducks, a pair of goosanders (that also very quickly flew off as soon as they spotted me), one or two mallard, a heron, and a couple of distant small ducks that were probably little grebes. A nesting swan graced the south shore. Her partner, wings raised elegantly as male swans are inclined to do, was swimming close by. Autumn, rather than spring, seems to be a much busier season on these lochs.

As I watched the waterfowl a female kestrel flew over my head, making towards the rough grass of Blairbell Moor. It's great to see one or two kestrels but whether they'll ever come back to their former numbers is doubtful, at least in the foreseeable future. Blairbell Moor, with its tussock grass should be a good hunting ground for kestrels, especially in a good vole year. As I stood at the open gate onto the moor two ravens were play-fighting over a stand of Scots pines ahead of me. From the same general area a green woodpecker was sounding his (or her) *kew kew kew* call. This is a really challenging call for the listener; the bird seems to be saying, 'I can see you but you can't see me'. I certainly get very exasperated with hardly ever being able to spot this bird.

I returned along the woodland track, again hearing the alarm call of the osprey as I passed the same part of the wood. There were also foresters working a quarter of a mile away so hopefully the osprey pair will accept the activity of its noisy neighbours.

My next stop was the River Earn at Forteviot. I drove through the farm steading of the former Milton of Forteviot Farm, seeing my first swallows of the year circling the buildings and flying in and out of a dilapidated shed where they will no doubt soon be nesting. I parked near the river, walking downstream. On a limb of wood in the centre of the river two common sandpipers were resting. I took a few photos but didn't realise until I looked at the photos later that they were facing away from me. Despite that they clearly saw me getting closer to them and they took off up the river in their typical stiff-winged flight, their wings barely more than flickering. I saw them – or other common sandpipers – several times after that on shingle banks of the river and later, on shingle banks of the May Burn.

I am well acquainted with this stretch of the river. In the 1970s when I was a police officer in Perth, I came out here any Sunday in spring, summer or autumn when I was day shift. In the early morning busloads of trout anglers descended on the River Earn. Most were genuine but a proportion were claiming to be after trout but using tackle appropriate for salmon fishing. It was legal to fish for trout without a permit at that time but to fish for salmon required a permit. Equally importantly, it was illegal to fish for salmon on a Sunday. The Sunday dayshift came around only once in every four weeks so the anglers never quite managed to work out the pattern as to the Sunday we would appear. We had very few Sundays when our checks were not successful and resulted in court appearances for one or more salmon poachers.

I continued down the river and saw a male and two female goosanders rising from the water and flying downstream. Am I seeing the same trio over and over again or do all male goosanders have two mates this year? I note several otter spraints in the same area of riverbank as I had seen on earlier visits. This must be their favourite pool and they have their territory well signposted. There was nothing particularly fresh but it was interesting to see that the grass was burned with an excess of nitrogen in the centre of the area marked by the otters and on the perimeter it was bright green with an additional, but moderate, amount of nitrogen.

On the bank of what I'll call the otter pool there were three pheasant eggs that had been taken from a nest and eaten by a carrion crow. Carrion crows, when they find a nest, will take every egg and often remove them to the same place to eat them. There was still some yolk in one of the eggs, meaning they were taken when freshly laid, though hardly surprising as pheasants have just started to lay. The robbed clutch may in fact not have been completed.

I met an angler, Bob, trying his luck for salmon and we had a blether. He had been fishing this part of the River Earn for many years and was well aware of the wildlife of the area. He said he had seen peregrines, ospreys and even a hen harrier while he was fishing, as well as otters, mink and water voles. Of the smaller birds he was aware of nuthatches in the area (which is only quarter of a mile from where I had seen them on 6th February), kingfishers, dippers, terns and even a purple sandpiper. He commented on the absence of singing willow warblers in the bushes lining the riverbank, a fact that I had wondered about as well. He'd had a blank day fishing and put the lack of salmon down to an increased number of goosanders. While there is no doubt that goosanders take salmon fry and salmon parr, migratory fish and fish-eating birds have co-existed for

Sand martins fluttered around the nest holes at the May Burn like a swarm of bees

millenia. The reduction in salmonids is much more complex than predation by goosanders.

There were two mute swans in the river but no swans where I had expected them to be nesting in the backwater further downstream. Like many big birds, mute swans don't breed until they are three or four years old. They may not breed every year, otherwise we would be awash with swans, so this pair may be having a gap year.

As I rounded a corner on the track a buzzard rose from a track-side fencepost. Almost at the same time an osprey appeared over the trees looking for a trout or grayling on the river. I could see it was intent on studying the water but it had no luck. It clearly had just tried for a fish as twice it shook itself in flight and I could see the water droplets against the sunlight in a halo around the bird. It circled higher and was harried for a while by a carrion crow. It crossed the river then circled over the centre of the estate. There are

some small ponds there but I would have thought its best chance of dining would have been from the river. Ospreys must have a difficult time in catching fish. Their success will be affected by discoloured water after heavy rain, bright sunlight reflecting off the water and strong wind causing ripples or even waves. Even if all these problems are absent there needs to be a fish of catchable size near the surface and then of course they have to get their talons into it. One of these talon-clad toes is also reversible, which means that instead of always having three toes pointing forward and one back (as most birds have), ospreys can also point two forward and two back. This gives them a much more powerful grip to prevent prey escaping.

I headed back towards my starting point by another route, passing another three pheasant eggs eaten by a carrion crow; like ospreys catching fish, nesting birds don't have an easy time either.

A male wheatear landed on a rotten tree trunk

A pied wagtail bobbed about the burn's edge looking for insects

From where I had parked the car I could see sand martins skimming up and down the May Burn. This area was worth investigating so I had a walk up the mix of shingle, rocky flood defences, rough grass and whin bushes adjacent to the burn.

My route rose a snipe from amongst some rushes and disturbed several rabbits which bolted for their burrows. I also easily identified where the sand martins are nesting. The bank of the burn on the far side is only about three feet high. About half way up in several places are lines of sand martin nest holes. The holes were so close to each other that I'd be surprised if in some cases one burrowing bird hadn't broken into the tunnel of its neighbour. Sand martins were fluttering around the nest holes like a swarm of bees. Very often a pair of sand martins were clinging to an entrance hole, though it was difficult to see if they were excavating. They were certainly busy birds and two settled on

a broken branch sticking out of the shingle for a well-deserved rest. They may not have started nesting yet, but if so it is likely the clutches of eggs will still be incomplete. I hope in due course than none of the hungry young martins fall out of the hole at the stage when they come to be fed: a drop directly into the burn would be the outcome.

Amid the hustle and bustle of actively-feeding birds one slightly bigger than a sand martin caught my eye. It landed on a rotten tree trunk just long enough for me to identify it as a male wheatear. I was doubtful of seeing a wheatear on the estate as they are mainly moorland birds, but the rabbit burrows and rocky flood defences will interest them as possible nesting places. I managed to take a few photos and when the wheatear flew off the tree trunk it was replaced a few seconds later by a meadow pipit. There were a good number of these pipits around, with probable nesting habitat on rougher parts of the grass field between the burn and the road.

The burn was also a popular place with pied wagtails and these relatively tame birds bobbed about the burn's edge looking for insects. Nearer the river a flash of canary yellow and grey signified the appearance of one of their more colourful cousins, a grey wagtail. It landed on a shingle bank just at the confluence of the burn and river. It hopped over a slight crest in the shingle to get to the edge of the river. It was a chance for me to get closer. When I did get closer it was gone. I was left wondering how such a brightly-coloured bird could disappear without me having seen its exit!

My last treat of the day, as I was walking through some permanent pasture adjacent to the burn, was hearing an ever so quiet alarm call, *pee weep*. I looked up to see two lapwings in the air just ahead of me. As they passed me I could hear the swish of their broad wings and see the orange-brown feathers under their tail. It is possible that the female had come off a nest in the rough grass at my approach and was joined by her mate. It's a while since I've encountered a lapwing's nest. It is a fairly simple affair: a scrape on the ground lined with some dry grass and maybe a pebble or two depending on whether it is on grass or cultivated land. The four green and brown speckled eggs are pointed and the points are always to the centre of the nest, making it easier for the bird to cover them. The lapwings landed at the other side of the burn and kept an eye on me. I sat on the bank of the burn a good distance away to see if either of the birds returned to a nest. There were many distractions though and I may have missed their return.

This permanent pasture was an area that I was not surprised to see lapwings; the surprise in fact was that there only seemed to be the one pair. It was also disappointing that on other permanent pastures I had seen no lapwings. It is sad that these lovely birds that used to herald the arrival of spring in substantial numbers, have all but gone from most of the Scottish mainland and are now on the red list of endangered UK birds.

New birds identified:
common sandpiper, ringed plover, wheatear, grey wagtail, lapwing
New mammals identified: none

CHAPTER 33

Monday 22 April. Glorious sunshine from early morning. 17°C.

Milton Den, The Parsonage

I'd an earlier start today, being on the estate for about 0730. Many of the summer migrants should have arrived by this time and I was keen to see which ones would be in Milton Den and The Parsonage. I parked at Munday House and as I was walking past the building I could hear a willow warbler singing from a tree with lovely heavy white blossom. It took me a while to locate this wee yellow and brown warbler. When I did pinpoint it, it was due to the movement of one of the large blossoms as the bird picked at it, probably having discovered a hapless insect. The warbler began to sing, and I could see its chest flickering with the effort. Its song is a series of thin and rapid chirps ending in a flourish. My enjoyment of the song was brought to a halt as a dog in a nearby garden started barking and a man came to the door in response. I didn't want him to think I was spying on the house, and anyway the dog was drowning out the natural sound of the countryside.

I headed down through a grass field to MIlton Den, with its lovely long, rectangular open woodland full of bushes, trees, a burn and a pond. As I went through the gate into the den I caught the whiff of where a fox had urinated, marking its territory. I met up with Stewart just after this, who told me that he thought a vixen had shifted her cubs to this area, possibly somewhere at the far end of the den.

After a quick chat I sat on the corrugated top of a structure about eighteen inches off the ground and used to give pheasants – and any other birds that partook of the seed left out – some protection from avian predators. Many of the trees were coming into leaf and there was a huge bank of hawthorn ahead of me, with its almost complete covering of white blossom making it resemble a giant snowdrift. The pond was behind me, only a short distance away. It was becoming more difficult to see small birds, hence my decision to sit, watch and, more importantly, listen.

Beside me a coal tit hung upside down on the branch of a willow, pecking at some unseen insect. A willow warbler sang from somewhere within the snowdrift of blossom. Again

Glorious specimen of cowslip, its yellow flowers just coming into bloom

unseen, a wren chattered and churred. They're feisty wee birds and it may have been alarmed at me being somewhere near its nest. As on my last visit to Milton Den there were a good few blackbirds around. A female flew into the hawthorn blossom, chattering as it went and continuing to chatter when out of sight. This was not a chatter of alarm at an avian predator nor the completely different pinking sound of alarm at a ground predator; it was more the sound given off by blackbirds as they are going to roost and may have simply been nothing more than letting other blackbirds know of its presence and location.

A chaffinch was singing from somewhere behind me, possibly near the pond, and a reed bunting perched momentarily on an overhead wire before it also headed in the direction of the pond. I'd now been sitting for about twenty minutes so I headed down to the pond, but it was absolutely empty, with nothing moving for the five minutes that I stood there. It seemed an ideal pond for moorhens and I was always expecting a moorhen to pop out of the reeds but drew a blank.

From the far end of the pond I could see a rabbit sitting under a bush, almost snoozing. I could see in the binoculars, and later in a photo that I took, that it was totally relaxed and that its eyes were almost closed. Nevertheless it was aware of me and as I took a step closer it was off to somewhere safer. Nearby was a glorious specimen of cowslip, its yellow flowers just coming into bloom. It is a relative of the primrose and this plant may have been brought here as a seed carried by birds. It is the only one I have seen in this woodland. Adding even more colour to the day was the plentiful supply of orange tip butterflies. There seemed to be more males, with their orange-tipped wings, than females, with their black-tipped wings, but maybe that was just because the males are more brightly coloured and more easily seen.

A robin viewed me from on top of a whin bush

I continued on to the end of Milton Den, then came back the track that skirts the south side of the wood. Further down the track I sat on a stile that provides reasonable comfort and a decent viewpoint. I could still hear much more than I could see. Top of the list was a song thrush. It was singing its heart out, with the repetitious song coming probably from near the top of several poplar trees. It was in competition with a couple of woodpigeons, whose lovely cooing song to me normally goes hand in hand with warm sunny days. Further off, outside the wood on the other side, a small flock of four or five black-headed gulls were screeching as if they were attacking something. Initially I thought they might be mobbing a fox that I had disturbed but then I saw a buzzard not far from the gulls. Would small black-headed bulls mob a bird the size of a buzzard? Possibly yes since there is safety in numbers. Black-headed gulls will be thinking of nesting now, with their usual date of laying their first egg being around 1st May. They would be much more likely to mob a buzzard if it was near the nesting colony but so far as I'm aware none nest in the area of Milton Den.

I was heading back to the car when I heard the *prukk prukk* of a raven coming from somewhere around Coldwells Wood. I'd heard ravens in this area several times now. They sometimes nest in a tree but other than trees there is no suitable nesting site near where this sound was coming from. I've never known of ravens nesting on this estate but Coldwells Wood is a large wood and could easily hide a raven's nest. It may well also be where the goshawks nest.

I moved on to The Parsonage next to spend half an hour sitting on a tree stump in the north-east corner. This corner has banks of rhododendrons and I always fancied it as a good place for small birds. I was hardly settled when a pair of bullfinches appeared. They separated (but not by much as bullfinches are real lovebirds) with the male on a tree and the female in amongst the rhododendrons. I wondered if she was looking for a suitable place to nest. They moved around a bit but by then my attention was taken by a singing whitethroat. Whitethroats and spotted flycatchers are the only summer migrants to frequent my garden and I have already heard the whitethroat singing from ash trees and bushes beside the burn that runs through my garden so I am well used to their song. I spotted it near the top of a tree but it soon moved on and sang from a tree a couple along. It seemed to be moving around, almost in a circle, probably delineating its territory for the summer breeding season. Its song comes in fits and starts and is maybe not the most eloquent of the migrants but it is a welcome sound of springtime.

Two dunnocks were next to appear among the rhododendrons but I heard no singing from them. A robin behind me made up for the lack of voice from the dunnocks and its song was sporadic but pleasant. A long-tailed tit perched briefly on top of a rhododendron *en route* to its nest construction with a small beakful of nest material. Two buzzards circled above, mewing angrily, possibly because I was too near their nest. The larger female floated over the tops of the trees a few times with her smaller mate high in the sky above her. There are regular stories about people being attacked by nesting buzzards but I think there needs to be two conditions present: there must be chicks in the nest rather than just eggs, and the person being attacked needs to be jogging or cycling rather than just walking or sitting. I've only once come reasonably close to feeling threatened when I was walking near a buzzard nest with chicks but the bird didn't come closer than about 30 yards.

I finished my half-hour on the tree stump by listening to a great spotted woodpecker drumming about a couple of hundred yards away through the wood. It was a determined bird and kept up this intermittent drumming for about ten minutes, remarkably all without getting a sore head!

I walked round the next part of The Parsonage keeping about 30 yards inside the wood and noticing a hare sitting just outside the fence. I managed to slowly get closer to it, and it seemed quite relaxed. It had been sitting hunched up but stretched to its full length and yawned. It then had a good scratch of its body with its hind legs, one side at a time, lifting its leg so high that I could see its enlarged teats. This confirmed it as a jill that would probably have leverets nearby. Next on the list of ablutions was a wash of the face, wetting its paws and even washing behind its ears. It was an entertaining ten minutes and I was pleased that I was able to back away and continue on my circuit of the wood without disturbing it.

As I passed the old wooden gate where the ladybirds had overwintered I could see that there were still some

The hare stood upright on its hind legs surveying me for several minutes

small clusters of ladybirds remaining in cracks and crevices, though most had scattered over a much wider area of the gate, Ladybirds are everywhere in the countryside and in gardens just now so hopefully we will have another good ladybird year. Aphids beware!

Not much further round the wood I could see the lovely russet colour of a red squirrel feeding on the ground. The squirrel had gone behind a tree so I gingerly stalked closer, getting to a few yards from where I had last seen it. I waited with my back to a tree for it to reappear but after five minutes I lost patience and moved forward. I could see it near the top of a conifer a few trees in front of me but I couldn't work out how it had got there unseen. My puzzle was solved when I saw a second red squirrel peering round the trunk of the tree beside me. It had been a double act to fool me.

Further still, when I was at the edge of the wood, another brown hare hopped a dozen or so yards across the field away from me but instead of taking flight it stood upright on its hind legs surveying me for several minutes. This is quite unusual for brown hares; often they sit upright but this one balanced on its hind legs, front paws held in front of its body and almost resembling a kangaroo, for nearly five minutes. Only when I moved away did it hop further out into the field. I suspect this was yet another jill with leverets nearby.

I was not finished with hares yet. As I was driving out of the estate I saw two hares in the field just up from Stewart's house. One was sitting up and the other was clapped flat to the ground. I am convinced these are the two hares that I saw and photographed on 18th March. They were in exactly the same place in the field and were behaving in an identical manner: one sitting relaxed and the other clapped down so tightly that I didn't even know it was there until I put the photos on to the laptop later in the day. Today was definitely a good hare day.

New birds identified: whitethroat
New mammals identified: none

CHAPTER 34
Wednesday 1 May. Dull with sunny intervals. 18°C.

Gloagburn Farm, Pond Wood, Back Hill, Garden Bank

Since 1st May 2019 is the date that beavers are added to Schedule 2 of the Habitats Regulations, protecting this industrious mammal, its lodge and dams, I made a check on the beaver (or beavers) at Methven Moss. The leaky dam is still intact and the water behind it is building up nicely, holding back some of the silt in the burn. At one end of the dam there is an area of mud worn smooth by the passage of the busy beaver and near to it there is a burrow just under the surface of the water. I'd always wondered where this beaver lived during the day but the burrow answered the question.

I don't fear illegal interference from the estate but I know the identity of the intruder to the estate who removed the dam at least once before. I intend to put an unobtrusive sign beside the dam warning of the new legal protection and of the potential penalty of a £5,000 fine and/or 6 months imprisonment.

My next call was to Gloagburn Farm, where I sat near the pond for a while hoping to photograph one of the pair of resident moorhens. There was no sign of moorhens – probably the female is on a nest – but unusually there was a heron at the far side of the pond awaiting a meal of fish or frogs. I've never seen either in the pond but the heron will know its territory better than me and would not waste its time at a restaurant with no food. The heron's food, of course, could also be in the shape of baby moorhens, but some survive every year, the parents sometimes even having two successful broods. Just before I left the pond a moorhen walked slowly and cautiously down to the water's edge so my wait at the pond was well worthwhile.

Leaving Gloagburn Farm, I drove through the centre of the estate, stopping for a while near the office and the buildings that form the core of Dupplin Estate and which all attract nesting swallows and house martins. Two or three swallows were catching flies around the trees in the field opposite but as yet there is no sign of house martins. The recent rain will benefit birds that use a lot of mud in

A Heron at the far side of the pond awaiting a meal of fish or frogs

the construction of their nest: swallows, house martins and song thrushes. In dry conditions I've seen them using cow dung as a mud substitute. It is equally effective but maybe less pleasant for the birds to work with.

I parked at the west end of Garden Bank and listened for a while to a distant mistle thrush, no doubt perched right at the top of a tree. It was too far away for me to attempt to write down my interpretation of its song. I was still keen to compare a mistle thrush song in this area to that of two mistle thrushes I regularly listened to on my last wildlife survey in Highland Perthshire. Even at a distance I could hear that it was nothing like those Highland Perthshire songsters. No better, no worse, just different.

I cut up through Lawn Park, intrigued by a lamb that appeared lost. It called in vain for its mother and ran back and forward between other ewes, but was rebuffed by all of them. Eventually it heard a ewe calling from 150 yards away and ran at full speed in answer to that promising call. Mother and lamb had identified each other's voices. They were reunited and after a brief nuzzling of noses the lamb was

Moorhen walked slowly and cautiously down to the water's edge

The front buck, being chased by a mature buck, was a yearling, scruffy-looking during its moult

underneath the hindquarters of its mother and suckling happily, tail wagging in satisfaction.

I walked up the ride between Harlaypoint Wood and Pond Wood, then cut left through a grassy track in Pond Wood towards the drive running north from Stewart's house. This track was bounded for about 30 yards on either side by young deciduous trees of mainly native varieties; birch, wild cherry, rowan and with a sprinkling of sycamore, all planted maybe 20 years ago and creating a much more colourful and interesting barrier between two dull areas of conifers. As I neared the end of the track I could hear a roe deer barking on my left. Until a few years ago I'd always assumed that the barking came from bucks; that was until twice during the month of May I saw and heard a doe barking because I was too near to where her fawn or fawns were hidden. Suddenly a buck and a doe ran across from left to right in front of me,

making it more likely that on this occasion it was the buck that had been barking at me. In any case, though May is the month for roe deer giving birth, 1st May is maybe still just a wee bit too early.

I reached the end of the track, exited the wood and walked up the estate road towards Back Hill. A brown hare sitting in the spring barley crop on my left looked suspiciously like one of the hares I'd photographed on two previous occasions, on each of which it was accompanied by a second hare. There was no second hare today but the hare I was looking at was reluctant to run off; even when it did so it was only for twenty yards before stopping and watching me. It was probably yet another hare with leverets hidden in the vicinity.

As I walked along Back Hill two roe

It had been pursued by a mature and strong-looking buck, still in its winter attire

bucks came running up the track leading from Pond Wood towards the track I was on. The front buck was a yearling, scruffy-looking since it was part-way through changing from its grey winter coat to its foxy-red summer coat. In hot pursuit was a mature and strong-looking buck, still in its winter attire. It was no doubt the master buck in the area and was seeing off the young pretender. The young buck came running past me at a distance of about 10 yards, close enough that I could see it had three points on its right antler but lacked the backward-facing third point on its left antler. It gracefully jumped the fence into Back Hill woodland and I turned my attention to the pursuer.

The mature buck saw me and jumped the fence on its right that bounded the track it was on. It had a thick neck and a lovely set of antlers. As it ran back down to the Pond Wood I could see that the butterfly-shaped

patch of white hair on its back end was flared out in display. By the time the breeding season for roe deer comes around in July it will have terrorised most of the immature or weaker bucks out of its area. One or two may even have been stabbed by the sharp points of the dominant buck's antlers, which can in some cases ultimately be fatal. My incidental presence may have saved the young buck an injury.

I walked along the ridge of the Back Hill woodland where there were several small patches of wood sorrel. This is an edible wild plant with distinctive leaves with three lobes. At night these three lobes fold up into a tepee shape, giving the plant protection. The delicate white flowers produced by the plant, which also close at night or in bad light, were just beginning to open up with a blink of sun. I continued my route towards the possible buzzard nest in the larch tree. I stopped before I came to the 'nest' to see if there was any activity but the more I look at it the more I think it is some sort of huge growth on the tree.

I took advantage of one of the few gates around the wood to get back to the field. It's not easy climbing a barbed wire and netting fence with a delicate camera and binoculars dangling round your neck and I try where possible to avoid that. From the field I could see four roe deer feeding at the top end of the next field. Three were bucks, with a distance of about 50 yards between them. The one furthest to the east had a doe beside it. I walked down to the fence dividing the two fields, keeping behind willow bushes growing in a narrow strip of bog land beyond the fence. If the deer had seen my approach they didn't appear bothered. I could now get a better look at them. The buck with the doe was the strongest of the three, with the best set of antlers, yet was nothing like the powerhouse of a buck I had witnessed earlier seeing off the yearling. If bucks are being culled the strong ones are the best to leave alone. They are the masters of their territory and if they are taken out an unnecessary power struggle develops, with injuries to deer and saplings getting thrashed and damaged by antlers in trying to mark territories.

I saw a brief movement of two birds in the willows. Initially I thought they were yellowhammers, but I then thought I saw a flash of red. I was looking into the sun which did not help. The birds had moved to another bush but even when I moved back I couldn't see them again. It was frustrating and the frustration was magnified when a green woodpecker called from the wood behind where the roe deer were grazing. *Kew kew kew kew*. It was a mocking call from a bird whose timing is always perfect!

Apart from these two unidentified birds there were no more along the ditch side, which was surprising as the wide area of rough grass either side of the ditch seems an ideal nesting place for many species. A hare sat dozing in the short spring barley crop just out from the fence. Again this hare was reluctant to move, and when it did so a second hare ran off alongside it. The second hare had been unseen by me in the grass at the fence side, and this was an area ideal for hiding leverets. As I reached the end of the field there was a lovely marsh marigold plant, a large buttercup-like flower with large, rounded, scalloped leaves, growing in the burn.

I made now towards Garden Bank, but as I was going down the estate track from West Munday towards my destination there were four suspicious piles of pheasant feathers near the edge of the track. Three were of cock pheasants and one of a hen pheasant. It looked like they had all been kills but what was the identity of the killer? Foxes will take pheasants but four in a straight line over 200 yards seems unlikely. Buzzards don't usually tackle full-grown pheasants. I've never seen any goshawks since August but they are extremely secretive birds. They would be more than capable of tackling a full-grown pheasant. I wonder if a goshawk had found an easy place on the estate to ambush pheasants?

Before I went down into Garden Bank I walked along East Drive, admiring the rhododendrons about to come into flower and the giant monkey puzzle trees. One of the monkey puzzle trees had grown dozens of little cones. It appears that monkey puzzle trees are either male or female. The male grows cones that are cylindrical and about three to five inches long. The female cones are spherical and when fully mature can reach six to twelve inches long. The cones on this tree were cylindrical and looked about four inches long so I concluded that they were young male cones.

Going down the slope into Garden Bank I passed through carpet after carpet of wild comfrey. This is a plant favoured by organic gardeners (myself included) to make liquid fertiliser or to add to compost heaps. Its leaves can also deter slugs. There would be a sufficient supply in just one of these beds of comfrey to keep my (substantial) vegetable plot in good health for a year.

Though there was plenty comfrey in Garden Bank there was a dearth of birds today. Apart from the mistle thrush that I'd heard at the start of my walk and which I could still hear singing in the distance as I neared my parked car, the only other bird I heard singing was the thin song of a willow warbler. It was now lunch time and maybe they'd all gone to dine. I was about to join them.

New birds identified: none
New mammals identified: none

CHAPTER 35
Friday 3 May. Dull with occasional sunshine 7°C.

Greenhill Farm

I was keen to see how the young rabbits in the burrow at Greenhill were faring. The field had been recently sown when I first saw the burrow on 10th April but there was now a good growth of spring barley. As I walked up the edge of the field I heard a willow warbler singing in a damp and rough area just outside the fence and went over to investigate. The wee light brown and yellow bird was perched right at the top of a small tree and was singing with gusto a series of notes that started off high in the scale and came tumbling down to a flourish at the end, rather in the manner of a chaffinch.

I walked up the field 30 yards out from the fence, knowing this was the line at which I would find the burrow. This must be about the favoured distance from the fence for rabbits digging their nursery burrows as I found another one before I got to the burrow I was looking for. The young rabbits in this burrow must have been recently born as the entrance was filled in to give them some protection against predators. Rabbits run in a series of hops, often landing in the same place as

they make their way to and from a particular area. There were three clear pads or hops off to the right made by the doe rabbit as it came and went from the burrow. The earth at these hops was smooth and shiny and the barley growing in the hops was flattened. It was a sure sign of activity at the burrow.

When I reached the burrow I had come to see, the entrance was now open, as I had expected. As in all nursery burrows the entrance was also much smaller in diameter compared to that of a normal rabbit burrow, only just big enough for the doe to squeeze through. There was clear evidence that it was still being visited nightly by the doe as the earth just outside the entrance was smooth and polished, caused by the doe sliding in and out. She obviously sat at the same place just outside the burrow, and this resulted in a rabbit-sized patch of flattened barley. Young rabbits start to come out of the burrow at four weeks of age. They were obviously not quite at this age yet as I would have expected to see the barley round the burrow nibbled as they were weaned off milk and onto vegetation.

Within the next few days they will be nibbling the barley and a week or two after that they will move from this short nursery burrow to a larger burrow in the bank of whin bushes beside the fence separating the barley field from the permanent grass of the moor.

On the subject of rabbits and their predators, it is really unusual that I have now been walking around this estate for nine months and have not seen either a stoat or a weasel. Stoats, in particular, depend on young rabbits as their main source of food. I have no doubt that when rabbit numbers crashed it would have had a knock-on effect on stoats.

I was pleased to hear the *coor-lee, coor-lee* call of the curlew emanating from somewhere on the moor. This is one of the loveliest sounds of the countryside but unfortunately curlews are yet another species whose numbers have crashed over the past decade or two. Nesting on the ground, their eggs and chicks are much more susceptible to predation and to agriculture than tree-nesting birds. The curlew is now considered by RSPB to be the bird of most conservation concern in the UK, its numbers having fallen by 43% since the mid-1990s. The sight of a nest of four olive green mottled eggs, exceptionally large for the size of the

bird, and all pointing inwards to the centre of the nest is something I have not encountered for many years. As I walked round the moor I was able to identify at least three different calling curlews. If there were three nests and even one brood survived to fledging that would be a real bonus.

I was sure there was at least one badger in the area (another predator of curlew eggs of course) and I came across a badger sett in amongst a bank of whin bushes on the moor. It looked like a very old sett, with more than a ton of earth at one entrance and other smaller entrances just visible in the jungle of whin bushes. There was evidence in the form of the marks of a narrow spade at the main entrance, though whoever had been digging had not gone in any distance. I wondered if it had been used by a fox at some stage and the superficial digging was an effort to block the fox in until a terrier could be brought to bolt the fox.

There was certainly no evidence of the sett being used by a fox as a cubbing den just now: no fox smell, no fox pad marks, no feathers or bones lying around. There was slightly more evidence of the sett being used by a badger. There was a partial pad mark in the soft earth at the entrance that was

Badger sett in amongst a bank of whin bushes on Greenhill moor

too broad for a fox but with insufficient detail to confirm as badger. There was also some dried grass near the entrance, which may well have been from a badger taking dried grass underground for bedding. I looked around the area for evidence of pad marks in mud or of a latrine, but there was nothing else that might have confirmed brock's residency.

This was just a short visit to Greenhill but as I was heading back to the car I was pleased to see a number of yellowhammers, linnets and meadow pipits amongst the whin bushes. One of the male yellowhammers was belting

out its song of *a little bit of bread and no cheese*. At one point I must have been too close to a meadow pipit's nest. It flew round me, landing several times on the top of whin bushes. A second meadow pipit joined in the attempt to harass me, though it kept its distance and seemed to be there more for moral support rather than as a determined participant. It was a great mix of wildlife over such a short distance, and all because of the habitat. While much of the estate, naturally, is utilised for intensive agriculture it still has sufficient wilder areas like this that allow wildlife to flourish.

One of the male yellowhammers was belting out its song

A meadow pipit landed several times on the top of whin bushes

CHAPTER 36
Monday 6 May. Sunny spells. 13°C.

Sauchie Farm, Sauchie Pond, River Earn

As I drove through the centre of the estate towards Sauchie Farm a red squirrel ran across my path towards the east end of Beech Alley. It had been completely out in the open 50 yards from the safety of trees and this is when it could become a victim of a predator such as a fox, cat, goshawk or buzzard. In this case it reached the conifers of Beech Alley safely and joined another red squirrel that was rooting about under the trees. It ran a few yards up a tree trunk and, clinging on vertically and effortlessly, gave me the chance of a lovely photograph.

I walked down to Sauchie Pond expecting to see many more birds, but some days they just seem to be either absent or quietly hiding. Some, of course, will be sitting patiently incubating eggs or keeping newly-hatched chicks warm. As I walked round the pond I heard a willow warbler ahead of me. It flew to a goat

A red squirrel ran a few yards up a tree trunk in Beech Alley

201

A willow warbler flew to a goat willow bush beside me

The Minister's Pool on the River Earn

willow bush, then flitted from branch to branch, still close to me. Like the actions of the recent meadow pipit at Greenhill I must have been close to its nest, and I was in little doubt that there was a well-hidden domed nest under a tussock on the ground close by.

The pond was rapidly being covered with the broad leaves of water lilies, though as yet no flowers. The only water bird I saw was a drake mallard, though from the far end I heard the distinctive *kurr-uk* of a moorhen. Apart from the presence of pike lurking below the water it would be an ideal place for moorhens and I was surprised that I couldn't see one. They are shy birds that often skulk amongst the undergrowth but I was satisfied that I knew at least one was present. I stood for ten minutes with my back against a tree and eventually a moorhen appeared at the edge of the rushes. My patience was rewarded, but if it breeds on the pond any wee fluffy black moorhen chicks would just be an aperitif for a pike.

I climbed out of the wood over the stile at the far end. The first house martins of the year were swooping on flies over the grass field. The east end of the field was separated from the west end by an electric fence, with sheep in the part on the west side. Strangely the house martins were restricting their flycatching activities to the clean east side, whereas I would have thought there would be many more flies over the part where the sheep were. No doubt the birds knew best.

I made now for the River Earn at Minister's Pool, walking through an area of bog on the way. I was hoping there may have been snipe, oyster-catcher or lapwing in the bog but the number of sheep and lambs in the field that also had access to the bog maybe made this a less-suitable place to nest. A heron landed on a tree at the riverside but had barely touched down on one of the higher branches when it saw me and flew off again, landing somewhere further downstream. A dozen or so mallard plus a male and female goosander were at the far side of Minister's Pool and quickly flew upstream at my approach.

I passed the anglers' hut and headed upstream, crossing a boggy area via a raised and impressively well-constructed slatted walkway for the anglers. Footprints on an area of mud at the riverside interested me, especially when the trail ended in the river. It was an otter track, though all but one of the prints were on drier mud and were unidentifiable. I could hear a willow warbler singing on my right and a warbler of some sort, probably a garden warbler, at the far side of the river. It was a good place to stop for something to eat.

I sat on a wooden bridge over a ditch, seeing more otter tracks in the mud below me. The willow warbler had stopped singing and I was distracted from the as yet unconfirmed warbler on the far side because of a much louder bird song almost in my ear. A sedge warbler was in the willow just behind me. This bird has a loud, much deeper sounding song than the other warblers. It is a very distinctive song with a wide range of notes, sometimes going from a very low note to a note at the top of the scale. It has lots of *churrs* followed by repetitive *cheeps* rather like a sparrow. I listened intently for a while then stood up to try to see the bird. It must have been deep in the willow but though I couldn't see it, it must have been aware of my movement so close to it and that, unfortunately, was the end of the song. I sat down again to finish my sandwich. Sitting there amidst birdsong, the occasional quiet *baa* of a blackfaced ewe making contact with its lamb and the higher-pitched *meh* of its lamb in return, and with the quiet gurgle of the river running by, was idyllic.

I walked further up the riverbank and was amazed at a huge carpet of the wild flower summer snowflakes. It is a flower of wet areas, particularly woodland bordering rivers that periodically flood over the bank. It grows to about two feet high and resembles a giant snowdrop, with bright green stems and white bell-shaped flowers trimmed with green. It brightened up the woodland, as did carpets of comfrey, a larger variety with what promised to be purple flowers and a shorter variety with white flowers. Unfortunately the woodland, like many other riparian woodlands, has been invaded by the dreaded giant hogweed. Enormous serrated leaves of this plant covered a large area, and its eight-foot-high stalks and umbrella-shaped skeletal flowers from last year were still in evidence. It is a horrible toxic plant, extremely difficult to kill off, and I doubt we will ever be rid of it. I remember none of these riverside

The male bullfinch posed on a sycamore stump

invaders – giant hogweed, Japanese knotweed or Himalayan balsam – when I was trapping here in the 1970s. A whitethroat sang briefly from a tree just above the giant hogweed, unaware of the blight on the ground below.

I retraced my steps and continued downstream past the anglers' hut, walking on top of the floodbank and glimpsing a hare that loped off ahead of me, disturbed from its riverside bed. Much further ahead I could see a heron standing on a shingle bed, back a couple of yards from the river and probably digesting an earlier piscine meal. I sat on the riverbank for a while listening to yet another warbler on the other side of the river. It was a continuous song, less staccato than some of the warblers, and I thought it was either a blackcap or a garden warbler since both have a similar song. I couldn't see the bird but made a guess that it was a garden warbler since its song was more flowing than that of a blackcap. As I sat there enjoying the unidentified bird's music a pair of bullfinches flew across the river and landed near me on a sycamore tree that

had been cut back almost to ground level, probably to facilitate easier salmon fishing, but was beginning to grow again.. The male posed for a photograph, while the female flew back over the river, joined seconds later by her mate.

I continued on. The heron had been joined on the shingle by a bird I could just make out at the distance: a grey wagtail, identification made easier by the constantly flicking tail. Beyond that a single swan cruised in a corner pool. Around the corner was a huge shingle bed where some of the gravel had been removed for use on the estate, and many tons had been piled up for future use. An oystercatcher flew off the shingle, and though I couldn't see a nest I found four or five nest-shaped scrapes where an oystercatcher had experimented with the site but had failed to add the smaller stones and dried grass that would have completed the nest. The river was really low, making the shingle bank much more extensive than usual and showing bits of branches above the surface from trees that had been washed down by annual floods and which normally lay completely hidden.

When I went around the next bend in the river I was surprised to see a pair of greylag geese, then another two and yet another two, each with a larger gander and a smaller goose. I was quite surprised at how approachable they were; wild geese from Iceland or Greenland would have flown off at the first sight of a human yet these geese happily swam within 40 yards of me. I suspect that they would have hatched somewhere on mainland Scotland since they appeared as used to people as their relatives on the Western Isles. Greylag geese on this estate in spring, maybe even breeding here, is yet another new concept since the 1970s. There were plenty of sand martins flying above the geese, yet I couldn't see a sand bank where they might have been nesting. There are suitable sites further downstream and that's where they probably came from.

I was intrigued by another warbler singing from the far side of the river and had to have another seat on the riverbank to listen. The advantage in spring and summer is that I can plunk my backside down almost anywhere, whereas in winter almost every otherwise-suitable place to sit is always wet. The warbler had been singing for nearly five minutes before I managed to locate it in a willow tree. It was too far away to identify even through the binoculars so I decided to try to take a photograph at almost maximum zoom for my Canon bridge camera. I was sure that the songster was either a garden warbler or a blackcap and the photo,

once on to my laptop, clearly showed it as the former. I double-checked the song with the RSPB Birdguides bird songs and was 100% sure of my identification of the bird.

I hiked back up the hill to my car, passing a couple of new-born lambs that had died. One had its eye pecked out by a carrion crow, most likely after death. Eyes are always the first to be taken by carrion crows, though they'd had a bigger feast on the second dead lamb that may have been lying in the field longer. On the way back through the centre of the estate in the car two jays flew across my path. Jays must be one of our most beautiful birds. They certainly take some eggs and chicks from songbird nests but their main diet is acorns. I suspect that they are on the verge of having full protection in England and I strongly suspect that approach will be taken in Scotland as well. After the announcement of UN scientists on 6 May 2019 that nearly a million species of plants and animals are on the verge of extinction, mostly because of the activities of humans, we need to look much more closely at how wildlife can be conserved, which most certainly includes far less emphasis on the supposed need to 'control' or 'manage' wildlife.

New birds identified: moorhen, sedge warbler, garden warbler
New mammals identified: none

205

CHAPTER 37
Farming and Wildlife – John Hogg, farm manager

I had a chat with John Hogg, farm manager of the 3,600 acres of Dupplin Estate that is farmed in-hand. The estate runs over 2000 breeding ewes, a small number of breeding cattle and grows primarily grain and oil seed rape. My main interest was in the wildlife-friendly aspects of farming and I was delighted to learn of the estate's plans to expand these considerably.

We've seen that there are many parts of the estate sown with wild bird seed mixtures. For the year 2019/20 John plans to have 25 plots of wild bird seed sown covering a total of 42 acres. The seed mix includes sunflowers, chicory, linseed, quinoa and barley. These varieties seed at different times, with some holding their seed longer than others. This gives an almost all-year-round banquet of seeds for wild birds. While some of these double as game crops for feeding and sheltering pheasants and red-legged partridges, many are different from other game crops that I have seen in that they are not always attached to woodland, widening or lengthening the area from which to drive birds for shooting; and some of these seed mixes are in plots

entirely unconnected to pheasant drives.

In addition to the 42 acres of plots under John's management, the estate gives wild bird seed mix to some tenant farmers, thus expanding the winter food available to wild birds over a wider area of the estate. Little wonder that I saw so many flocks of small birds on the estate over the winter time.

I had noticed some areas of phacelia growing, particularly at Nether Keir and John explained that this is grown to attract pollinators. Phacelia is highly attractive to honeybees and bumble bees, which are valuable pollinators. It is also reputed to attract other beneficial insects, such as parasitic wasps. Phacelia provides both pollen and nectar and can be sown at the optimum time to build up beneficial insect populations in anticipation of their requirement to control a crop pest.

The estate now sows vetch and clover amongst their oil seed rape, which increase the amount of mycorrhizal fungi. Mycorrhizas are beneficial fungi, growing in association with plant roots and exist by taking sugars from plants in exchange for moisture and nutrients gathered from the soil by the fungal strands. The mycorrhizas greatly increase the absorptive area of a plant, acting as extensions to the root system and also seems to give some protection against root diseases. A perfect example of symbiosis.

I asked how the use of pesticides on crops works alongside all this much more natural and scientific method of growing crops. The answer, I was pleased to hear, is that pesticides are now only used as a last resort.

John and I discussed skylark plots, where every so often when sowing winter cereal, small gaps are left unsown that allow the skylark to land, where otherwise it would be reluctant to in well grown cereal in spring and early summer due to the height of the crop. John is aware of skylark plots but wonders if patches of bare ground might be a magnet for foxes, which would then predate any skylark nest nearby. He put a counter argument that skylarks land in the tramlines and generally their nest is within a few feet of the tramlines. Tramlines are the regular route taken by a fox through a field of cereal so there is still a

possibility that a fox could predate skylark nests near tramlines. Maybe a skylark plot right in the middle of the grain between, but stopping well short of, the tramlines could be the best solution.

Nests in growing crops are difficult to see from a large tractor with a cab. In my day they were more easily spotted from a small tractor without a cab. But John was pleased to tell me that one of the tractor drivers spotted an oyster-catcher nest in one of the fields this spring, marked it and worked round it with any further operations. He is also aware of a curlew which fledged two chicks in a winter wheat crop in 2018.

I raised two negative issues with John: removing existing fences to increase the size of fields and the late rolling of spring cereal that I saw in some fields this year. In relation to the fence removal, these are fences that were old and were bare or almost bare, in other words did not have hedges or any other cover alongside the fence. Their removal in every case is counterbalanced by a four to six yards wide strip up the side of the field. John stated that in the six years he has been on the estate this is the first time they have had to roll cereal fields after the grain was through the ground, and it was caused by being caught out by wet weather immediately after the crops were sown.

On plans for the future, the estate is about to embark on an agri-environment climate scheme (EACS). I'd to look this one up. This scheme provides payments to farmers who subscribe, on a voluntary basis, to environmental commitments related to the preservation of the environment and maintaining the countryside. Farmers commit, for a minimum period of at least five years, to adopt environmentally-friendly farming techniques that go beyond legal obligations. In return, farmers receive payments that provide compensation for additional costs and income foregone resulting from applying those environmentally friendly farming practices in line with the stipulations of agri-environment contracts. Agri-environment payments encourage farmers to adopt agricultural activities or levels of production intensity that deliver positive environmental outcomes, while not being necessarily the first choice from the point of view of profitability.

Examples of commitments covered by national/regional agri-environmental schemes are:

- environmentally favourable extensification of farming;

- management of low-intensity pasture systems;

- integrated farm management and organic agriculture;

- preservation of landscape and historical features such as hedgerows, ditches and woods;

- conservation of high-value habitats and their associated biodiversity.

So far as the estate is concerned there will now be more over-winter stubble, which provides feeding for birds that otherwise would have been ploughed in. There will also be more wild bird seed crops and green manure sown after a crop has been harvested, with the green manure ploughed in before it seeds in spring time. At least as important is the plan for a massive increase in the number of hedges. To comply with the scheme the hedges have to be of native species so most likely will be of hawthorn, but interplanted with native trees.

CHAPTER 38
Wednesday 15 May. Hot and sunny. 22°C.

Wester Cairnie Farm, River Earn

I was still keen to establish what species of summer visitors come to the estate and today I decided to walk round the river area of Wester Cairnie. I drove down to the small brick shed near to a boggy patch of tall reedy grass adjacent to the river and parked there, though not too close to seven or eight beehives that had been placed next to a field of flowering oil seed rape. The bees were busy flying to and fro collecting the yellow pollen from the plants and carrying out a great pollination job while doing so. A swallow flew out of the brick shed but when I investigated inside there had been little change since my last visit. Two complete swallow's nests and one tattered one were glued to the rafters. There was no addition of mud to the completed nests since they didn't really need exterior improvement. I gently felt inside the nests expecting eggs to be in at least one of them. They were empty and as yet had no interior enhancement by way of a new lining of feathers. The disused wasps' bike was still clinging to the window frame and the only change to the inside of the shed was a dead and desiccated hare. I think it unlikely that

any predator would bring the hare into the shed and I suspect it had been a sick hare which had simply gone in there to die.

I was pleased to see that there was still plenty water in the two large pools in the wet area of tall grass. When I first looked at this part of the estate in Autumn 2018 the pools were completely dry and I was concerned this was a permanent change. In effect the pools were simply dry because of the long dry summer of 2018. They now seem to be back to normal. Half a dozen mallard erupted from the first pool, as did a pair of shelduck. I suspect the shelduck were those that I saw in pools of water in a grass field further down the river on 5th April; it seems a pity that they don't appear to be breeding this year. The shelduck were keen to get back on to the pool and made a couple of passes as if about to land, but aborted when they saw there were no mallard, and eventually landed on the river.

I was hoping that I might see reed buntings, a species that were present on every other visit, but there was neither sign nor sound that indicated they may have been breeding there. A wren flew in short bursts along a ditch side keeping just ahead of me. Its wings were whirring at top speed and it occasionally gave a quiet *churrr*, which helped me keep track of it. Because it was such a sunny day there were hundreds of butterflies around and the wee wren seemed little bigger than its more colourful lepidopteran flying companions.

As I scanned the tall grass I could see that I was being watched. A yearling roe buck was keeping a close eye on me from the depths of the grassy jungle. He had short spiky antlers typical of a roe buck of his age and he seemed to have a white blaze on his forehead, similar to that of many horses. A closer look revealed that the 'white blaze' was in fact the seed heads of one or more stalks of grass in front of him. I've never seen a roe deer with any white colouring on its head but I have seen a red deer with such a white blaze. Some individuals within a strain of red deer on the south side of Loch Tay have white blazes and white patches. Several years ago I was lucky enough to see one of those, plus, for good measure, a newly-born red deer calf hiding in the heather, on a walk with the estate gamekeeper as part of the Tayside

Police initiative to prevent and detect wildlife crime, Operation Countrywatch Partnership.

I'd reached the river now and walked slowly upstream. I could see the two shelduck ahead of me on a sandbank on the far side. They saw me at the same time and slipped into the river, swimming upstream for a short distance before taking off and circling back towards their original pond. Despite twice flying over the pond they were wary because of the absence of any other wildfowl and diverted back to the river, landing still further upstream. Had there been mallard or other ducks on the pond I'm sure they would have landed but they are rightly suspicious, despite not being a species that is hunted.

When I reached where the shelduck had been, there were dozens of sand martins swooping low over the river feeding on flies. Some were obviously entering holes in the overhanging bank at my side though I couldn't see the nest holes for the overhang. With interference of these hardy wee migratory birds at their nest sites at sand quarries it is good to see that they also make use of any suitable sandy riverbank for nesting, and there are plenty of these on this estate.

Drake of the pair of shelducks on the River Earn at Wester Cairnie haugh

As I approached a wide bend on the river further upstream I was puzzled at what I thought were half a dozen shelduck on a gravel bank in the centre of the river. When I got closer I saw that there was only the pair of shelduck that I'd been annoying for half an hour plus three great black-backed gulls – an easy mistake to make as at a quick glance the gulls are of a similar colour and size. The shelduck took to the water again, floating downstream with the current, while the more wary gulls flew off.

I gave the harassed shelduck time to get past me and out of sight before moving forward to the river. When I did so a common sandpiper, which had been sitting below the bank, flew across to the shingle bank and watched me from there. The grass in the field was quite long as there have been no sheep in it since the autumn, and the sandpiper may well have had a mate on a nest in the grass near the river side. An oystercatcher, which I think came off a nest on the shingle bank, ran quickly along the shingle then stopped and observed me after a 30-yard sprint. Even though it was safe at the other side of the river it had diverted attention away from its nest, knowing that a predator, in this case and in the bird's opinion, me, would make towards it rather than the nest.

A common sandpiper was sitting below the bank of the River Earn

Sedge warbler singing from within a bush on top of the flood bank of the river

Mixed herd of red and roe deer feeding on West Cultmalundie (photo: Bill McIntosh)

On my last visit to this part of the estate on 22nd February two dead swans, one whooper and one mute, lay under the power lines that cross the field. I walked over to see what was left of them. The swans were desiccated and though they had probably been predated by crows and gulls they didn't seem to have been predated by foxes, otherwise bits of the swans would have been chewed off and removed or lying around near the carcass. Unfortunately another two swans had also hit the wires since my earlier visit and lay dead near the original two. These power lines are on a direct approach to the river and are at the exact height that the swans would be if gliding in to land on the water.

I crossed a fence to the edge of a field of oil seed rape, in fact diagonally opposite where the beehives were. As I walked up the edge of the field I could hear a sedge warbler singing up ahead. I then saw the bird rising out of the oil seed rape and making for a bush on top of the flood bank of the river. Had I not heard the song and in fact managed to photograph the bird in the bush, where it again began to sing, I may have thought it to be a pipit. The warbler, flying above the height of the bush, suddenly fluttered down in the manner of a tree pipit to land on the bush. I'd never seen this of a sedge warbler before, but of course when walking in the countryside every day is a school day.

New birds identified: none
New mammals identified: none

A relaxed brown hare was sitting in the sun surrounded by succulent food

CHAPTER 39
Tuesday 21 May. Dull with odd sunny spells. 14⁰C.

East and West Cultmalundie Farms, Greenhill Farm

I hadn't been to East and West Cultmalundie Farms for a while and as I drove up the farm road I noted two fields on East Cultmalundie that hadn't been sown or planted with any crop. The fields were still in plough and with a substantial covering of weeds. These are the kind of fields that lapwings, oystercatchers, curlews and grey partridge are attracted to but there was no signs of any of those species on or over the field. The later-sown crops are normally peas and beans and there are already several fields of peas on these two farms with the peas through the ground. I'm sure these fields will be destined for a later crop of peas.

Further up the farm road two separate pairs of goldfinches flew across in front of me, then it was the turn of a small flock of six goldfinches (a *charm* of goldfinches being the collective noun). This was maybe a brood from this year, which I could have established from their plumage if they had landed but they flew behind me after they crossed over the road. A succession of rooks was also flying back and forward across the road, many landing at puddles on the road to get a drink or to bathe. Their origin is a small conifer wood behind West Cultmalundie Farm, which I had now reached. Parts of East and West Culmalundie are now derelict, which suits the swallows, and they were swooping in and out of old buildings or perching on wires around the farms.

I was now a mile or so from the public road at West Cultmalundie Farm. At this point the farm road degenerates into a farm track and my destination was yet another mile along this track. I passed a field of peas on my left, where a very lucky and relaxed brown hare was sitting in the sun surrounded by succulent food. It gave some good photo opportunities and in fact turned from side on to almost head on to watch me. I left the hare undisturbed – observe, photograph and move on – which is the way I try to operate when possible.

I parked where the top end of a strip of elderly Scots pine trees meets

Cultmalundie Woods. A willow warbler which had been perched on top of a whin bush rose into the air towards another willow warbler and the pair interacted for a few seconds in the air before fluttering down to land on top of separate whin bushes. I'm not sure whether this was a male/female pre-breeding display or whether it was territorial but this is the second time I've seen warblers (last time it was a sedge warbler) flutter down and land in the manner of a pipit.

Behind me at the edge of the birch woodland a garden warbler was singing. I think this is my favourite warbler as its song is much less of a series of fits and starts than some of the other warblers. It continues its song for a decent length of time, even though in this case it was flitting from tree to tree in a rough circle which I assume would be around its territory. It was quite difficult to see, though when it moved from one perch to another it gave me an opportunity to home in on it.

I walked down the line of Scots pines, which had almost complete ground cover of whin bushes underneath. A male yellowhammer landed above me on a thin branch of the only oak tree in the strip and watched in concern that I might be a threat to its mate somewhere on a nest

underneath. I note that bird books nearly always state that yellowhammers nest on the ground though in my youth I found them quite regularly in whin bushes. This seems a far more sensible place for a yellow bird to nest; as well as the benefit of camouflage and thorns it is off the ground and slightly less susceptible to predators. I walked on for 50 or so yards to the end of the line of pines and turned back. The yellowhammer was still on the same perch, and was now singing.

I walked up the edge of a field of spring barley to Cultmalundie Wood then headed west along the wood edge. There were still obvious signs of roe and red deer coming out of the woods and feeding on the barley, which will not please the person who leases the land from the estate. I walked down the far end of the field, which is bordered by yet more whin bushes. A pair of linnets sat on top of the whins, with the male closest to me and easiest to photograph. When photographs of the male were in the bag I turned to the less colourful female. She had disappeared!

I was now at a small wood with the eastern half primarily birch and alder trees and elder bushes which had been fenced off at one time as a pheasant release pen. The western half

A male linnet sat on top of the whins

comprised Scots pine trees. I walked down the east side, seeing a sedge warbler with its distinctive eye stripe skulking about in the undergrowth. Further along, a whitethroat perched obligingly atop a hawthorn bush. This was a real treat for me as whitethroats are my nemesis, always heard, seldom seen and if seen only for seconds. It sat for at least a minute, which was the highlight of my day. I continued around the three acres or so of woodland disturbing the rooks from their nests in the Scots pines as I walked underneath. It was a small rookery by most standards with probably about 50 nests, which might fledge around 150 young rooks. These baggy-trousered corvids always seem to do well at nesting time. Pity that curlews, lapwings, skylarks and grey partridges can't be trained to nest up trees and in colonies.

Leaving the rookery wood I continued west along a track at the edge of Cultmalundie Wood which led to the fields of Westmuir and Greenhill. I remembered an interesting phone call that I had concerning Westmuir when I was wildlife crime officer with Tayside Police. Anyone operating a crow cage trap must apply to the police for a code number. The code number and the contact telephone number of the local wildlife crime officer must be displayed on the crow cage when it is in use. A caller made the following request:

'My name is Farmer Bloggs. I'm needing to put cattle on to Westmuir. Could you come and take your trap away please?' I asked what trap he was meaning. 'It's the crow trap in the strip of trees – it has your phone number on it.'

I replied that it wasn't my trap, and that it was operated by Raymond, who was the keeper on the estate at that time. 'But it's got your phone number on it.' I explained that the details

A whitethroat perched obligingly atop a hawthorn bush

shown on the trap are what is required as a condition of the general licence under which the trap is operated so that anyone coming across an illegally-set trap can report it to the police. Farmer Bloggs was not going to give up easily.

'Anyway, could you come and take it away before I put my cattle out?' I explained that what I would do was to phone Raymond and make him aware of the situation. Farmer Bloggs was not best pleased, gave a grunt and the phone went dead.

Returning to real time, at the end of the track and as I reached Westmuir there was a strong smell of something dead. I looked around inside the wood, expecting to find a dead roe deer, but drew a blank. I crossed the gate on to Westmuir then turned right through another gate on to Greenhill, then continued walking westwards towards a narrow area of birch and oak woodland at the western estate boundary. I turned right (north) when I reached this open woodland and walked quietly through it. I could hear a song thrush singing loudly on my left and a warbler singing ahead of me which I suspected was either a blackcap or a garden warbler. I slowly got closer to the singing warbler but had difficulty locating it because of the volume of the song thrush on my left and a very low-flying aircraft with RAF markings that had suddenly appeared on my right. Once the plane had passed I could hear the singer right ahead of me and at possibly no more than head height. It was a lovely song and I stood for a few minutes enjoying the sound. Still not seeing the bird I took another few steps forward and disturbed a blackcap, which immediately ceased its aria and flew off. Damn!

It was beginning to rain lightly so I headed back up towards Cultmalundie Wood. I had hoped to see curlew in the field as I had heard them there on a visit on 3rd May to an area of Greenhill Farm just north of this. It was disappointing that there were none today but there may well have been one or more unseen and sitting on a nest in some of the damper areas of the field. At the top of the field I discovered what the smell had been. A dark brown calf lay dead in a dry ditch. Clearly the mother had been standing by the calf wondering why it didn't rise and follow her as the ground was well trampled. There was no obvious reason why the calf had died; the ditch was wide and shallow so there was no reason that the calf could not have got out. It simply reminded me that where there is livestock there is also dead stock and was a sad end to the day's walk.

New birds identified: blackcap
New mammals identified: none

CHAPTER 40

Wednesday 22 May. Dull with odd sunny spells. Moderate wind. 14°C.

Aberdalgie Mains Farm, Sauchie Farm, River Earn, Milton Den

The farms of Mains of Aberdalgie and parts of Sauchie were where I headed today. I parked on a track that runs between the two farms and was immediately treated to the song of a whitethroat as I stepped out of the car. I listened for a while but, as is very often the case, I was unable to locate the songster. Slightly disappointed, I walked down the track on the east side of an attractive strip of woodland that held some conifers, but mainly oak, beech, ash and wild cherry. Under the trees the ground was a lovely blanket of pink campion. I was bounded on my left-hand side by a hawthorn hedge. I'd seen five or six old nests in this hedge in winter and I'd hoped, come spring, to see what species of birds nested there. Unfortunately (for me but not for the nesting birds) the hedge was now so dense with leaves I was unable to see anything in its inner sanctum unless I took it very slowly and had my nose almost right up against the hedge, which I was not prepared to do.

As I emerged from the track there was a field of winter wheat, now about a foot high, which had been behind the hedge, and a field of spring barley a few inches high on my immediate left. On my right was about half an acre of scrub land and a pile of old fencing and other discarded wood. I walked on for 20 yards and saw a hare hopping purposefully from the scrub land and crossing the path I had just traversed. The hare hopped into the young barley and I could see that it had a large patch of fur missing on its upper right back leg. The skin on the bare patch looked yellow and had possibly suppurated after a fight with another hare.

The hare stopped to survey the scene, then continued on along one of the tramlines in the field. Halfway along the field I could see another hare nosing about near the field edge bordering the winter wheat. 'My' hare stopped opposite and thirty yards from this second hare but for whatever reason did not approach it. My assumption was that they were both males. The second hare slipped through the fence into the winter wheat and emerged minutes later along with

The jack hares ran in close convoy after the female

another two hares. One of these must have been a female and 'my' hare was now interested. It joined the cavalcade and there was considerable kicking and boxing taking place within the group, with the hares jumping into the air and running in close convoy as if jockeying for closest position to the female. This continued for a good five minutes before the hares disappeared into the next field, and without any of the hares managing to mate with the female. Procreation for many wild species is fraught with danger, and hopefully the hare with the injured leg will recover.

As I was watching the hare, I was aware of a skylark singing in the sky above me. I was lucky it was quite close with my age-related difficulty hearing skylarks and other birds with high-pitched songs. As the skylark sang it gradually lost height and eventually landed in the spring barley field. I wondered if it had a nest near where it landed but I suspect the barley was still too short to give sufficient cover for a nesting attempt. The field had also recently been rolled, which would have put paid to any nests or chicks of any species, maybe even leverets.

The next field was in grass, with some rushy, formerly wet but now dried-up areas round the edge. Several

meadow pipits rose from the rushes and flew to the field next door, which was also spring barley. I was surprised at such a number of meadow pipits – eight or nine – being together at this time of year as I thought they would be in pairs nesting. This was certainly a good nesting area for them but nesting meadow pipits would not flush in a large group such as this. It's possible of course that they could have been a family group from an early nest.

I reached the River Earn and walked upstream. Dozens of sand martins were swirling low over the river catching flies and at a bend further ahead eight or nine mallard, mainly drakes, sat on shingle beside two female goosanders. The wary and much persecuted goosanders did not hang around long after they spotted me and were soon off, flying upriver. The mallard dallied slightly longer then they also took off. The reason for the number of sand martins was clear: round a bend in the river and at the far side was a virtual sand martin city. Dozens of holes had been excavated in the sand bank with a white splash of droppings at several of them, confirming occupancy. Many sand

The female grey wagtail came to feed the chick at least fifteen times in five minutes

A female swan sat patiently on a neat nest of reeds at the edge of the pool

martin colonies are in an almost straight line in the sand where the birds have found a striation in the sand that is most suitable for digging. In the case of this colony the holes were scattered over a large area of the sand bank, one or two dangerously near the waterline. Chicks will only be reared successfully in these second-class tenancies if there is no sudden rise in the water level. The birds are certainly lucky in the meantime as the water level is very low.

A pair of grey wagtails were flitting over the river clearly on serious fly catching expeditions. I saw the reason why as the female of the pair landed on a branch at the side of the river. A young grey wagtail waited patiently there for his breakfast. As I watched, the female (the one without the black bib) came to feed the chick at least fifteen times in five minutes. The chick was content to wait on the branch, knowing that he or she was being well serviced with a favourite meal: flies. I'd lost sight of the male, though he was most likely feeding another chick elsewhere. It was a lucky, and lovely, insight into the private world of birds.

Before I left the river to head to some marshland I watched a common sandpiper probing for sand-dwelling morsels on a sand bank upstream of the sand martin colony. It seemed to be having success as I saw its beak open and shut a few times as it guzzled some delicacy. A blackfaced ewe had not had the same level of luck. It had fallen into the water and now lay dead against the bank. There were blackfaced ewes in the field where I was but I'm not sure if this was one of that flock. The sheep in the field, so far as I could see, had yellow ear tags while the unfortunate drowned sheep had an orange ear tag. It was not in particularly deep water but it may have fallen in further upriver and in any case its fleece would soon become sodden leaving it with little chance of reaching the bank.

I headed now for a wet area with several permanent pools of water and surrounded by willow and alder trees. I'd noticed a mute swan in the field (again spring barley) and could now connect it with one of the pools of water. A female swan sat patiently on a neat nest of reeds at the edge of the pool and the swan in the field was the male standing guard. He was a pretty poor guard as he never came near me, even when I was quite close to his mate on the nest. Swans can have a big brood of cygnets: from four or five up to nine. I'd be surprised if there will be enough food in and around this wee pool and I suspect shortly after hatching the family will move to the river.

The trees and bushes here are ideal habitat for warblers and I could hear the distinctive sound of a sedge warbler coming from just beyond the swan. Further round the marsh a willow warbler was singing and as I came to the area of scrub and old fenceposts near the start of my walk a warbler of some sort took on an intruding warbler, probably of the same species. They had a very short tussle just above the level of the rough grass and one of them, probably the intruder to a nesting bird's territory, took off into some trees. As I walked through the scrub area in the direction of my car a warbler, probably a willow warbler, rose almost from my feet. I had a gentle look around where the bird erupted from to see if there was a nest but my search was short (and unsuccessful) as I didn't want to trample or damage a nest.

I drove round to have a quick look at Milton Den as I had some spare time.

I parked at Munday House and as I walked under the old walnut tree I was scolded by a great tit, mouth full of caterpillars. I was clearly near its nest with chicks, probably safely ensconced in a hole in the ancient tree, and the bird didn't like my proximity to its nest one bit. It sat on a selection of branches not far above my head and chattered at me until I moved on.

I walked down the grass field to Milton Den, hearing the loud boom of a gas gun going off in the field of peas just beyond the den. I was quite surprised to see a roe doe run from a dip in the den, where it had been unseen by me, into the thick blackthorn bushes in the centre of the den. It was closely followed by a buck. These two were obviously accustomed to the regular loud report of the gas gun and hadn't paid the last loud report any attention whatsoever.

Further along the den I sat on my regular and comfortable seat: a corrugated plastic sheet on four legs used to give cover to pheasants and partridges. I was sitting watching and photographing a willow warbler on top of a hawthorn bush when suddenly a streak of black shot past me through the grass. A mink was chasing a young rabbit, which it caught and quickly killed, giving the unfortunate rabbit time only for a single scream. I moved forward to try for a photograph but the mink saw the movement, abandoned the now-lifeless rabbit and headed towards the pond.

The mink cut right before it came to the pond and headed along the side of a pheasant release pen. I couldn't see it after it fled from the rabbit but I could follow its progress by the reactions of the birds. A blackbird and chaffinches were sounding their *pink, pink, pink* alarm calls for a predator on the ground as opposed to in the air; a song thrush followed the route of the mink, flying from bush to bush in pursuit, and a pair of dunnocks, normally birds that are on or near to the ground, flew to the top of a bush to keep an eye on such a dangerous predator. Even a single mink like this will cause untold devastation to the eggs and chicks of nesting birds, and if it is a female with young to feed, even more so. I passed the sighting to Stewart and hopefully he may be able to trap this non-native invasive menace.

I walked down to near the edge of the pond and spotted a heron at the far side. Unlike many of the herons I have been close to over the past couple of weeks, which have been young ones, this was an adult. I was surprised it

didn't notice me but it was busy feeding on something at the edge of the water and was partly hidden behind a bush. It was so engrossed in its feeding that I managed to back out from my position and walk past the pond without it even being aware that I had been there. This was very unusual for such a sharp-eyed bird.

As I headed back to the car I thought about the origin of the mink in the wild and the devastation they have caused. The mink locally were originally released by animal rights activists from a mink farm near Comrie in Perthshire, probably in the 1960s. I certainly don't agree with farming mink for their fur, but I don't agree either with releasing non-native predators from North America into the wild in the UK. Mink have almost exterminated our native water voles – Ratty from *Wind in the Willows* – which had absolutely no defence against the onslaught of these deadly mustelids, and the efforts to kill off the mink has cost a huge amount of public money and has only been partially successful. I was still thinking about mink as I passed under the walnut tree. The great tit was chattering at me again.

New birds identified: none
New mammals identified: mink

CHAPTER 41

Tuesday 28 May. Dull with sunny intervals. 11°C.

River Earn at Forteviot, May Burn

My route today took me past the spots notorious for flytipping. The roots of four large conifers had been dumped in a layby near to the hamlet of Tibbermore, while further along that road, near to the A9, a truck load of branches had been dumped in a field entrance. In the first case the local council would have the responsibility to lift the waste, but in the second case, it being in a field gateway, the tenant farmer has the responsibility unless the council workers felt inclined to assist. Not only that, the farmer was left meantime with a blocked entrance to his field. I really wish someone could be caught for this criminal act and the case given maximum publicity.

There are a number of immature herons from this year's progeny about just now and one stood on the bank of May Burn as I drove towards my parking spot beside the River Earn. They are much less cautious than adults and this one simply flew 100 yards into the field as I drove past. It was the first of three that I saw in different locations this morning and they may well have all been from the same brood. I regularly have a visit from young herons to the burn that runs through my garden. There are plenty small trout in the burn for them but I particularly remember one heron that was having a really bad day. The rain was pelting down and the burn had risen considerably, making fishing more difficult. This young heron had moved on to the grass bank at the side of the burn and stood there hunched up, its normally long neck folded up and with a regular drip at the end of its dagger beak. It looked absolutely miserable. In poor fishing conditions I'm sure many of these first-year birds succumb to starvation unless they learn to adapt their feeding to worms and other morsels that can be found in a wet grass field.

I parked and walked over to the river. Two female goosanders swam upstream away from me. I've often wondered about goosanders, since I see far more females than males. Could there be a natural preponderance of females in a brood of youngsters? At least twice I've seen broods of goosanders fledged to the point that the sexes can be differentiated where there

Roe deer with fawn at Woodhead
(photo: Bill McIntosh)

have been far more females than males. During the 10 months so far on this estate the ratio has been at least two females to one male, and that is also taking account of the moulting period when the males' pelage is temporarily similar to that of the female.

I walked along the riverbank, yet again enjoying the lovely melody of a song thrush that was sitting like a Christmas fairy right on top of an ash tree. On my last visit here on 17th April there was a distinct lack of warblers, a fact also commented on by the angler I chatted with. Today the situation was completely different with warblers singing everywhere. Garden warblers were the most common, then willow warblers and with sedge warblers and

whitethroat about equal. For the second time in the past couple of weeks I must have stopped near to a willow warbler's nest. The displeased wee bird flew back and forth from bush to bush, quite close to me, until I moved on. Frustratingly it gave no opportunity for a photograph.

With the river still on my left, I came to a clearing on my right where the willows, alders and other bushes and trees gave way to long grass. A roe doe was sitting in the grass but immediately saw me and ran into thicker cover, closely followed by a buck. The clearing gave perfect cover to hide fawns and I wondered if she maybe had a fawn or

The young goosanders' dappling matched perfectly the light and shade of the river

fawns nearby. If so she may have given a bark, but she was silent. I've only twice before stumbled upon a roe deer fawn lying hidden. In both cases I was only a few feet from them and they absolutely froze, not even blinking or moving an ear, until I moved on. Their dappled coat as fawns gave them perfect camouflage and I felt it a real privilege to have seen them.

I returned my gaze to the river, just in time to see the electric blue of a kingfisher darting down the far side. It was about six feet above the surface and I hoped it would land on the branch of a tree. Its mind was made up that it was heading elsewhere but nevertheless it was an exciting glimpse. There are suitable sandy banks on the river for a kingfisher nesting further upstream and further downstream though I couldn't think of any within half a mile or so. I disturbed a sandpiper now, which flew upstream, and at almost the same time a great-spotted woodpecker crossed from my side diagonally upstream and

landed in a tree 150 yards further up. It would have been unidentified but for the two white patches on its wings and its undulating flight: a few flaps of the wings, then wings closed, a few more flaps and a repeat of the flight process. Shortly after there was the sound of drumming coming from the area the woodpecker landed.

I'd to leave the riverbank now for a short distance because of dense trees, shrubs and other vegetation and could now hear the strident *wee, wee, wee; wee, wee, wee* of a nuthatch coming from my right as I moved out of the trees. I stopped and tried to locate the sound but could see no bird. I moved forward a few feet and watched and listened again. Still the *wee, wee, wee,* but no bird. I moved again and so did the nuthatch; it had been right in front of me but about twice as high as where I had been looking. I am not too familiar with nuthatches since it is only recently that they've moved into

Scotland but I suspect this was an alarm call and there would be a nest in the vicinity.

I returned to the river at the point where there is an anglers' hut. A loud croaking sound caught my immediate attention: it was a female goosander with a smallish flatfish firmly held in its serrated bill. It was fifteen or twenty yards out into the river and suddenly seven young goosanders, grey/brown bodies dappled with white patches and with the same chestnut brown head as their mother, swam as fast as they could to catch up with her. Their dappling matched perfectly the different light and shade of the rippling river. The croaking sound was clearly a call to the youngsters to come to her but was it the true sound or was it distorted because of the flatfish in her bill? In any case it had worked and the convoy swam further over the river, gradually coming downstream past me. The mother dived several times, a regular means of escape used by diving ducks, but came up seconds later as the young had possibly not yet learned to dive. After the third dive she eventually managed to swallow the flatfish. I wondered about the goosander swimming downstream past me, which she would not normally have done. She maybe realised that it was far easier for the troupe of followers to swim with the current rather than have to paddle their wee legs like hell against the current of the river. Whichever way they went it was a lovely sight, though this might be disputed by some anglers.

I passed several large patches of dame's rocket

It was a busy ten minutes. There were a few sand martins flying low over the river catching flies but higher in the sky there were two scimitar-shaped swifts. I'd looked at some old properties on the estate where I might have expected to see swifts but nothing, then here, where I least expected to see them, there they are. They were less than a mile from Forteviot village; older

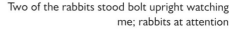

Two of the rabbits stood bolt upright watching me; rabbits at attention

houses there may afford them nesting opportunities.

I passed several large patches of dame's rocket, wild flowers that grow about three feet tall and come in white, pink and purple. All three colours were included in these patches, though white was the most prevalent with purple the least common. The flowers, like night scented stock, give off a perfume at night and are a host to the caterpillars of various moths and butterflies, including the lovely orange tip butterfly. As I looked at the flowers an osprey came flying over the fields in the direction of a small wood near Kildinny Farm. This is the second time I've seen an osprey flying towards that wood and there may well be a nest in that vicinity.

Nearer the car I disturbed a leveret, possibly a month old and already self-sufficient, which ran off up between tattie drills. It's an amazing fact of nature that, because they are born above ground, brown hares give birth to miniature versions of themselves, complete with fur and with their eyes open. Rabbits, on the other hand, as I've earlier described, give birth underground to naked and blind kits that don't even venture out of the burrow until they are four weeks old and still depend on their mother for a

couple of weeks after that. Shortly after the leveret sighting a litter of about six young rabbits ran over the track from a field of spring barley to the woodland. Two of the rabbits stopped short of entering the thick cover and stood bolt upright watching me, rabbits at attention, making a great photograph.

I had a quick look over at May Burn, where a shelduck was bathing and feeding. There are plenty rabbit burrows here, which is where shelducks like to nest, and I was hoping this was a male since there might be a female nesting nearby. The bird flew off while I was still some distance away but from its size and the fact that I couldn't see a knob on its beak, which the male has, I suspect it was a female.

I was hoping to see lapwings – or even better, be mobbed by a pair with their *pee-weep, pee-weep, pee-weep* alarm call in defence of chicks. A couple of oystercatchers slunk away on the opposite side of the burn as if one of them had come off a nest but didn't want to give its location away, but there was no mobbing of oystercatchers either. If there had been chicks around the parents would have been screaming round my head with their *peep peep peep* alarm call.

New birds identified: kingfisher, swift
New mammals identified: none

Woodpecker's nest hole in a dead oak tree

CHAPTER 42
Monday 10 June. Sunny and calm. 15°C.

Woodhead, Garden Bank, Lochs, Peel Farm

Today I popped in to see Bill MacIntosh, the retired keeper of the eastern part of the estate, at his house at Woodhead. Bill had found a woodpecker's nest a day or two before the chicks fledged and was keen to show it to me. The nest was in a dead oak tree and was obvious by its neat circular hole in what was quite a narrow trunk. In fact there were three holes at different heights and I wondered if the other two were nest holes from previous years. The nest holes were all facing approximately west, which was unusual since that is the direction of the prevailing weather. The middle hole of the three was that of this year's nest.

One of the chicks from the nest high in a Scots pine tree

The chicks had fledged the day before but I managed to track one down high in a Scots pine tree, alerted to it by its regular calls for food, since it was still very much dependent on its parents. The chicks constantly call for food while they are in the nest, which is a dangerous practice as the sound could attract a predator such as a squirrel or pine marten.

227

Osprey nest in Garden Bank decorated with sheep's wool and baler twine

From Woodhead I moved along to lovely Garden Bank and was hardly into my walk along the track through the centre when a roe doe trotted through the trees on my left followed by two fawns, sometimes known as kids. The fawns had left the ungainliness of their first few days of life behind and were roe deer in miniature prancing along behind their mother. They still had their spotted coats, which are an aid to camouflage when they lie in dappled woodland, and which they retain until about two months old. Though twins

Pine marten scat
on one of the tracks to the lochs

are not uncommon this is the first time I have seen twins as young as this, probably around a month old.

Further along the track I heard an osprey alarm call on my left. I looked round, to see it fly off a nest at the top of a high conifer. My previous visits to Garden Bank were on March 25th and May 1st, yet I saw no sign of ospreys. On the earlier date they had possibly started nesting but on May 1st they would most certainly have eggs in the nest. Had the osprey not alarm-called on this occasion I would not have known of this nest. Chicks in the nest may now be about half-grown. The nest was unusual in that it was decorated with sheep's wool, orange baler twine and with a substantial length of blue baler twine that someone had tied up neatly but which may have fallen off a tractor or trailer. This nest decoration is much more in keeping with the habits of red kites when they build a nest.

Leaving Garden Bank I went to the lochs. On these walks it's always difficult to know whether to look on the ground, look ahead or to look up. Depending on the habitat it is often a combination of all three and I was lucky to be looking down on to the ground on my way along the track to the lochs when I spotted a pine marten scat on

one of the tracks. It was absolutely fresh and was the typical black colour of carnivore poo but fading to a light brown at one end. Whatever the meal or meals had been, there were some small bones visible. This is ideal woodland habitat for pine martens and I'm surprised this is the first time I've seen their scat on the estate. I was reminded that in the autumn of 2018 I found a pine marten scat in my garden not ten yards from my hen house (though my hens and ducks are locked inside at night) and probably only four miles as the crow flies (or the pine marten runs) from the lochs. The difference in that case was that the poo was almost red in colour as the pine marten had been feasting on berries, which they love.

Further up the track the ospreys I had seen on one of my last visits and which I thought were nesting at the top of a trackside conifer were still there, both of them lifting quietly off the tree at my approach. It was interesting that there was no alarm call from these birds, which may be because they will be put off the nest every time someone walks or takes a vehicle up the track. They may now be well used to brief intrusions into their domain.

Mallard duck with a brood of five half-grown ducklings, line astern, on Dupplin Loch

I had a look at the waterfowl on Dupplin Loch, which still consists mainly of mute swans. On a previous visit there had been a swan on a nest at the far side but there was no sign of it today, nor could I see a swan – or more likely a pair of swans – with cygnets. From the boathouse the only other waterfowl I could see was a mallard duck with a brood of five half-grown ducklings, line astern, proudly swimming down the centre of the loch from west to east. The ducklings were still covered in down but with hints of feathers staring to appear. Most mallards start off with about eight ducklings but, mainly due to predation, they are whittled down to a smaller number, with sometimes even all of the brood being lost. This duck had done well to rear five to this size and they should now be much more likely to reach adulthood.

As I reached Pitcairnie Loch I experienced a fantastic mix of sounds of the countryside. First into the orchestra was a pair of ospreys with their *pieu pieu pieu* alarm call. The fact there was a pair and alarm-calling indicated yet another nest, though from the track I could see nothing obvious though there was a great choice of conifers. Joining in now was a buzzard, which circled just above tree height over my head. It was mewing anxiously, *peee-uu, peee-uu*, an indicator that I was not too far from a nest. If I had been a jogger or a cyclist it may even have attacked me, though buzzards with chicks in the nest don't seem to attack people walking. Next in the mix was a green woodpecker, with its *kew kew kew* call, which was coming from somewhere on a birch tree at the lochside. I'd to side-step round a conifer to try to see the bird but as usual we saw each other at the same time and it flew off. A heron now flew off from a small pond on my right, giving a loud *kaark* as it did so. I've often wondered if there are trout in that pond but there must be something that attracts herons, though maybe just frogs and minnows. The penultimate addition to the ensemble was a moorhen with its harsh *kurruck*. I'd actually heard it a few times but was paying much more attention to the other sounds. Remarkably it was just a few yards in front of me at the side of reeds at the lochside. I flicked my camera on but when I looked up again the moorhen had vanished into the reeds. Lastly, the chorus was being sung by a chaffinch. It was a wonderful few minutes of sound, all within about 10 yards. All of these sightings and sounds were right beside the graves of a former

owner of the estate and his wife. When I walked round the graves someone had been sitting where I sometimes sit at the fence between the graves and the loch. Regrettably they had left behind an empty juice tin, yoghurt carton and chocolate bar wrapper.

Turning my attention back to the loch, a Canada goose that on my last visit on May 13th had six recently-hatched goslings, now only had one. She had a mate at that time and the two were never apart, but he seemed to have disappeared as well. I wondered about the fate of the goslings, which would have spent a good deal of their time on the loch, and suspected that the predator may well have been either an otter or a mink. I'd hoped to see young tufted ducks but they nest slightly later than mallard and the ducks may still be incubating. There were plenty tufted ducks on the loch, though about three quarters were male, which tended to confirm my thoughts of incubating females.

Further along the loch, there was a bed of short reeds just out from the bank, which was almost hiding a pair of resting little grebes. They're lovely colourful wee birds but frustratingly they always seem to be at the opposite side of the loch from me. Further along still the mute swan remained patiently on its nest in the reeds. It was standing

Canada goose with brood of 6 goslings and tufted ducks on Pitcairnie Loch

up, so it's possible the eggs were hatching or had recently hatched. The dutiful male was also in attendance beside her. Swans are great parents and it will be interesting to see how many cygnets they manage to rear.

I walked back through the wood to the tall reeds at the east end of Dupplin Loch to see if there may have been any small birds using the reeds as nesting places. There were no small birds that I could see but there was a commotion on the water that I could just about witness over the top of the reeds. Two little grebes appeared to be having a fight. There was plenty of splashing going on and a lot of whinnying, which is their unusual call, especially in territorial disputes. This time, instead of being 100 yards away they were less than ten yards from me. I took some photos, which I was excited about and which I hoped would have shown their battle. What I got was reeds in perfect focus and two dark blotches behind them. Damn! The good news was that

slightly further out on the loch a little grebe was feeding a recently-hatched chick. The chick was not at the diving stage yet but swam to meet its mother (or father) every time she surfaced and was fed a morsel gathered from the bottom of the loch. I had a good look around expecting to see the other parent with a chick or chicks but if there were any more they must have been in the reeds.

I came home via the farm tracks through Peel Farm. I'd entered the farm via the track opposite Cotton Farm and had a wry smile at a memory of that location in the early 1970s. At the time I was a police constable in Perth and on night shift. One of my colleagues, Jim MacDonald, had stopped a suspicious-looking car about 4.00am. The two occupants ran off but Jim, being a fit chap who did lots of swimming, managed to catch one of them. It transpired that the car had been stolen in Glasgow and had been used to commit a crime in Aberdeen. The rest of us on night duty searched the area for the second fugitive but by 6.00am there was no sign of him. Some of the night shift remained on duty to continue the search to allow the day shift to carry on with their normal duties but I had snares to check on Dupplin and went back to the office to finish duty.

The day shift sergeant at that time was Jock Thomson, who left the police shortly after that incident and went on to be a solicitor, then a well-respected QC. He said to me jokingly that I had no interest in the job but that they would try to manage without me. I drove home, got changed and headed out the A9 to Dupplin Estate.

As I approached Cotton Farm road end a figure appeared from the woods and started thumbing a lift. He fitted the description of the missing fugitive and his trousers and shoes were soaked from traipsing through long grass and crops. I stopped beside him and he jumped into my car, saying, 'Thanks pal, just drop me anywhere in Glesca.' I wheeled the car about and headed back to Perth, much to the astonishment of my damp and exhausted passenger. I revealed my identity and told the Man from Glesca that he was under arrest. I suspect he was too tired to attempt another escape from the law but, just in case, I never stopped my car till I got to the police station, including going slowly through a set of traffic lights at red. I was really chuffed to present my prisoner to Sgt Jock Thomson and ask him, 'Who has no interest in the job now?'

I had seen plenty of evidence of red deer on the estate in the form of footprints, hair and crop damage but I had never yet seen a red deer. Today on the Peel Farm there were two, a hind and her calf from the previous year at the far end of a barley field. They kept an eye on me, even though I was more than a quarter of a mile away and in my car. The farmer wouldn't be pleased at deer eating their way through crops but I was pleased that there were red deer within about two miles of my house.

And I was still smiling thinking about the Man from Glesca.

New birds identified: none
New mammals identified: pine marten

Update on the swan breeding success on Pitcairnie Loch: The pair of swans failed to rear any cygnets. The eggs may have been infertile or the eggs or cygnets may have been taken by predators. The two swans remained on the loch.

CHAPTER 43
Tuesday 2 July. Sunny with some cloud. Breezy. 17⁰C.

Aberdalgie Mains Farm, Sauchie Farm, Forteviot Farm, River Earn, May burn, West Cultmalundie Farm

I have been a bit more limited in the places I can walk of late as there has been thick cover almost everywhere, whether that be the crops in the fields or the length of the grass in rough areas and in the more open woodland. Two or three shorter walks in more accessible places has been the norm rather than one long one. Today though I was on a mission and heading on to fairly open land down near the River Earn at Aberdalgie Mains Farm. The mission was (hopefully) to see a cattle egret that Stewart told me he had seen there a couple of days earlier. I parked at Sauchie Farm to do a quick circuit of the river and the flooded pools on adjacent Aberdalgie Mains. I was barely half-way to the river when an osprey wheeled from the river over my head. Its fishing trip so far had been unsuccessful but it looked like it was making further upstream to try its luck there. There is a good chance it is from the nest in Garden Bank.

My egret-spotting trip was also unsuccessful. The bird had maybe moved to pastures new but my walk round the flooded pools was enjoyable despite the absence of the reward I was seeking. What I did manage to see and photograph was a lovely painted lady butterfly. I had just been reading about this species. They're fascinating butterflies, usually arriving here from North Africa in June. The caterpillars from the eggs they lay turn into butterflies by the autumn and most emigrate to Africa for the winter, with any that remain here dying since it's too cold for them. It is apparently the most widespread butterfly in the world, inhabiting every continent except Australia and Antartica.

As I walked up the side of a wood on Sauchie Farm, which is farmed in-hand by the estate, I also saw an unusual mix of young birds. The first I spotted in a wild cherry tree was a young long-tailed tit. It was joined by several others, then some young blue tits then some young coal tits. There would be at least a dozen flitting about but none would stay still long enough for a photograph. I'm not sure what would have attracted such an assortment of birds to the wild cherry tree but it was a delightful sight.

I'd looked at the decent crop of wild cherries on the tree but slightly further on there was a domestic cherry tree with a lovely crop that was starting to colour to red. This tree will need a return visit when they are ripe. I was surprised to see a well-defined rabbit run coming from the wood near the cherry tree, across drills growing artichokes as a game/wild bird crop and finishing at the edge of a field of wheat. It was reminiscent of the runs that were on many parts of the estate prior to VHD. The fact that a significant area of wheat at the edge of the crop had been eaten confirmed the volume of rabbits.

Having failed in my egret mission I moved on to the River Earn at Forteviot where I sat for half an hour at the mouth of May Burn. The water in the Earn was low and I was quite surprised at the amount of weed in the river, which will provide great hiding places for trout and salmon parr and smolts. Several wee fish, probably trout, were making concentric circle designs on the calm water as they sucked in a drowning or hatching fly. It was a lovely peaceful place to spend half an hour, with relaxing music being provided free of charge by blackbirds, song thrushes

and a garden warbler. At one point, as nearly always happens when I am at the river, an osprey came flying upstream looking down at the water in the hope of seeing a fish just under the surface. I have watched ospreys looking for fish dozens of times now but have yet to see one making a dive for a fish. Frustrating!

I wandered up the edge of the burn to see how the sand martins were faring. There were plenty around and they were making regular visits to the nest holes. They are the earliest of the hirundines to finish nesting and head back to Africa but that will be in early August and most should have managed to rear two broods by that time. Flying amongst the sand martins, and sometimes confusing me for a second or two with their similar colours, were numerous pied wagtails; black and white adults and grey and white youngsters. They seem to have had a successful breeding season as well.

Three, or maybe four, common sandpipers were regularly flying ahead of me on stiff wingbeats and landing at the side of the burn about 50 yards ahead, then repeating the exercise as I got closer. I was a bit surprised that none of the birds were exhibiting any alarm behaviour, in particular their *tee*

A common sandpiper
landed at the edge of the burn

wee wee call as they would do if they had young to protect. It's possible that they had bred earlier and the young were now self-sufficient.

With the help of my walking stick to steady me I waded the burn with its slippery pebble bottom and headed back downstream on the far side. A pair of oystercatchers rose at the point I crossed the burn and though they gave a shrill *peep peep peep peep* alarm call they did not keep it up and fly around me as oystercatchers with dependent chicks always do. I suspect they had no young. There is no question that ground-nesting birds have a hard time in breeding successfully. I'd also hoped to see evidence of lapwings breeding in the rough grass field which the burn bisects but of that increasingly rare bird there was no sign.

It is difficult to determine what may have been the cause of the lack of breeding success of these birds (if indeed I am correct). There had been sheep in Forteviot Haugh, which is the name of the field, during the main breeding time though they are unlikely to have caused any problem. The shepherd drove around the field every day on his quad bike checking the sheep, but the birds would get used to that. Possible predators of eggs or chicks may have been rooks from a nearby rookery which were regularly in the field in large numbers, but much more likely could have been carrion crows, which are incredibly intelligent and experts at finding nests. Eggs and chicks can also be affected by adverse weather. Waders have coped with all of these problems for millenia but the difference now is that the numbers of some of the species is so low, mostly caused through intensive agriculture, that predation or adverse weather can have a much more serious effect and drive their numbers down even further. The lapwing is already red-listed, while the common sandpiper and oystercatcher are amber-listed. None of

Three rosy-faced swallows
rested on the top wire of the fence

them have a rosy outlook unless agriculture practices change. As I drove out of the farm road I was cheered up somewhat by the sight of three rosy-faced swallows resting on the top wire of the fence

My next stop was West Cultmalundie Farm, where I drove the two miles or so along the farm track almost to its boundary with the fields of Greenhill Farm. Despite the growth of the crops I was amazed at the number of hares that I saw, either running in front of me at various stages along the farm track or diving into tattie drills or wheat fields or fields of peas. At the end of the track I stopped at the small square piece of woodland that holds a small rookery. It was silent since all the rooks had left to forage elsewhere. I walked down the east side of the wood, where two whitethroats took an interest in me, *churring* with annoyance at my proximity to their nest. They *churred* from deep within the bushes, occasionally flying to a different bush

but never more than 10 yards from me. I waited for about five minutes and finally the female came out into the open where I managed a decent photograph. That was enough for me and I left the pair to get on with their busy lives.

I'd intended next to have a walk around the rough pasture on Greenhill. The field was full of cows and calves, maybe up to seventy cows with their followers, and when I got to the gate I could see that they were very unsettled. Normally cows with calves are content to quietly eat grass or sit and ruminate, unlike younger cattle which are much more likely to run after a person entering the field, bucking and snorting and farting, generally being a damn nuisance and certainly not being conducive to quiet wildlife-watching. These cattle were not at that stage but there were two Aberdeen-Angus bulls in the field and they were pestering the cows since one or more of them was certainly in season. I couldn't see me getting peace for a walk there and decided to move elsewhere.

I drove back to West Cultmalundie Farm and spent some time parked at a large and muddy puddle since I'd earlier seen a house martin gathering mud. I had a good view of what might be taking place but was not so close as to put off any birds that wanted to use the puddle. It turned out to be quite a popular spot, with both swallows and house martins stopping off to gather mud, and swallows swooping down to take a quick sip of water on the wing. I watched a pair of swallows regularly accessing a shed via the narrowest of gaps above the door, despite the fact that many other sheds on the partially derelict farm were wide open. The swallows had their entrance down to a fine art, closing their wings just as they

reached the door and shooting through the gap with the grace of a goshawk flying between the tiniest gaps in woodland branches. Other visitors for a drink or a bath were chaffinches, a house sparrow, a goldfinch and tree sparrows. Tree sparrows were in abundance and I think I had parked beside their favourite bush, which they seemed to use after their ablutions as an ideal place to dry off.

As I drove out of the farm road I had the car window open as it was a lovely day. Just before I reached the main road I braked quickly, as a linnet was singing loudly from somewhere within the hedge on my right. I looked and looked for this lovely songster but it was well hidden and in fact I didn't see it until it flew from the hedge and crossed the public road. It was a good end to my day.

New birds identified: none
New mammals identified: none

CHAPTER 44
Little ringed plovers

As in my previous job in policing I always expect the unexpected. In late April an interesting pair of birds flew in front of me on one of my walks. They looked brown and white in flight but when they landed on shingle and I got the binoculars on to them (with some difficulty because of their camouflage) there was a proportion of black in the plumage on the head and neck. I was thrilled to see that they were ringed plovers but I had to get closer to identify which of the two types they were: ringed plovers or little ringed plovers. I was delighted to confirm them as little ringed plovers.

This short chapter covers my sightings of these two little ringed plovers, which are rare breeding birds in Scotland. Here the birds are found mainly on the east coast where they breed on shingle banks and islands and in gravel pits. There are possibly not many more than a dozen breeding pairs in Scotland though considerably more in England.

I have kept the detail on these birds separate from the information gleaned on the rest of my walks. My fear is that if they return in future years and their location is well known their presence might attract numerous birdwatchers. Although most of these folks would be well-meaning, there are always one or two who would try to go a stage further and disturb the birds at a nest. As has happened already with capercaillie on this estate they could therefore reduce their chance of producing chicks. The little ringed plover is listed on Schedule 1 of the Wildlife and Countryside Act 1981. As such it is an offence to intentionally or recklessly disturb the bird while it is nesting or has dependent young unless in possession of a licence from Scottish Natural Heritage to do so.

I moved a wee bit closer to take a photograph of one of the birds. The photos turned out to be reasonable enough, but I never noticed that the second bird, which to my surprise was in one of the photos, had been much closer to me than the one on which I was focussing. I didn't realise this until they flew off again and can only say that their camouflage is absolutely incredible. The photographs I took showed four clear identifying points. This bird had a very distinctive yellow eye ring; it had a white band between

One of the pair of well-camouflaged little ringed plovers

the black band over its forehead and its brown – almost gold – head; it had a dark coloured bill rather than the orange and black bill of the ringed plover, and it had flesh-coloured legs rather than the orange legs of its larger cousin. The dainty little ringed plover is yet another of our summer visitors and this pair will not long have arrived from their winter quarters in Africa.

When I first saw the little ringed plovers it was a tad early for nesting but I gave them almost six weeks of peace and quiet before I went back to the area, leaving my visit until mid-June. I hoped by that time the female may have either been sitting on eggs or have small chicks. I kept well back from their most likely nesting areas bearing in mind their Schedule 1 status. There was no sign of them where I saw them before, but at one point one of the little

ringed plovers flew over my head and landed on a small shingle bank. Despite only seeing one the chances are they were both still in the area. I hoped it was the male that I saw and that the female was sitting somewhere incubating a clutch of eggs.

I returned to the area in July. The two little ringed plovers were back in the shingle patch where I first saw them in April. They appeared relaxed and made no effort to alarm at my presence. My conclusion was that they did not have young although they had probably nested, but for whatever reason the nesting attempt failed. I suspect they will be off on their migration to Africa shortly after this sighting. What a pity that this pair were not able to increase the population of this lovely wee bird.

CHAPTER 45

Tuesday 22 July. Cloudy with sunny intervals. Breezy. 21°C.

Wester Cairnie, Bankhead, Methven Moss

Wester Cairnie was my destination today, though I knew many parts of the farm would be unsuitable for walking because of the height of the crops. I drove through the farm steading and down a track towards the huge bog that lies between the farm and the River Earn. The grass in the centre of the track was getting higher the further I drove down the track and by half-way the grass was higher than the bonnet of my car. Had I not known the track well I would never had attempted this route with an ordinary car. Suddenly there was a very young pheasant chick running along the right-hand track in front of me, then two, then three. I stopped and the mother pheasant appeared from the long grass and ran with them. I was hoping that they would run into the long grass at my side of the track but they kept on going. I followed slowly behind and it was a good forty yards before they eventually abandoned the track and took cover in the grass. I passed them safely but I could only hope that none were left at the starting point since pheasants are pretty hopeless mothers. As she had some chicks with her she'd be quite happy to continue and be unaware if some had been lost.

I parked beside the small brick building that houses the swallow nests and the wasp bike. I was keen to check inside to see what the current position was but the building was surrounded by waist-high thistles and I knew that somewhere hidden in the depths of the thistles was a ditch. I therefore abandoned that idea.

I walked towards the first of two ponds in the bog, rising ten quacking mallards. Two mallards remained in the pond and as I watched them I was aware of another bird in the middle distance. This was one of the few times that I have seen a snipe before it has flown off. It was partially hidden by grass but it most certainly saw me. Nevertheless it decided to be a model snipe and posed while I took several photos, only flying off when I chanced a step or two forward. There was a *buff* behind me which I initially thought was

One of the few times that I have seen a snipe before it has flown off

someone coughing. When I turned it was a yearling buck, maybe even the one I had seen and photographed on my last visit here. It ran off into the adjacent crop of oil seed rape, giving a final *buff, buff buff buff* from the depths of the tall crop.

I moved forward to the pond to see what footprints there might be in the mud of its receding waters. Most prints were of waterfowl, with an odd roe deer print. A freshly-dead mallard duckling lay upside down on the mud. If it had been killed by a predator it would have been eaten. It was maybe a weakling and had died. I have also seen a weakling duckling killed by its mother. We had a brood of mallard ducklings years ago in which there was a weakling. The mother tried several times to drown it despite our rescue attempts, including gently pressing it to empty its lungs of water. The mother duck was determined and won in the end. In the case of the dead duckling in front of me, where were its siblings? Had they all been lost or were they hiding in the grass at the edge of the pool along with the mother. Hopefully the latter.

I walked down between the edge of the bog and the field of oil seed rape. It was a struggle, with some of the grasses more than six feet high. I could hear the chirping of young birds in the reeds and grasses calling on their parents to provide food. I suspected they were mostly reed buntings but one young bird's *cheep* is much the same as another. Apart from when birds were flying over the reeds they were mostly deep in the undergrowth. Thankfully, at one point, a male reed bunting perched near the top of a reed and I was able to confirm the identify at least one bird frequenting that dense jungle.

It was hard going with the height of the grass, reeds, thistles and nettles to get (almost) to the river. My last obstacle was the flood bank and the fence on its far side. At my side of the fence it was the normal height but there was a drop on the far side of half as much again, plus the grass obscured any possible hidden rock, bump or hole that could twist my ankle on landing. Furthermore, there had been no stock in the field since last autumn and the grass was thigh height; not pleasant for walking. I'd twisted my ankle years ago

241

Spotted flycatcher on favourite perching place from which to launch aerial sorties

in almost identical circumstances and the injury limited my walking in the countryside for several weeks. I must now be getting much more cautious in my old age and I turned about and made my way back to the car.

I moved on to more central parts of the estate, parking at The Parsonage and photographing an obliging brown hare that was hopping slowly towards a field of barley, but intermittently stopping to wash its face with its front paws. I walked down the estate road at the west end of The Parsonage then down the side of the Factor's Strip. A roe fawn trotted down the outside of the deer fence on my left, then turned and came back. It stopped for a few seconds, not long enough for me to get a photo, then turned again and trotted down between the deer fence and some broom bushes. The fawn was too young to survive on its own but there was a good chance its mother – and maybe even its twin – was not far away.

On my right was a field of barley with a 30-yard strip of phacelia on the west and south side. It's great to see much more use being made of these lovely purple flowers that are such a great attraction to pollinators. The phacelia was alive with bumble bees, white butterflies and several of the much more colourful small tortoiseshell butterflies.

Beyond the Factor's Strip I continued on down a strip of mainly mature oak trees, the purpose being to check yet again for the presence of nuthatches since this is where I first saw them on the estate. Two buzzards were circling in the sky, alternating between the air space over the strip of trees I was walking in and Beech Alley to the east, all the while calling to each other with their melancholy *peee-uu* call. Part of the way down the strip of oaks, a small brown bird flew off a thin dead branch half way up one of the trees. It caught a fly and returned to the branch. A second identical bird was perched on another dead branch nearby. The two spotted flycatchers then gave me a lovely demonstration of how to catch flies – not that I was interested in doing so myself. The two dead branches were clearly their favourite perching places from which to launch their aerial sorties and to which they returned with their catch of the day. Photographing small brown birds against the sky on a breezy day is not easy but I did manage to get one or two reasonable photos.

Beaver's muddy slipway at Methven Moss

I walked up one of the farm tracks leading to Bankhead Farm. I'd not been on this track for years and was pleased to see it was now lined on both sides with an unruly hedge consisting of a mix of hawthorn and wild rose, both great for cover and food for wild birds. At Bankhead Farm sheep were being sheared and one of the men shearing was pleased with progress, telling me that there were only 1,200 still to be done out of 3,500. He also said that maggot infestations had been bad this year since we'd had more spells of damp muggy weather, though they had not lost any sheep to fly strike.

From Bankhead Farm I headed up another farm track leading me back towards my car. I caught a glimpse of a small flash of white at a gap in the grass under the fence. Suspecting a stoat or a weasel I made a squeaking noise like a rabbit in distress and a small brown and white triangular face appeared briefly at the gap again, the first weasel I had seen on the estate in almost a year of walks.

I came home via Methven Moss to check on the beaver in the ditch near the Moss Road. After an absence of about eleven weeks since my trespassing suspect removed the dam, the beaver was back again. There were now rudiments of a new dam in the same place, a very obvious run through the long grass made by the beaver leaving the ditch to come up to a willow tree on the bank to feed, and a muddy slipway on the far bank where the beaver had also been exiting the burn to feed on nearby willows. I would have been happy with this ending to my morning's walk but as I walked back to my car parked at the roadside a red kite floated over my head from the woodlands of Methven Moss and landed on a strip of grass which was part of a field of barley on Merriness Farm, a tenanted farm on the north boundary of the estate. In the past I've often seen a pair of red kites in this area and suspected they were nesting in the trees of Methven Moss. I had given up hope of seeing a red kite during my year's walking on the estate but, maybe like the beaver, they had been there all the time.

New birds identified: red kite
New mammals identified: weasel

CHAPTER 46

Thursday 1 August. Cloudy at first then sunny. Calm. 19°C.

East Lamberkin Farm

I thought it appropriate to finish these Chapters on Dupplin Estate with one on East Lamberkin Farm, where I spent the happiest days of my young life from aged about seven until I started work aged seventeen.

I had meant to walk over East Lamberkin in the spring, my only other walk over the fields and woods having been the previous October. Time and the growth of greenery had caught up with me and when I walked 'Down the Strip' today it was overgrown and barely accessible. I turned back before I was even at the half-way point and had a look at the relatively new strip of trees that replaced the former old oaks and beech trees that made up the part named 'Up the Strip'. It wasn't quite as impenetrable, with a sea of long grass, but it didn't look too inviting. It's a problem at this time of year finding a walk through fields or woods that are not knee (or sometimes waist) high with either grass, thistles, nettles or crops.

I was reminded when I looked 'Up the Strip' of a time when it comprised

ancient trees and grass kept short by the regular presence of stock. It was a favourite place for us to drive an old car that Jimmy Robb's father, Bill, had bought for us to drive around in. I forget the make of car now but it was black and probably a Ford or Austin of some kind. Jimmy Robb, his brothers Alex and David and I would all be aged somewhere between 13 and 15 and were competent drivers already, being well used to driving tractors and the farm Land Rover. We had great fun driving between the trees but there was a problem. It was a serious health problem, though we didn't realise it at the time: the significant noxious fumes from the car exhaust somehow came right in through the floor of the car. We learned to keep the windows open, but that didn't make a great deal of difference. We could only drive the car for a short time before we had to abandon our otherwise enjoyable pastime and get some fresh air outside.

We put up with the exhaust fumes for a few weeks but it got to the stage that there was no pleasure in using the car. We decided that was the end of the car adventures and, as wild teenagers sometimes do, we trashed it by jumping on the roof and bonnet. At the same time as we were bouncing on the car roof Jimmy's father, knowing of the potentially lethal issues with the car, had been seeking a buyer. He did manage to find someone who was interested and told him quite honestly about the issue with fumes. The answer was along the lines, 'That's OK, I can soon sort the exhaust out. Just as long as the bodywork is in reasonable condition. . .'

By the time I had come to this part of the car's demise in my thoughts I found myself back in the farmyard. I wandered past the barn, a two-storey building with the upper part most often used for storage of hay. The exception was one evening when there was no hay in the barn, the floor was swept and a barn dance was held, to the great delight of the considerable crowd that attended.

In the lower part of the barn oats were run through clanking, dusty belt-driven machinery every few days so that the grains were flattened converting them to bruised oats, which were much better for the digestion of the cattle to which they were fed. There was often a pile of biscuit meal for mixing with the bruised oats. Within this pile of biscuit meal we often found a treat in the form of a complete or almost-complete biscuit, which we munched with great pleasure, and in hope that mice or rats had not had an earlier share.

The far end of the lower part of the barn was fenced off for the hens, which had access to the stackyard outside via a window with a ladder on the outside to allow them access again when they wanted to return. The hens spent a lot of time pecking round the stackyard, especially after the grain in the stacks had been threshed. From memory there was capacity for about sixteen stacks, and they were built of the sheaves of grain immediately after harvest. Each round stack was about 12 feet in diameter with vertical sides up to a height of about 10 feet, then graduating to a point at the top.

The stackyard was always a hub of wildlife, some welcome, others less so. Those not welcome were the rats that always infested the stacks, feeding in relative safety on the grain in the stacks' interior. Occasionally their peaceful life was upset by a stoat or weasel, since these mustelids can easily reach where any rat can go, and both can make an easy meal of a rat. They, like buzzards, are for the most part a farmer's and forester's friend, controlling numbers of rats, mice, voles and rabbits. It is a real pity that all farmers don't recognise that.

Finches of all sorts welcomed the spilt grain in the stackyard, with chaffinches, greenfinches, linnets, goldfinches, yellowhammers and siskins being joined by hordes of house sparrows. In times of prolonged snow in winter, flocks of woodpigeons descended on the stackyard, with some grain around the stacks and, in nearby fields, turnip leaves peeping out the snow about all that they had to eat until the thaw arrived and revealed a much wider variety of food.

The hundreds of sheaves remained in the stacks until the travelling threshing mill could attend. This was a massive machine, belt-driven with the power coming from a tractor, which threshed the sheaves, separating the grain from the straw. The grain, depending on which stack, would be wheat, oats or barley, was then bagged. The straw was tied by the threshing mill into bunches, which were then stacked for use in the 'reeds' or cattle courts for bedding or feeding the cattle, or for insulating tattie or neep (turnip) pits so that these root crops could be stored free of frost over the winter. The bags of oats or barley weighed a hundredweight (112 lbs/50kg) though the bags of wheat were a hundredweight and a quarter (140 lbs). For youths of 15 or 16 to carry these for even part of a day was really hard work. It was even harder when these were being stored in the loft above the cart sheds as that meant climbing a dozen or so steps with them on our backs.

Just beyond the cart sheds was the stable. Inside, the stable had a loose box at either end and stalls in between. Bess, the black draught horse, was stabled there and was a great substitute for a small tractor. She was especially good at haytime for pulling the hayricks onto a flat trailer. As the farm workers, Jim Ogg and Bob Clark, drove the hay to the farm Jimmy and I looked after Bess in the hayfield, often climbing on to a hayrick to give us the height to get on to her back. With us perched there, well above ground level, bareback and Red Indian style, the gentle giant would walk slowly around the field.

I've mentioned 'bunnets' – all of us, farmers, farm workers and laddies wore a bunnet, slanted mostly to one side of the head, though there was no practical reason for this and may have been the way it was naturally placed on the head with the right hand. However there were many practical uses for a bunnet, and these were described in a poem by Jimmy's father, Bill, who was a prolific poet and regularly and cleverly converted to verse many unusual or amusing situations. For all the good times and all of the knowledge I gained at East Lamberkin Farm I think it is appropriate to end these chapters on Dupplin Estate with one of his poems.

A New Year Toast to the Bunnet

You may wonner what's happened tae the man o' the hoose
He's sair perplexed and fu' o' abuse
Sae listen tae me and I'll tell ye whit's done it
The pair auld soul has lost his bunnet.

Noo we hear o' inventions near every day
Many clever things have come our way
But just think for a minute – a' the things that's done wi' it
An ordinary plain and simple bunnet.

Tae cover a heid, it was really intended
But to so many things, itself has lended
It skites the rain frae aff your pow
Or may wipe the sweat aff your brow.

Should the sun be strong and get in yer ee'
Pu' doon the skip and then ye'll see
Or if on your neck the water runs doon
Just tak and turn the skip aroon.

There's aye a chance you'll fin' some day
A wheen o' eggs a hen has laid away
You gether them up, but yer hands are too sma'
So tak your bunnet and you'll manage them a'.

And when you find a pot ower het
Ye'll tak yer cap, it is my bet
Likewise should ae thing be frozen stiff
My hoo a bunnet can save your niff.

And if a cork be screwed on ticht
Ye fecht awa wi' a' yer micht
Then aff yer heid intae yer haun
It gie's ye twice as muckle braun.

When kneeling down as you can see
Mak's much more comfort for yer knee
And when a wasp hovers near your ear
Your headpiece helps to keep him clear.

Sometimes a tractor or motor will stall
Tae ca' the handle, the bare mitt's nae use at a'
Just tak your cap, it's grand protection
Three snappy burls and you've got connection.

Then if your team is doing well
Up goes the bunnet as you cheer like hell
But if all is wrong and they can't do a thing
Sure as fate, it's your bunnet you'll wring.

And on meeting a lady in the street
You touch your cap and smile so sweet
Or in remembering those now sadly passed on
You remove it respectfully as you carry on.

Whatever the future we cannot say
But the guid auld bunnet is here to stay
And here's hopin' it won't be needed tae wipe a tear
Frae mony eyes throughout this year.

William Robb

CONCLUDING THOUGHTS

The year walking on Dupplin Estate has been fascinating. There have been many changes in habitat since I frequented parts of the estate in the late 1950s and early 1960s, and even since I carried out rabbit trapping over the whole of the estate in the 1970s and early 1980s. While the farming aspect of the estate has swung slightly away from sheep, cattle and winter fodder such as turnips in favour of grain, oil seed rape, peas and winter sheep fodder such as kale, there are plenty of places for a variety of wildlife to thrive. These wilder areas are known and appreciated by the estate and there is no plan to alter them. They are supplemented by game/wild bird seed crops and these are well enough described in the body of the book that I need say no more except that Stewart would like even more of them. I suspect that there will be few estates in Scotland, maybe even in the UK, that cater as well, either consciously or incidentally, for wildlife. I must also give credit to most of the tenant farmers, who also have odd corners of their farms left rough, or wet, or sown with wild bird seed crops.

The rarest birds – at least for this part of Scotland – that I encountered were the little ringed plovers, the nuthatches and the Mediterranean gull. In addition to my sightings of the nuthatches, Stewart has seen one near the office in the centre of the estate. Of the other birds in the list it was heartening to see the numbers of whooper swans that spent at least part of their winter on the river or lochs. Skylark and yellowhammer flocks were impressive and I was pleased to see that a reasonable number of these species remained on the estate as breeding birds during the spring and summer. Hopefully a decent proportion was successful.

Of the waders, I saw no indication that there were any signs of a recovery to even modest numbers. Oyster-catchers and probably common sandpipers seemed the most successful but numbers of curlews remain depressingly low and I would be surprised if there were any lapwings at all that successfully fledged young over the whole estate.

There are a handful of grey

partridge, one of my favourite birds, on Dupplin. The habitat that favours the grey partridge is beginning to return: miles of hawthorn hedges, game/wild bird seed crops, wide field margins, reduced spraying and, under the proposed agri-environment climate scheme, the ploughing of stubbles left till spring. I suspect grey partridges may need a boost by way of a few reared and released birds to bolster their numbers.

Dupplin Estate, unlike many estates, has a relaxed view of raptors. I'd suggest that numbers of buzzards are quite high and although I saw no indication of predation either to gamebirds or to wild birds by this species, Stewart tells me that he sees young pheasants killed on a regular basis. Numbers of other raptors are moderate to low: kestrels, ospreys, sparrowhawks, merlin and goshawks. Some predation by goshawks on reared and released mallard was reported by Stewart and there is a possibility that the remains of four pheasants that I found over an area about 200 yards in length between East and West Munday and the East Drive *may* have been caused by a goshawk. I have not seen the goshawks after September, my second month on the estate, but Stewart still sees them regularly. He said

I need to get up earlier in the morning.

The estate has issued clear instructions that any losses of game birds to raptor predation will be accepted as part of the natural predator/prey relationships, a position under which both Stewart and the estate can operate in a much more stress-free atmosphere given the law of vicarious liability in Scotland. This is also in accordance with the point made in 2018 by Roseanna Cunningham, Cabinet Secretary for the Environment, climate change and land reform, who stated that predation of game birds 'is a business risk that must be accepted and managed within the law'.

I had some fantastic views of hares and roe deer. There is an excellent brown hare population, though still nothing like what it was in the 1960s. The change in farming practices is the only reason I can think of for the reduction, nevertheless brown hare numbers are still healthy. Roe deer are now everywhere, even from time to time in my garden. They have few risks of a natural death on low ground estates, with their only risk, as fawns, coming from foxes. Many are killed by vehicles yet their numbers still seem to be on the rise. Despite regular culling by Bill, Stewart and guest guns, their numbers on Dupplin appear to be much higher than I remember them on any of my former visits to the estate.

Red deer numbers have burgeoned, as the number shot by Bill shows. In my earlier years at Dupplin I only remember one red deer stag at rutting time in October being seen on the estate yet now there are tracks everywhere and though I only saw two red deer hinds during the year there is evidence of them on all of the farms on the north side of the A9 dual carriageway.

The dearth of stoats is a bit of a mystery. There is no doubt they would have suffered from lack of food after the elimination of rabbits on the estate, but stoats are opportunists and many would have survived on mice, voles, rats and nestling and fledgling birds. To have walked round Dupplin over the course of a year and never seen a single stoat (and only one weasel, though they are much less visible in any case) is puzzling, particularly as there is no tunnel trapping carried out on the estate.

What's equally puzzling was the absence of the cuckoo; no sight or sound of one throughout May and early June. Cuckoo numbers are falling and it

has now joined the red list of birds of conservation concern. The cuckoo concentrates on particular bird species as its host in hatching its egg and rearing the emerging parasitic, but nevertheless amazing, young cuckoo. The main hosts seem to be the meadow pipit, reed warbler, dunnock and redstart. There are no reed warblers on the estate, there are few redstarts and there are not huge numbers of dunnocks or meadow pipits so cuckoo numbers are never going to be high. I would have thought there were sufficient meadow pipits nesting in the area of Blairbell to sustain one or two cuckoos (especially since that was where the unfortunate cuckoo was shot by the wife-beating Mr Nasty) but I found absolutely no trace of them. I asked Stewart if he had heard or seen any cuckoos. He had heard only one but by the time I spoke with him he couldn't remember where he'd heard it. I know there are also stonechats in the Blairbell area as I've seen them there in the past, but unfortunately not during my year on the estate.

I had no night-time visits to the estate so my chance of seeing owls was limited. There are tawny owls and some barn owls present, and Stewart sees and hears them regularly at night. Since short-eared owls are diurnal I was disappointed that I didn't see at least one. I picked up a long-eared owl as roadkill at the side of the A9 at Broxden Farm many years ago but I've no idea if this owl species is still on the estate and I have not spoken to anyone who has seen one.

Returning to mammals, I've been told there are otters on the lochs – the disappearance of some of the young Canada geese did support this – yet I never saw one or even found an otter spraint on the perimeter of the lochs. I never saw an otter on the River Earn, but at least there were plenty signs of them in the form of footprints and spraints.

Dupplin is a wonderful estate with a wealth of wildlife to see, as well as some majestic ancient woodland. Wildlife tourism is popular yet few estates become involved in this important and potentially lucrative industry. In Scotland of course responsible access to almost all land can be taken by individuals and some might prefer to walk on their own. On a tour guided by someone who knows the land, flora and fauna there is much more chance of seeing wildlife of interest, learning of its ecology and of how it fits in with the estate. There is no

reason I can see why the commercial activities already undertaken by an estate – farming, forestry and game shooting – would not slot in with the addition of eco-tours; they can all complement each other. In particular the value of hedges and game/wild bird seed crops can be appreciated as both cover and food for wildlife. Readers of this book will already be aware of the numbers of passerines that feed on this additional habitat over the winter time.

The risks to wildlife through eco-tourism are that they may either inadvertently or carelessly be subject to disturbance. However this can be minimised by a professional guide and also balanced against the benefit to wildlife by the increased knowledge of the visitors and their subsequent enthusiasm in protecting wildlife for further generations.

To assist and encourage wildlife and also to improve tours for visitors the following could be considered:

- A variety of nest boxes that could encourage owls, kestrels, swifts, and a variety of small birds. Nest boxes for goldeneye (on top of plastic poles to prevent raids by pine martens) might encourage goldeneye to breed on the lochs.

- Though there is a very good chance of visitors seeing red squirrels, strategically-placed red squirrel feeders could increase red squirrel sightings as well as providing an additional food source for them.

- Nuthatches come readily to bird feeders. Bird feeders over the winter months in the general area of the Factor's Strip, Beech Alley and the River Earn banks from Kildinny to the May Burn may encourage this new visitor to Scotland and make it more easily found.

- Hides from which to observe wildlfowl at both lochs would be a real boon, especially if they can be sited at the north east and south west shores of Dupplin Loch and south east or north west shore of Pitcairnie Loch.

- John Hogg, the farm manager, made

valid points about the ability of skylarks to access winter cereal crops via tramlines, but skylark plots are worth considering.

I would envisage wildlife tours being of two types. The first would be where the guests could be transported for most of the route but walk short distances to relevant points of main interest, such as hides or along the riverside. The second would be where the whole tour is carried out on foot, though this could only cater for a very small group because of the heightened risk of noise.

Lastly, because of the swan strikes on electricity cables crossing the River Earn at Wester Cairnie Haugh, it would be worth asking the electricity supplier to place baffles on the wires to alert the swans to their presence.

APPENDIX

Birds

R – Red-listed birds

A – Amber-listed birds

** – Schedule 1 birds

blackbird	
blackcap	
brambling	**
bullfinch	A
bunting, reed	A
buzzard, common	
chaffinch	
chiffchaff	
coot	
cormorant	
crossbill, common	**
crow, carrion	
curlew	R
dipper	A
dove, collared	
duck, mallard	A
duck, tufted	
dunnock	A
fieldfare	** R
flycatcher, spotted	R
goldcrest	
goldeneye	A
goldfinch	
goosander	
goose, Canada	
goose, pink-footed	A
goose, greylag	A
goshawk	**
greenfinch	
grebe, little	
gull, black-headed	A
gull, common	A
gull, great black-backed	A
gull, lesser black-backed	A
gull, herring	
gull, Mediterranean	** A
heron	
jackdaw	
jay	
kestrel	A
kingfisher	** A
kite, red	**
lapwing	R
linnet	R
magpie	
martin, house	A
martin, sand	
merlin	** R
moorhen	
nuthatch	
osprey	** A
oystercatcher	A
partridge, grey	R
partridge, red-legged	
pigeon, feral	
pipit, meadow	A
pipit, tree	R
pheasant	

plover, little ringed	**	warbler, willow	A
raven		wheatear	
redstart	A	whitethroat	
redwing	** R	wigeon	A
robin		woodcock	R
rook		woodpecker, green	
sandpiper, common	A	woodpecker, great spotted	
shelduck	A	woodpigeon	
siskin		wren	
skylark	R	yellowhammer	R
snipe	A		
sparrowhawk			
sparrow, house	R	**Mammals**	
sparrow, tree	R	badger	
starling	R	beaver	
swallow		cat, feral	
swan, mute	A	deer, red	
swan, whooper	** A	deer, roe	
swift	A	fox	
teal	A	hare, brown	
tit, blue		hedgehog	
tit, coal		marten, pine	
tit, great		mink	
tit, long-tailed		mole	
thrush, mistle	R	otter	
thrush, song	R	rabbit	
treecreeper		squirrel, grey	
twite	R	squirrel, red	
wagtail, pied		weasel	
wagtail, grey	R		
warbler, garden			
warbler, sedge			

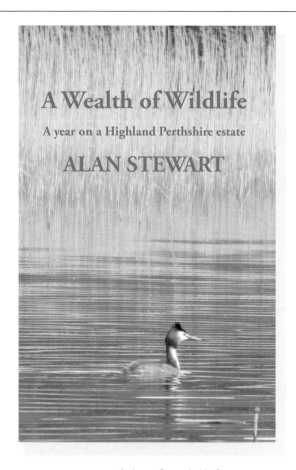

A Wealth of Wildlife

a companion volume by Alan Stewart

Published in 2015, *A Wealth of Wildlife* takes the reader north of the Highland line and provides a fascinating an account of a year walking on a Highland Perthshire estate. The unnamed estate is run jointly for farming and shooting. Once again the author demonstrates that a vast range of wildlife can thrive where conservation is embraced within careful land management practices.

Signed copies available from the author at
wildlifedetective@gmail.com
or copies from Thirsty Books at http://www.thirstybooks.com/

Follow Alan Stewart's blog:
https://wildlifedetective.wordpress.com/